HOME WITH A GOOD COMPANION

Five amateur pantomimes and related short stories for the New-Year season when it snows cats and dogs. These are all suitable for reading aloud and are mainly of interest to the young, although farce and heartwarming stories are often equally of interest to adults in the cold days. The lyrics and basic music are in tonic sol-fa, for camcorder, DVD, CD, film. For use on stage, schools, halls, colleges, hotels, gardens or in your own home. These stories include humorous tales of many different types – skits, farces, sketches, slapstick, witty humor, sharp satire. Stories and pantomime scripts include:

❀ *Little Boy Blue*
❀ *Mother Goose*
❀ *Old Working Dog*
❀ *Santa and the Nursery Rimers*
❀ *Professor Luck*

LIFE OF DREW CARSON
Storyteller and Songwriter

Sam Drew Carson was born in the North of Ireland and educated there at Wellington College and the Ulster Polytechnic. He completed his education in the USA at New Mexico Highlands University and the University of Arkansas. He has traveled widely in Europe, around the Atlantic and in North America.

Carson worked as a seaman and fish-gutter in Vestmannaeyjar off the coast of Iceland.

He has lived and worked in the Irish and Western Isles Gaeltachts and was married in Welsh-speaking Carmarthen after which he honeymooned in Belfast.

He has told his stories, composed and sung his songs, seeking storylines in Bristol and the English Westcountry.

Carson has also lived and written in Nashville, Tennessee, in the wooded hills of Mid-America and from the Appalachians to the Ozarks. This was the culture that gave rise to the now worldwide Scotch-Irish country music.

In the USA, he has also worked beside the bayous of the French-speaking Cajuns in the South and among the Western Spanish-speaking Navajos,

Apaches and Pueblos of the Sangre de Cristo Mountains in New Mexico.

Carson has sailed far into the seas of old Gaelic and Oriental legend. After many years searching for inspiration for story and music, the author is still traveling and writing.

BOOKS BY THE SAME AUTHOR

SAGA OF TSUNAMI –
the Trilogy, 2nd edition

ZENISUB –
Fun and Games in Businezz

GOOD FOR A LAUGH –
Six Funny Playscripts for Amateurs

HOME WITH A GOOD COMPANION –
Amateur Pantomime Scripts for a Merry Winter

BACK TO THE GOOD OLD DAYS –
Miracle Plays of Sunlight and Shadow

Home with a Good Companion

Amateur Pantomime Scripts
for a Merry Winter

DREW CARSON

Order from: https://www.createspace.com/3505803

Legals

Published by S. A. Carson,
29 Northleaze, Long Ashton, Bristol BS41 9HS, UK
Publisher's email: verygoodreading@googlemail.com

STORIES/PANTOMIMES:
Little Boy Blue, Mother Goose, Old Working Dog,
Santa and the Nursery Rimers, Professor Luck

Amateur Productions: ten percent of all monies received
should be sent, a.s.a.p., to the copyright holder.

ISBN: 978-0-9561435-4-9

ALL FIVE MUSICAL PLAYS ARE PANTOMIMES

WHAT IS PANTOMIME?

Children's farce can be a very popular genre. One of the great forms of farce for children is Pantomime which, after centuries of development, still draws huge audiences to British theaters. The traditional British Pantomime is a farce, particularly popular at Christmas, mainly for young children but also for adults or teens with an unspoilt sense of humor. It has the following ten main elements:

1. Songs:
Traditional or traditional-type singalong songs.

2. Join-in:
Audience participation such as 'boo-the-villain,' join-in singing, answering questions with yes or no, etc., and similar. If a large print copy of the words of each song are made available to the audience, this will encourage both children and adults to join in the singing.

3. A Silly Plot:
A racy, rescue-the-heroine type plot with a happy ending. No serious love interest or serious anything else for that matter.

4. Fun:
Humor, usually simple and uncomplicated although subtle satirical humor (e.g., Alice in Wonderland or Wizard of Oz) is often hugely

appreciated by young audiences. Always a little (sometimes more) slapstick. Characters laugh at each other and with the audience.

5. *Principal Boy:*

An important, but not central, character from nursery rhyme or fairy tale - known as the principal boy. This character is traditionally acted by a casual, tall, elegant young woman.

6. *Grand Dame:*

The central character - the grand dame is a figure of fun and frolic in a frock and is traditionally acted by a male comedian. This comedian is often a famous and celebrated comic in some of the larger productions.

7. *Comics:*

Additional major comic characters backed up by several minor funsters.

8. *The Principal Girl:*

A pretty but weak, compliant young lady much given to being kidnapped by the villain and rescued by the Principal Boy.

9. *The Villain:*

Much booed and jeered by the audience is at once the essence of pure evil and often (for young audiences) a loveable old softie. Just a fraud at heart.

10. *Zany Fantasy:*

An other-worldly, irrational zaniness typified by way of weird costumes, bright colors, fatuous humor, running back and forth, absentminded double-takers and changes of mind on the part of the characters - all of whom are way out of tune in one way or another. Notwithstanding their consistent success on stage, these old traditions of the British stage need not necessarily all be followed in the diverse cultures of the international theater. It may well be that videos, plays or tapes will achieve great success when modified for local audiences. Write to the kindly and friendly old publisher about any such proposed modifications.

––––––––––

TABLE OF CONTENTS

Little Boy Blue

Short Story and Three-Act Pantomime

The Story

It was Christmas Eve, Father Christmas (aka Santa Claus) decided to visit his old flame Ma Kelly. At the same time, the evil Firebug also paid a secret visit to the Kelly household. Firebug snuck around the house and then set it on fire. He also set fire to Santa's white furry bottom.

Father Christmas jumped around like he was possessed by the return of youth before Ma Kelly could put out the fire on Santa's white rim of fur. But while she was dowsing Father Christmas' flames, her house began to catch fire quite badly. The flames shot high into the air and were soon lapping around her stairs and landings.

During this commotion, Firebug grabbed Ma Kelly's daughter Daisy and hauled her off, clamping a set of handcuffs on his own and Daisy's wrists. Daisy screamed, called for help and surenuffski Little Boy Blue ran up to try to rescue her. However, the Firebug trailed Daisy away and hid in the shrubbery.

Ma Kelly grabbed her mobile phone and called the fire brigade, screaming that someone had set fire to her home. At the fire station, the phone was answered by Henry the Eighth who was the Fire Chief at the time. Henry the Eighth asked Ma for some information, "All crimes must be reported first to the police," he said. "They will direct you as to whether you need to call other emergency services. Otherwise, you could be charged with wasting firemen's time – a serious crime."

"Look-ee here Mr. Fire Brigade - Santa Claus has just set my house on fire. What - a case for the police? No, it was an accident. I'm sure it wasn't his fault. What? You say that's for a jury to decide? Are you giving me the runaround? I need to go to the police first? Before you can act? Oh boy, here I come. Wait there for me . . no, I mean YOU come here - don't you understand? My house is on fire!"

"Now there's no need to shout, ma'am," responded Henry, "You know these brief formalities are for the benefit and protection of all taxpayers. I know your house is on fire - you've mentioned that dear lady. Now ma'am, I just need to know for the fair use and purposes ordinance - has this house of yours ever been used to discriminate against any class, color or creed?"

"But my house is burning down. You must come right away," screamed Ma Kelly.

"That would be fine, ma'am," agreed Henry the Eighth, "if your house had just burnt down by accident or lightning but you reported arson and this is a crime – which must first be reported to the police. Obviously, they must be informed right away. We cannot deal with crimes – that is clearly a matter for police. I'm sure you're a fine citizen. I don't need your address, just yet, not until we know if you're eligible for use of our municipal firebrigade. Do get back with me when you've cleared it with the police. You must get a clearance for action from the police."

Little Boy Blue volunteered to help rescue Daisy. So he and Ma Kelly dashed down to the police station to try to speed up the claim for a firetruck.

Police Chief Joshua had recently been elected Sheriff because of his hard line on criminals, including arsonists. "Step One – the Tower. Step Two – Chop off their heads. Step Three – Conduct a fair inquiry to establish any possible guilt." This had been his campaign platform, designed by his friend Fire Chief Henry VIII. He had been elected Police Chief or Sheriff with a landslide vote over Jack the Ripper who had been considered soft on offenders by comparison.

When Ma Kelly and Little Boy Blue arrived at the police station they were ushered in to Police Chief Joshua's office. Joshua immediately started into a barrage of questions. "House set on fire? Who dunit? Don't know? How can I catch the firesetter if you can't name him? Am I supposed to be a mindreader? Only Santa Claus? We'll look up his rap sheet. You want permission to use the firebrigade? Are your taxes paid up? Are you a legitimate citizen? Who owns the house anyway? Oh, you do . . hmm . . too bad. Well, you'll need to identify the suspect. I'll get you to look over some mugshots."

Ma Kelly yelled, "Don't you understand – my house is on fire?"

Police Chief Joshua continued to fill in a few forms. "Let me check your credit rating, Ma, just in case we have to bill you for the use of the firemen or other public services like first aid, clean up, utilities such as hose water and so on."

"My house is on fire," Ma Kelly tore her hair. "My house . . and my daughter Daisy is missing. I need permission to use the fire service."

Joshua neatly filed away his last form, "O very well," he grunted. "I know it's an urgent matter. So go ahead. See Henry the Eighth, but first I need a description of the suspected arsonist – Father Christmas. Was he dressed like a priest?"

"No," replied Ma Kelly, "he was wearing a white beard and a white and red fur suit."

"Great," said Joshua. "We should soon find an eccentric character like that."

A policewoman spoke up, "Police Chief Joshua, I saw him today at a large store downtown. In fact, I saw more than one person dressed like that."

"Go get him," ordered Joshua.

The policewoman left.

"Hold on until we see if you can identify him, Ma Kelly," suggested Joshua.

Ma Kelly and Little Boy Blue were at their wits end. "Her house is on fire," cried Little Boy Blue.

Just then the policewoman returned with half-a-dozen Santa Clauses and lined them up in a row for Ma Kelly to identify one of them.

"No, no, no," moaned Ma, "Father Christmas never set fire to anything."

Little Boy Blue spoke up, "I saw Firebug hanging around Ma's house. I suspect him. He has red skin and face, two horns and a long black tail. He carries a pitchfork and a box of matches."

"Oh, we'll soon find a strange bird like that." Joshua was delighted. "Go ahead and talk to Henry the Eighth."

Ma Kelly and Little Boy Blue dashed across the road to the fire station. "Where's my daughter Daisy?" she asked Fire Chief Henry. "I thought she'd come here? Didn't she report the fire?"

"Oh no ma'am, there was no young woman here. No ma'am - no one reporting a fire here. No, only an horrible old doll on the phone."

"Hey, that was me," responded Ma. "How dare you. Oh dear, I wonder what happened to poor Daisy. Hey, Mr. Fire Chief, my daughter is missing."

"Ma'am this is the fire station," said Fire Chief Henry, "Try across the road at the Police Missing Persons' Desk."

"Don't you dare give me that old runaround again. The police sent me here. My house is burning down. Oh, I'm so upset.," cried Ma Kelly.

"The Police Chief has cleared my complaint for action."

"Oh has he indeed?" replied Henry the Eighth. "Well that's alright for him. But we're the ones who have to clear government regulations and fill in all the forms."

"Why can't you just send a fire engine to my house?" asked Ma Kelly.

"Now it's not as easy as it was in the good old days before the war, ma'am. Why, just forget it my dear lady, your house must be a goner by now. I'm sorry, you know, it's not my fault, it's just that we've so many psychological profiles and forms and reports to fill in, we get lost in the red tape. Really it's the government's fault. Like everything else!"

"Oh, but if Daisy didn't come here, where did she go?" asked Ma Kelly. "Oh, I'm so confused."

"Well, dear lady, next to the police, ahem . . who likely wouldn't help much, the best thing to do about your daughter is to have a good worry about her," suggested Fire Chief Henry. "WORRY, WORRY! If you worry hard enough about a thing, the scientific facts prove, the thing you worry about hardly ever happens. So let's have a good worry - just to head off the bad luck."

"Oh, my poor little Daisy. I'm so worried. First her romance with that Italian rogue got broken up and then she goes missing. Maybe she got burned up in the house. Oh . . boo, hoo, hoo, ohhh my. I'm so worried."

"Yes, I'm so worried about your dear darling daughter. That she's been burnt up. I'm afraid your poor house has been burned down too and that's even worse," said Fire Chief Henry. "Dear, dear, to lose a daughter is bad enough but a whole house. Yes, I'm so worried."

"Oh burnt out! Poor Daisy, oh, oh, oh," cried Ma. "Oh I'm so worried! Poor Daisy gone forever!"

Long about then, Firebug took his captive, Daisy, back to Ma Kelly's house – just to see it burn. He promised her, "I'll let you go if you promise to split the royalties of your book 50/50 with me." He urged Daisy.

Daisy replied, "What book?"

"The story of your kidnap by wicked ole me, of course! Why do you think I'm making all this happen – just to remember it all in my old age! Don't be dumb. I want you to write a book and I want a 50/50, fair shares, honest split between us. O.K?"

"O.K." agreed Daisy.

Firebug set her loose at once.

After Ma Kelly and Little Boy Blue got back home to view the smoldering ruins of the home, Little Boy Blue married Daisy and they all lived happily ever after on Daisy's book – the Firebug, Joshua, Henry the Eighth, Ma Kelly, Daisy and Little Boy Blue.

END OF STORY

Contents of Pantomime

PRODUCTION SPECIFICATIONS

Actors:

Eleven Actors - seven male, four female.

Age Groups:

Audience - all ages, mainly young children.

Actors - all ages.

Music:

Eight old music hall choruses (refrains):

Kelly; Antonio; Little Boy Blue; Henry the Eighth; Joshua; Let's all Go Down the Strand; On Mother Kelly's Doorstep; Daisy, Daisy.

Audience participation. Singalong and responses.

Stage Time:

About 140-150 minutes depending on the treatment of the songs.

Sets:

Four Sets: (1) and (2) Ma Kelly's House - inside and outside; (3) The fire station; (4) The police station. A full Three Act - Seven Scene production.

CHARACTERS

DAISY:

Principal Girl, daughter of Ma Kelly. A pretty, somewhat weak but loveable rescuee.

MA KELLY:

The Grand Dame, traditionally (but not necessarily) acted by a male comedian. An old mater familias, in shawl and bonnet and long skirts, excitable, hard-nosed but sentimental at heart. The central humorous character of the pantomime.

SANTA CLAUS:

Sometimes known as Father Christmas, in red, white-trimmed jacket, hood, trousers and white boots. Bumbling, bungling and shortsighted.

FIREBUG:

A devil-like Villain in red leotards, red shirt, red cloak and red boots. Pointed beard, moustache, and ears. Short or tied back hair. Carries a pitchfork. Sometimes wears short horns.

FIREBUG MINIONS:

These optional extras, male or female, are adults: or children of all ages, who support, follow and dance after the Firebug. They are dressed like the Firebug and join in the chorus at times.

LITTLE BOY BLUE:

The Principal Boy, traditionally (but not necessarily) acted by a tall, elegant girl. The fairytale character who rescues Daisy. Wears a shirt, short jacket, cocked hat and tights, all blue.

FIRE CHIEF HENRY VIII:

In charge of the city fire brigade. A loveable buffoon of a procrastinator and red-tape addict.

DEPUTY DALMATIAN:

A sycophantic assistant to the fire chief, is a dog, i.e. an actor in a white coat with black spots. He salutes frequently and continually repeats phrases such as: Aye, Aye, sir. Anything you say, sir.

CHIEF CONSTABLE JOSHUA:
A not-too-bright follower of all the rules. A suspicious-minded bungler.

SERGEANT SALLY:
Joshua's assistant and the new sweetheart of Antonio.

JACK AND JILL:
Strays from another nursery rhyme, who have lost their way, but who are only trying to be helpful.

ANTONIO:
An ice-cream seller and Daisy Kelly's former suitor - brings ice cream to the cast (and audience?)

SANTA CLAUS EXTRAS:
About half-a-dozen male or female, anonymous department store Father Christmases (or Santa Clauses) much suspected by Chief Constable Joshua, because of their weird red and white garb.

OUTLINE

ACT ONE: MA KELLY'S VISITORS
Scene One: Santa Drops In
Scene Two: Firebug and Little Boy Blue Arrive
ACT TWO: GET THE FIREBUG
Scene One: Fireman Henry VIII
Scene Two: Chief Constable Joshua
Scene Three: Back at Ma Kellys
ACT THREE: AND HAVE FUN AT THE FIRE STATION
Scene One: Daisy, Daisy
Scene Two: Mother Kelly's Doorstep

STORYLINE:
Ma Kelly's visitors get the firebug and have fun at the firestation.

———————

ACT ONE
MA KELLY'S VISITORS
SCENE ONE: SANTA DROPS IN

It is Christmas Eve. Anywhere in the world. The inside of Ma Kelly's living room in her old fashioned farm-style home. Ma Kelly is dressed as a farming wife with a long skirt, bonnet (traditionally the Grand Dame is acted by a male comedian).

Center back there is a huge range of roaring coals and flames surrounded by tongs, a coal shovel and poker set. On the left, a huge bellows and a large caldron on the right. A wide mantelpiece is set above bedecked with Irish bric-a-brac (e.g., pictures of shamrock, or saints, framed prayers, statuettes of leprechauns or crocks of gold).

The rest of the room is cluttered with two rocking chairs with cushions, a couch with cushions, dining table, tablecloth and chairs, also littered with cushions. There is a large dresser or display cabinets also filled with bric-a-brac and thick scatter rugs all over the floor. There is a telephone on a small table, right. Daisy, a young attractive lady in long skirt and blouse is sewing in one of the rocking chairs, head bent over.

Enter Ma Kelly, from right stage, *carrying a saucer of milk.*

MA KELLY: *(preferably in a slight Irish accent)* I'll just leave this outside the door for the fairies. The wee folk can't be left thirsty on Christmas Eve or there's no telling what bad luck they'll bring. *(pauses, listens)*

Now what's that noise in the chimley *(thinks, shakes her head)* no it couldn't be that old fool unless he's in his dotage - sure all the children are long, long gone their own way *(sigh)* except Daisy who's grown up. Aye, it was so nice when Father Christmas used to visit us.

She leaves stage left. *There is the sound of a door opening and closing. Then **Ma Kelly re-enters from left stage** minus the milk. As she does so Santa appears in the* *fireplace in full red and white costume, white beard and carrying a large bag over his shoulder.*

SANTA: *(bumbling and near-sighted as Ma Kelly hides behind a chair playfully)*

KELLY
Sung:　Fast and Funny

l_1　d - d - d - d - d　taw$_1$　l_1 - d
Has　anyone here　seen　Kelly?
l　l　s - f　r - r
K - E - Double L - Y
l_1　d - d - d - d - d　taw$_1$　l_1 - d
Has　anybody here seen　Kelly?
1 - 1 - 1 - 1 - 1　s　f
Kelly from the Isle of　Man.

Has anyone here seen Kelly?
K - E - Double L - Y
Has anybody here seen Kelly?
Kelly from the Isle of Man.

She's not here is she?

AUDIENCE: *(in unison)* YES!

SANTA: *(scanning the audience)* Oh no she's not!

AUDIENCE: *(in unison)* OH YES, SHE IS!

Repeat once or twice.

Santa looks around but Ma Kelly follows behind him giggling as they walk around stage singing: ANYBODY HERE SEEN KELLY?

SANTA: *(to the audience)* She's not here at all, at all, is she?

AUDIENCE: *(in unison)* OH YES, SHE IS!

SANTA: Oh no she's not!

Finally, Ma Kelly steps in front of Santa, her arms akimbo.

MA KELLY: Oh, all right, here I am Father Christmas. Now what is it?

SANTA: Ho, ho, ho. A merry Christmas to all the little ones. See what I've brought you all.

MA KELLY: *(horrified)* What are you doing here you old imbecile? The children are all grown up and all gone except poor Daisy.

DAISY: *(hearing her name and looking up)* Oh, hi Santa.

SANTA: Oh, gee I forgot. Yea, hi Daisy.

A puff of smoke floats across the room.

SANTA: *(to Ma Kelly)* I was hoping you would be pleased to see me, after all we're old friends and you're a widow, maybe we can have a date, you and I, after all my Christmas chores are over.

MA KELLY: *(sniffing suspiciously but unaware of smoke, due to her being caught up in memories)* Oh no, Nicholas *(coyly)* I couldn't allow another suitor in my life ever since my daughter's last gentleman friend so cruelly deserted me.

Ah . . . *(she sighs and dabs her eyes. Then fiercely)* Oh yes, the fiend, the monster, the Italian rascal. Nick, he was a self-employed ice-cream manufacturer. He seemed so respectable. Poor Daisy trusted him .. but he was no good - he left.

SANTA: The brute, but she's better off without the stuff. The ice-cream I mean. It's, why, it's freezing all the time. What was his name? *(outraged)* Tell me his name and I'll never visit his house.

DAISY: O I could never trust another man. O, O, Antonio how could you!

MA KELLY: Anyway, Nicholas, I'm sorry I can't date you, just now. The memory of Antonio is too bitter. *(she hangs her head)* You men are all the same. We trusting girls *(coyly)* only get left behind.

SANTA: That's all right, Mary Majella, maybe next year, when you've all got over the shock.

Light whiffs of smoke still continue to rise from the various parts of the stage.

MA KELLY: *(weeping and angry sings)*

ANTONIO

Sung: Slow and with Humor

m   m   r - r   d s_1
Oh,   Oh,   Antonio
d   d t_1 l_1
He's   gone   away
f   f   m - m   r l_1
Left her   alonio
t_1 r t_1 l_1 s_1 - s_1
All   on   her   onio
m   m   r - r   d s_1
I'd   like   to catch   him   with
d   d t_1 l_1
His   new   sweetheart
d   f   f - f   m - m   r l_1
Then   up   will   go   Antonio
t_1 d   m   r   d
And   his   ice-cream cart

Oh, Oh, Antonio
He's gone away
Left me alonio *(points to Daisy)*
All on her onio
I'd like to catch him with
His new sweetheart
Then up will go Antonio
And his ice-cream cart *(kicks her legs up)*

Repeat with Santa, Daisy and Audience.

<u>Curtain</u>

ACT ONE
MA KELLY'S VISITORS
Scene Two: Firebug and Little Boy Blue Arrive

MA KELLY: *(moaning loudly)* *(aside to Audience)* Do you smell something?

AUDIENCE: *(in unison, prompted by exhorters planted in the audience)* YES.

MA KELLY: Oh, Oh, Antonio - how could you do it? *(to audience again)* Do you smell something?

AUDIENCE: *(in unison)* YES.
Enter the Evil Firebug from front left, hidden to stage by the curtains. Red tights and shirt, pointed beard and ears, red cloak and gloves, holding red pitchfork. Unseen, he creeps up to Santa and sets fire to his rear end.

FIREBUG: *(to Audience, in stage whisper)* No, no. Tell her no. Ha, ha. See how I, the Firebug, set fire to Santa's tail. But he didn't see me. Hee, hee. Soon I'll have the whole house burned down. Say no, no, to Ma Kelly.

MA KELLY: *(to Audience, as she cups her hand to her ear, puzzled)* Do you smell something?

AUDIENCE: *(in unison)* YES, YES.

MA KELLY: *(to audience)* Did someone say 'Yes'?

AUDIENCE: *(loudly, in unison)* YES!

SANTA: Oh gee. Yea *(scratches his head as he sits down on sofa - smoke and sparks or flame flies from the cushion as he sits. He jumps up and hits himself on the bottom and goes to sit on a rocking chair. It too begins to go up in smoke)* I forgot. Heck. Hi, Daisy - these seats of yours are hot for some reason, Ma Kelly. You keep this room well heated.
(he sits on armchair where smoke also appears)

> *By now, it should be clear to the audience that Santa's rear end is smoking and on fire - a fact of which, however, he is still unaware.*

Little Boy Blue

Enter from right-stage, Little Boy Blue,
tall, slim with shoulder-length hair -
traditionally but not necessarily a girl -
dressed in 16th-17th century jacket, cocked
hat and tights, elegant high heeled boots, all
blue. Carrying a French Horn.

DAISY: *(looking up, with interest and admiration)* Who are you?

LITTLE BOY BLUE: I am Little Boy Blue.

MA KELLY: Little? *(looking closely)* Boy? Really! *(thinks)* Hmm, well you're blue alright. *(to Audience)* Oh yes he's blue - very true. I'll give you that. And so am I, I'm blue about *(hand on heart, coyly sighing)* Antonio. He's broken up with Daisy. *Ma Kelly folds her hands and gazes up. Santa looks around, shortsightedly and sniffs and blunders about in the smoke suspiciously.*

DAISY: *(jumping up and curtseying to Little Boy Blue, playfully. It is clear that Little Boy Blue and Daisy take great interest in each other)*

LITTLE BOY BLUE
Sung: Cheerful and Perky

VERSE ONE:

d - d - d   m
Little Boy Blue
    m   f   f   s
Come blow your horn
d   d   d   d   m - m
The sheep's in the meadow
   s   f   r - r t_1
The cow's in the corn
   d   d - d   m
Where's the small boy
  m   m   f - f   f   s
Who looks after the sheep?
  s d^1 - s   s   s - f
He's under the haystack
  m   d - d
Fast asleep.

VERSE ONE:

Little Boy Blue
Come blow your horn
The sheep's in the meadow
The cow's in the corn
Where's the small boy
Who looks after the sheep?
He's under the haystack
Fast asleep.

VERSE TWO:
Little Boy Blue
Come out and play
Hold up your horn
And blow away
Little Boy Blue
Come blow your horn
O lead us all in
A dance today

LITTLE BOY BLUE:
Where is the leading girl? *(Daisy curtsies)*
And the grand dame? *(Ma Kelly curtsies)*
Back in the farm house
Going up in a flame

They laugh and repeat the last four lines - giggling and dancing around. Then Ma Kelly and Santa look around and notice the smoke for the first time. They jump in the air, open-mouthed. Ma Kelly jumps into Santa's arms and screams.

DAISY: *(to Little Boy Blue)*
Little Boy Blue
Come blow your horn
Quick - blow it to get help

Little Boy Blue raises his horn, somewhat casually, to his lips and blows it, in all directions, in a decorative, slow, stylized way.

MA KELLY: *(to Santa)* Oh, you've done this, you old blethering halfwit. You must have caught your tail on fire coming down the chimley.

SANTA: *(feeling his bottom)* Well, I did feel a little hot, come to think of it.

More smoke or flames appear from some of the furniture. Smoke gets a little stronger and everyone begins to panic.

DAISY: Where's the fire extinguisher?

She rushes around the room, looking, her hands outstretched in a searching gesture. Comes close to Firebug, beside the curtains, front-stage left, who, leaving his pitchfork aside, pulls her over by the hand, grabs her by the arm, then puts one hand over her mouth and the other around her waist.

FIREBUG: Ah, ha, my lovely. I'll treat you to a good house burning party. You'll just love it - we'll burn the house down around us to a cinder and you can be Cinderella.

(to audience) You'd like to see Cinderella - yes?

AUDIENCE: *(in unison)* NO.

FIREBUG: *(laughs)* Burnt to a cinderella. Ha, ha.

DAISY: *(weakly but struggling slightly)* Oh, mother. Little Boy Blue. Santa Claus. Help.

Panicking in smoke, Little Boy Blue, Santa and Ma Kelly, do not notice that Daisy is missing.

SANTA: *(to Ma Kelly)* Ma Kelly, no one will hear Little Boy Blue's horn. They won't know what it means. Quick, call the fire brigade on the phone!

Ma Kelly rushes over to phone, picks it up, flustered and panicky.

MA KELLY: *(on phone)* Help. Get me the fire brigade. My house is on fire. My name? What does it matter? Kelly. No . . . KELLY. *(shouting to Little Boy Blue)* Shut up blasting that silly horn - you bluebottle. Can't you see I'm on the phone. <u>Shut up.</u> *(to phone, nicely and softly and politely)* Oh no, not you, sir. I was just speaking to a friend. *(suddenly, screaming and sniffing the smoke.)* Get that fire brigade round here right away. MY HOUSE IS ON FIRE. Of course my city taxes are paid up . . of course my lawns are weed-free, according to city regulation # 2778. No, we're not overcrowding . . . Will you listen to me?

Santa leaves via chimley, waving goodbye.

FIREBUG: *(to Audience)* Ha, ha. I could have 20 houses burnt down before she'd get any help from THAT fire brigade. Ha, ha. All they do is fill in forms and ask questions. They are getting more like the police everyday. Hee, hee. So here's my chance to show my beautiful bride-to-be what a lovely house-burning is all about.

(to audience) She should marry me - shouldn't she?

AUDIENCE: *(in unison)* NO, NO.

FIREBUG: Oh yes, she should.

AUDIENCE: *(in unison)*
OH NO, SHE SHOULDN'T.

FIREBUG: Oh yes, she should.

AUDIENCE: *(in unison)*
OH NO, SHE SHOULDN'T.

FIREBUG: *(muttering to himself)* All they can say is "Oh no she shouldn't." They don't understand.
(brightening with an idea and addressing audience)
She shouldn't try to leave me, should she?
(grins hopefully)

AUDIENCE: *(in unison)*
OH YES, SHE SHOULD.

FIREBUG: *(disappointed)* She should be mine. Yes?

AUDIENCE: *(loudly, in unison)* NO.
Firebug pulls Daisy offstage left as she struggles tearfully and somewhat weakly. Little Boy Blue, Santa and Ma Kelly get obscured by more smoke.

MA KELLY: *(still on phone to fire brigade)* Look-ee here Mr. Fire Brigade - Santa Claus has just set my house on fire. What - a case for the police? No, it was an accident. I'm sure it wasn't his fault. What? You say that's for a jury to decide? Are you giving me the runaround. I need to go to the police first? Before you can act? Oh boy, here I come. Wait there for me . . no, I mean YOU come here - don't you understand? My house is on fire!

<u>Curtain</u>
End of Act One

ACT TWO
GET THE FIREBUG
SCENE ONE: FIREMAN HENRY VIII

This scene takes place in the main hall of the firestation. On the backdrop there are fire engines and a pole down which firemen arrive for their fire engine duties. A spotted Dalmatian is also on the background. At each side, left and right-stage, there are offices, doors and windows and bulletin boards.

The stage is paved with clean tiles so that the stage is fairly clear. Left stage there is a small desk and chair containing books, paper, pen and a telephone hanging off the hook.

As the curtain rises. Fire Chief Henry VIII is standing by the desk with the telephone in hand taking the call from Ma Kelly. He is a large, middle-aged or older man, naive, painstaking, slowmoving and slowerthinking. He is holding a pen and is taking notes. He wears the Fire Chief's helmet and uniform.

FIRE CHIEF HENRY: *(standing but taking notes on the desk)* Hmm. let me see now . . form number seven. Details of request for service - yes, that's it. *(Picking up the form and slowly* *approaching, then raising to his head the hanging phone)*

DEPUTY DALMATIAN: *(an actor in a coat of white with black spots)*   Woof, woof, truth, truth - Aye, Aye, sir. *(he salutes)* Are you O.K. boss?

FIRE CHIEF HENRY: Shut up you dopey dog.

DEPUTY DALMATIAN: Anything you say, sir, but please don't behead me, Henry VIII.

FIRE CHIEF HENRY: Are you still there, Ma'am? *(Puts one finger in his ear and grimaces)* Now there's no need to shout, Ma'am. You know these brief formalities are for the benefit and protection of all taxpayers. I know your house is on fire - you've mentioned that several times dear lady. Now Ma'am, I just need to know for the fair use and purposes ordinance - has this house of yours ever been used to discriminate against any class, color or creed? *(winces)*

Now lady there's no need to get hot under the collar. You know we can't send out city equipment to just anyone. We've already - let me see, yes, covered taxes, weeds in the garden and overcrowding according to city ordinance # 2278. Has fair use? . . Yes . . I think there's just one or two more forms and you've agreed to report it <u>first</u> to the police as a case of suspected arson?

(nods approvingly) I'm sure you're a fine citizen. Your name's Kelly with an 'e' - no I don't need your address just yet, not until we know if you're eligible for use of our municipal firebrigade. My name? Oh, I forgot to introduce myself. I'm Fire Chief Henry VIII. Yes Mrs. Kelly, I'm Henry the Eighth. Really I am. Here, hold on while I prove it to you . . .

Lets phone hang again off the hook, faces the audience, prances up and down proudly and sings.

HENRY THE EIGHTH
Sung: Jaunty and Jolly

```
d   r - d - l₁  taw₁   d    l   f
I'm Henry the Eighth I am
f - f - f   f     s     f   r   f   d
Henry the Eighth I am I am
d   d   r - d   l₁  taw₁  d - d   l      f
I got married to the widow next door
  s     s     s - r   m - f   l    s m d
She'd been married seven times before
 f s - l    f - f   m - f - s
Everyone was a  Henry
 l   taw - taw   s - s   l - l   f - f   s
She wouldn't have a Willie or a  Sam
 d   f   s   l   f   s   m     f - r - d
So I'm her eighth old man named  Henry
 f   s   l - f - l   f   s   m   f
So  it's Henry the Eighth I  am
```

I'm Henry the Eighth I am
Henry the Eighth I am I am
I got married to the widow next door
She'd been married seven times before
Every one was a Henry
She wouldn't have a Willie or a Sam
So I'm her eighth old man named Henry
So it's Henry the Eighth I am

(He pauses, goes back to phone, lifts it up)
Can you still hear me singing. *(cheerfully)* Oh
good, good. *(irritably)* Yes, you told me about

your house. I know. Do get back with me when you've cleared it with the police. You must get a clearance for action from the police.

Oh, but really I must introduce myself in the interests of good official relations with the public - after all we're your <u>servants</u> Ma'am. You're our boss, see. O.K. *(sweetly)* Listen.

He sings again, strutting flamboyantly and manfully up and down the stage while encouraging the audience to join in.

I'm Henry the Eighth I am
Henry the Eighth I am I am
I got married to the widow next door
She'd been married seven times before
Every one was a Henry
She wouldn't have a Willie or a Sam
So I'm her eighth old man named Henry
So it's Henry the Eighth I am

Henry repeats this performance, goes back to phone, lifts it, smiles.

HENRY: Ma'am, did you hear that? That's funny, it's gone dead . . . *(puzzled)* Gee, I could've sworn there was some old doll there complaining about her house . . . catching fire or something . . . *(scratches his head, lifting off his helmet and shaking his head)* Strange, hmm. See . . there you are . . that's the thanks I get for being nice and introducing myself. She's hung up on me . . some people just don't care how they waste the time of hard-working public servants like me . . dear, dear. *(scratches his chin)* Now let me see, what form was I filling in?

He peers shortsightedly at his papers then.

DEPUTY DALMATIAN: I promised my Mum that I would never lose my head.

HENRY: Oh, I must take a break from all this backbreaking work.

DEPUTY DALMATIAN: *(saluting)* Yessir, Nossir. Three bags full sir. You need a rest sir!

*Henry straightens his back - sings **HENRY VIII** again as before. On the final "I am"*

Henry kicks up his legs, throws wide his arms and stares crazily cross-eyed at the audience as

HENRY: Oh, shut up! You dopey dog.

<u>Curtain</u>

ACT TWO
GET THE FIREBUG
Scene Two: Chief Constable Joshua

Scene Two is set in the great hall of the local police station. Left-stage center there is a large desk and chair covered in papers and rolled up wanted posters. This desk belongs to Chief Constable Joshua, a thin older man in blue uniform and police peaked cap, who has a habit of peering suspiciously forward and then jerking back his head, eyes slanted, for a better focus.

On the walls, right-stage and left-stage, are wanted posters of criminals. Covering the whole length of the back stage area in front of the backdrop is a large lineup platform in front of which are a few empty chairs (or benches) facing the platform. Right-stage back is a smaller desk with a few photos and papers on it, belonging to Sergeant Sally.

As the curtain rises, Joshua and Sally, a young lady with long blonde hair, also in blue uniform, are sitting at their desks hunting through papers so assiduously that at first it is difficult to attract their attention.

Sally has a habit of scratching the side of her face occasionally, in wonder at what is going on.

Enter Ma Kelly running from right, followed by Little Boy Blue *with his horn.* Ma *Kelly skids to a halt in center stage and looks at first one and then the other of the two police officers, neither of whom look up. Ma Kelly clears her throat briefly but still neither look up.*

MA KELLY: Hey quick, my house is on fire.

JOSHUA: *(still peering at his work)* This is the police not the fire station. Try across the road.

MA KELLY: But they sent me here. What is this - the runaround? Look, I pay my taxes - my house was just set on fire by Santa Claus.

SERGEANT SALLY: Ah, set on fire - suspicion of arson eh Chief Constable Joshua?

JOSHUA: Yes, quite right Sergeant. *(to Ma Kelly)* Who is the suspect, this Santa fellow?

Joshua rises from his desk suspiciously, notepad and pen in hand and looks Ma Kelly and Little Boy Blue up and down.

MA KELLY: Oh, I'm sure it was just an accident. Santa would never *(places her hand in front of her mouth and titters)* set a fire on purpose. He's such a nice . . but *(getting urgent again)* look MY HOUSE IS ON FIRE, Officer. Can't you send the firebrigade round to my house.

JOSHUA: Certainly, Ma'am, certainly, no problem . . *(Ma Kelly looks relieved and blows)* but first I need to fill in my suspicion of arson report.

MA KELLY: *(to Little Boy Blue)* Suspicion of parson, oh it wasn't the parson I'm sure.

LITTLE BOY BLUE: No, arson. They think the fire was set on purpose.

MA KELLY: Why can't he say so. Oh no *(to Joshua)* it was only an accident, Officer.

JOSHUA: That would be for a jury to decide, Ma'am. Now give me a description of the suspect. *(writing)* Suspect's name?

MA KELLY: This is ridiculous. Santa's name. Oh, Chief Constable, my house is on fire. Can't I get the firebrigade? Please?

JOSHUA: Just a few details, Ma'am. First, name of complainant?

MA KELLY: *(turning to Little Boy Blue in confusion)* Who? Me? You? Santa?

LITTLE BOY BLUE: It's you, Ma Kelly.

JOSHUA: Right, Ma Kelly. Location of house?
    Joshua looks close-eyed, peering at Ma Kelly in suspicion.

MA KELLY: *(turning about in confusion)* Third from the corner.

Joshua writes on his pad, slowly. Sally is also taking notes. Joshua looks up suspiciously, peers at Ma Kelly and jerks his head back.

JOSHUA: Third from corner. *(peering closely again at Ma Kelly and jerking back his head for a better view)* Which corner?

MA KELLY: *(almost in tears and counting on her fingers)* The fifth one along. But see here, my house . . .

JOSHUA: Yes, yes. I heard you, it's on fire. I know - but others need to be protected. *(self-righteously)* My job is to apprehend the suspect . . .

Ma Kelly looks blankly at Little Boy Blue and shrugs.

LITTLE BOY BLUE: He means "catch the villain."

MA KELLY: *(relieved)* Oh, yes *(fixes her hair)* of course. Hey! Santa's no villain.

JOSHUA: Ma Kelly. Full name of suspect - that is <u>VILLAIN</u>?

MA KELLY: *(flustered and confused)* Antonio - why he just up and broke off with my Daisy.

JOSHUA: What's that got to do with the house on fire.

SALLY: Oh, I know such a nice young man *(dreamily)* called Tony.

MA KELLY: *(suspiciously)* Oh, yeah, do you indeed? If I catch you with that Italian two-timer, why I'll . . . *(she lifts her boot)*

Joshua is speechless and open-mouthed and peers, jerks his head back.

LITTLE BOY BLUE: Ma Kelly, the Chief Constable has just one more question. Don't you sir?

JOSHUA:*(recovering himself)* Name of suspect?

LITTLE BOY BLUE: *(to Ma Kelly, in stage whisper)* He means Santa.

MA KELLY: Yes, Santa Claus - sometimes known as Father Christmas.

JOSHUA: *(writing it all down with satisfaction)* Good. Got him now! *(mumbling as he writes)* Alias Father Christmas, eh? Masquerading as a priest, eh? The rogue . . . *(to Ma Kelly)* Description of villain - I mean suspect.

MA KELLY: *(incredulous)* Don't you know what he looks like?

JOSHUA: *(irritably)* How would I know? I wasn't there, was I?

MA KELLY: *(confused and scratching her head)* No, I suppose not. O just, he was just dressed as usual.

JOSHUA: *(at a slight loss)* Oh as usual eh?

MA KELLY: Yes.

JOSHUA: What . . dark suit and tie? Usual type suspect sets fire to third house from the fifth corner over, dressed as usual. Hmm, that doesn't give us much scope for intelligent police work.

MA KELLY: *(sardonically)* No it doesn't, does it. Certainly not. *(shakes her head)* Look, I meant as usual for Santa Claus - see - red suit with white fur trim and a white beard - Father Christmas - get it?

JOSHUA: *(pleased)* Ah, now we're getting somewhere. A unique character like that should be easy to find, eh?

SALLY: *(interrupting and scratching her face)* Chief, I agree with you. Downtown today I saw an old codger just like that . . .

JOSHUA: You saw this priest masquerader who looked like <u>that</u>?

SALLY: Yes he was sort of fat . . . *(she holds out her hands)*

Ma Kelly is almost in tears.

JOSHUA: *(to Sally)* Well, what are you waiting for? Bring him in on suspicion quick . . right now.

SALLY: Yes SIR. *(salutes and **leaves stage right**)*

MA KELLY: *(agitated and prancing up and down)* All right, Chief Joshua, now you've got your report will you tell the firebrigade to come out and save my poor house - you see my house . . its . . . *(weeps bitterly)* Oh, oh, oh . . .

JOSHUA: *(absently)* Yes, I know, it's on fire . . . *(he shuffles some papers)* This suspect, this fat red and white guy, did he strike you?

MA KELLY: *(still weeping)* No, no, he's only a kind old man.

JOSHUA: *(disappointed)* Well, that's a pity in a way - if he had hit you we could have got you into the woman's shelter, hmm . . too bad . . no house, no shelter . . let me see . . you're upset, badly upset.

Ma Kelly nods tearfully, hopefully.

MA KELLY: *(with hope)* My house . . .

JOSHUA: *(interrupting her)* Yes, it's on fire - that must have been a great trauma to you. I'll put your name down for counseling. We have a police psychologist here who is just terrific, why she could take a nincompoop apart in 30 seconds.

LITTLE BOY BLUE: *(boldly)* Lookee here sir, Ma Kelly does not need a psychologist. What she needs is a firebrigade.

MA KELLY: *(brightening)* Oh well said, son, thank you.

Joshua now looks at Little Boy Blue with new-found suspicion.

JOSHUA: How do I know you didn't set the fire, boy?

MA KELLY: Oh, he didn't. He only arrived later. I can swear he didn't.

JOSHUA: O can you now? How can you be so sure? Maybe you have inside information you're not giving me? Maybe <u>you</u> set the fire yourself to collect the insurance money? Eh?

MA KELLY: *(weeping)* It wasn't insured.

JOSHUA: *(sternly)* Ma'am do you know it's an offense not to have third party insurance. Now, if you want to burn your house down that's your business. But innocent visitors must be protected. Subsection 2 of Section 5 of City Law 33247 states clearly . . .

Enter Sally from left, interrupting Joshua and saluting him, smartly.

SERGEANT SALLY: Chief Joshua.

JOSHUA: Yes, Sergeant. Have you caught him?

SALLY: Well . . yes sir, in a manner of speaking.

JOSHUA: *(delighted and preening himself and jerking suspiciously offstage left, rubbing his hands)* Bring him in. *(to Ma Kelly)* We have your suspect, Ma Kelly.

MA KELLY: *(ranting and stamping her feet and thumping her fists in the air)* I don't want a suspect. I just want the fire put out.

Sally hesitates.

SALLY: Chief, I have a shock for you.

JOSHUA: *(sternly)* Bring in the suspect!

Sally goes to left-stage entrance and crooks her finger. A Santa Claus looks into the stage and at the audience, timidly.

SALLY: *(barking out orders, army style)* All right, enter station! Quick march.

As a line of phony looking, guilty faced Santa Claus' (4, 5, 6 or more) slink in miserably, looking around scared and nervous, carrying bags over their shoulders

Follow me. Right wheel.
As they follow her to the steps of the line-up platform and climb the steps and line up facing the audience.

Present bags.

As they hold their bags in front of them and stand still.

Company halt. All right Santas, at ease.
The Santas droop down and look extremely intimidated and miserable. Joshua ushers Little Boy Blue and Ma Kelly over to the seats facing the line up. Sergeant Sally stands in front of the lineup, saluting Joshua.

JOSHUA: *(to Ma Kelly and holding up a magnifying glass towards the lineup)* Take a look - pick out the villain.

He remembers something, goes to his desk, returns with a card which he reads from stiltedly and myopically and mechanically

Oops, I meant to say - from this group of randomly selected diverse individuals, is there any one who closely resembles the alleged perpetrator of the crime. *(looks around and smirks with great self-satisfaction)*

Pauses till audience stops laughing.

MA KELLY: *(to Little Boy Blue)* What's he mean?

LITTLE BOY BLUE: He means - pick out the villain.

MA KELLY: The villain. Santa is no villain. It must have been an accident. But anyway the real Father Christmas isn't here. These are just department store phonies. Can't you see they're fakes?

JOSHUA: Ah, ha, phonies. Sergeant Sally arrest them all for - let me see - impersonating a fat man in a red and white suit.

SALLY: But Chief. They actually are fat men in red and white suits.

JOSHUA: *(blustering and at a loss)* Oh, well. Send them home, then let their wives arrest them. What do they think this place is anyway? A Santa Claus rest-home. Why, when I first came on the force, we would have arrested those layabouts for public begging or limping, landlubbering, loping, landloping, loitering, looting, layabouting, leering, laughing, lingering, lagering, louting, lunatiking, loopie looing. *(aside - get it?)* What the "L", arrest them for anything, anything.

The Santas begin to file out the way they came in but do not yet leave the stage.

MA KELLY: Look Chief Joshua, give us a policeman to help us fight the fire and give me permission to go fetch the firebrigade. We may be in time to save part of my house. I think my daughter Daisy may have gone to the firestation. *(looks around)* I don't see her here.

JOSHUA: *(morosely, but weakening)* Oh, Ma Kelly, it's tough not to make an arrest . . .

SALLY: O go on *(winningly and coaxingly)* Chief Joshua - do let me go and help.

All sing winsomely and pleadingly, JOSHUA, with help from the Santas.

JOSHUA
Sung: Cheerful and Rousing

d   d - t₁ - d   d - t₁ - d
Oh Joshua, Joshua
d - r   m   l m   s   f   d
Sweeter than lemon squash you are
 l   l   l   s   r
Eee, by gosh you are
 s   l - s   l - s   f
It's Joshu - osh - uah

Oh Joshua, Joshua
Sweeter than lemon squash you are
Eee, by gosh you are
(winking at audience and jerking thumbs at Joshua)
It's Joshu - osh – uah

JOSHUA: *(flattered)* Well, very well. Sergeant Sally - you go with Little Boy Blue to the site of the fire and see what you can do and Ma Kelly, go tell the Fire Chief Henry the Eighth *(smugly and self-satisfied)* that I've, ah, ha, released the report for action. *(hands on hips, he beams on them munificently)*

OTHERS: About time!

Little Boy Blue

Santas and Joshua are joined by a chorus dressed for a walk down The Strand in hats jackets and boots. Arm and arm with the Santas, the Chorus dance or walk around the stage or around the theatre. The audience joins in as they sing:

LET'S ALL GO DOWN THE STRAND
Sung: Happy and Marching

f   d   taw₁ l₁   taw₁   d
Let's all go down the Strand
r   l₁ s₁ f₁ s₁   l₁
Let's all go down the Strand
r - r - r   m   r - d   l₁
Put your hats and jackets on
r   r - r   m - r   d l₁
Tell your mother you'll not be long
f   d   r   l₁   s₁   f₁
Let's all go down The Strand.

Let's all go down the Strand
Let's all go down the Strand
Put your hats and jackets on
Tell your mother you'll not be long
Let's all go down The Strand.

Ma Kelly *beats the air, writhes and twists in frustration then* *dashes offstage right* *while* *Sally and Little Boy Blue dash off the stage left.*

Joshua, the Chorus and the Santas continue to dance or walk around as audience joins in.

Curtain

ACT TWO
GET THE FIREBUG

SCENE THREE: BACK AT MA KELLYS

The scene is set outside the still smoking house of Ma Kelly. The house is just beginning to blaze up with some flames leaping from windows and roof. It has a large slab of stone as a front porch, all of which is seen on the backdrop, while the rest of the stage represents the garden outside the house with bushes, flowerbeds and trees.

There is a path up center-stage leading from the house's large stone porch to the roadway. All of the upstage, or apron if any, from left to right, is a roadway and sidewalk (or pavement). The front and center-stage should be kept fairly clear for action.

Enter Firebug, *right as before, a red pitchfork in his right hand threatens his captive - Daisy - who walks in front of him and beside him,* *but always within reach. Surrounding them and following (depending on the numbers) are Firebug's minions. These may be children or adult actors but should all be smaller than Firebug. They are dressed like him but do not carry pitchforks. They crouch down at times, moving their red-gloved hands up and down, imitating flames but also in order to give the audience a clearer view of Daisy and Firebug.*

The numbers of Firebug minions is discretionary - (2-12) is suggested - depending on the size of the production and stage area available. If extras are not available, the minions may be omitted entirely without great loss of action or plot but in this case Firebug will be seen to exercise more close control over his captive Daisy since he will be without help from his minions. In any case, Firebug and his minions strut up and down the center garden. Firebug takes hold of Daisy by the arm.

FIREBUG: *(to audience)* Ah, ha. *(twirling his whiskers)* What a warm welcoming I have made and here I have the beautiful Daisy - her mother doesn't even realize that she's gone - soon she will be my bride. Don't you agree?

AUDIENCE: *(in unison)* NO. *(they hiss)*

FIREBUG: *(taken aback)* You want her to escape my clutches eh?

AUDIENCE: *(in unison)* YES. *(they boo)*

FIREBUG: Hee, hee. Well, she never will. By the time Ma Kelly gets through all the red-tape I'll have Daisy safely down in Firebugland from which *(he laughs)* from which she can never escape. Ha, ha. Nothing can ever defeat me except cold and icy water and Henry the VIII can never get here on time. Hee, hee. He's too fond of form-filling and singing about himself - hee, hee. I'm safe, safe, ain't I.

Daisy weeps and shakes her head.

AUDIENCE: *(in unison)* NO. *(hisses and boos)*

FIREBUG: *(looking first at Daisy and then around at audience suspiciously)* Why, no? You like me don't you? Show me how much you're on my side - just to encourage dear little Daisy, my future wife! *(he smiles with phony winsomeness and places his hand behind his ear, to hear better)*

AUDIENCE: *(in unison)* BOO. BOO. BOO.

FIREBUG: *(frowning and upset and grabbing Daisy by the arm)* In that case I'll just be off to Firebugland!

AUDIENCE: *(in unison)* BOO. BOO. BOO.

Firebug waves his hand, dismissing the audience and turns away, crouching down.

FIREBUG: Bah! Ahh, who is this coming? *(to audience)* Silence! Or I will run her *(Daisy)* through with this pitchfork.

AUDIENCE: *(led by **Little Boy Blue** as he **enters left**)* *(in unison)* BOO, BOO, BOO.

***Enter Little Boy Blue**, horn hanging at his waist and Sergeant Sally, slowly and stealthily from left, tiptoeing towards*

Firebug and his party (center), who are hidden by garden bushes.

SERGEANT SALLY: *(peering over a bush)* It's Firebug. We've tried to catch him for a long time and look, he's got Daisy as a captive. *(loudly and shaking her fist)* Oh, the scoundrel!

FIREBUG: *(glaring around suspiciously)* Who goes there? Friend or foe?

LITTLE BOY BLUE: *(taking out his horn and holding it up to his mouth)* Foe!

Firebug and his minions put Daisy behind them, crouch down and approach Little Boy Blue and Sally in a bold manner.

SERGEANT SALLY: *(tearfully and afraid)* Oh Little Boy Blue, why, why do you have to be so honest?

FIREBUG: *(to Audience)* Ha, ha, it's only Little Boy Blue and Sergeant Sally; not a fireman in sight.

LITTLE BOY BLUE: *(to Sally)* Don't be afraid of Firebug, a little ice cold water will soon knock him over.

SERGEANT SALLY: *(fearfully)* I know - but we haven't got any! And Henry VIII is probably looking at himself in the mirror!

Firebug and his minions jump out of the bushes just in front of Little Boy Blue and Sally. Firebug holds his pitchfork aloft; ready to strike. Little Boy Blue and Sally draw back slightly as Little Boy Blue sounds his horn.

SALLY: Help! Get the police, someone.

FIREBUG: But you are the police, Sally, eh?

SALLY: *(fearfully)* Oh, I meant the nasty ones. HELP.

Little Boy Blue and Sergeant Sally continue to retreat towards left stage as Firebug, holding out his pitchfork, glowering fiercely, advances towards them, followed by his minions.

Enter right front stage, Antonio, riding on his tricycle/ice-cream box. (the ice-cream box is part of his tricycle and is mounted on two large front bicycle wheels) Antonio is dressed in a white suit, white shirt, blue tie, white or light straw hat, white socks and shoes. He is young, slim, dark haired with a short neat hairstyle and carefully trimmed black moustache and short sideburns. A neat and trim figure, he sails in self-confidently across the front of the stage (on the roadway).

He smiles and raises his heavy dark eyebrows at the audience. Sitting bolt upright, he waves and raises his hat to the audience as he rolls past Firebug without taking the bug under his notice. While a real tricycle is not ruled out, safety would seem to prefer a simulated ice cream cart across front-stage, especially if the apron is being used.

Firebug and his minions crouch down behind bushes, center left, in puzzlement and doubt as Antonio (on either the real or the simulated tricycle) rolls past them and brakes to a sudden halt beside Little Boy

Little Boy Blue

Blue and Sally at extreme left stage where they have just retreated.)

ANTONIO: *(to Little Boy Blue)* Did you sound your horn, sir, can I get you an ice-cream? *(then seeing Sally)* Oh, hello Sally. I thought you were on duty.

> *He dismounts and bows to Sally, hat in hand and kisses her hand, nods to Little Boy Blue*

SALLY: I <u>am</u> on duty, Antonio, but I have bad news for you. Firebug has burnt down Ma Kelly's house and he's got your old girlfriend Daisy kidnapped over there. *(she points center)*

ANTONIO: *(looking towards center stage where Firebug and minions are crouched)* Daisy, where are you?

DAISY: *(faintly)* Help, Antonio.

ANTONIO: *(shouting)* Hold on, Daisy, we'll get you out!

FIREBUG: *(rising up, horribly - loudly and slowly)* Oh no you won't.

AUDIENCE: *(in unison, loudly and slowly)* OH YES WE WILL.

FIREBUG: Oh no you won't.

AUDIENCE: *(in unison, led by Little Boy Blue)* OH YES WE WILL.

FIREBUG: *(triumphantly)* Ha, ha. Nothing but cold ice water can turn me back and *(nastily and smugly)* they haven't got any. Ya, ya, ya. *(puts out his tongue)*

Audience hisses and boos.

ANTONIO: *(opening his ice-cream box and addressing Firebug teasingly)* I have something close. How about some ice Firebug?

Little Boy Blue, Sally and Antonio begin to throw ice at Firebug. He draws his cloak around him in discomfort at the cold. They shower Firebug with ice and then throw blobs of ice-cream at him and his minions.

Firebug advances once or twice towards his assailants but is turned back each time by a shower of ice and ice cream. The cold begins to cower and discomfort him but he fights bravely on. At this point it should not be quite certain, at least to the (young) audience, who is going to win.

The house is still smoking with the occasional flame shooting out. It appears that it would still be possible to save most of the house at this point.

<u>Curtain</u>
End of Act Two

ACT THREE
AND HAVE FUN AT THE FIRESTATION
SCENE ONE: DAISY, DAISY

This scene is set in the main hall of the firestation as in Act Two - Scene One. Fire Chief Henry VIII is already on stage, looking at himself in a hand mirror, strutting and preening himself cheerfully. He then dances up and down, lifting his knees and hands high in the air, his head thrown back smugly.

Henry VIII sings:
    I'm Henry the Eighth I am
    Henry the Eighth I am I am
    I got married to the widow next door
    She'd been married seven times before
    Every one was a Henry
    She wouldn't have a Willie or a Sam
    So I'm her eighth old man named Henry

So it's Henry the Eighth I am, I'm Henry the Eighth, I am and so on.

As Henry's song comes to an end, **Enter Ma Kelly** *from right, bustling and in a great fluster of a hurry.*

MA KELLY: *(looking around)* Where's my daughter Daisy? I thought she'd come here? Didn't she report the fire?

HENRY: Oh no Ma'am, there was no young woman here. *(shakes head)* No Ma'am - no one reporting a fire here. *(remembers)* No, only an horrible old doll on the phone . . .

MA KELLY: Hey, that was me . . how dare you. *(pauses)* Oh dear, I wonder what happened to poor Daisy. Hey, Mr. Fire Chief, my daughter is missing.

HENRY: Ma'am this is the fire station. Try across the road at the Police Missing Persons' Desk.

MA KELLY: Don't you dare give me that old runaround again. The police sent me here. My house is burning down. Oh, I'm so upset. The Chief Constable has cleared my complaint for action.

HENRY: Oh has he indeed? Well that's alright for him. But we're the ones who have to clear government regulations and fill in all the forms.

MA KELLY: Why can't you just send a fire engine to my house?

HENRY: *(kindly)* Now it's not as easy as it was in the good old days before the war, Ma'am. You know I think I recognize you, Ma'am,

from somewhere. Why, you're Mother Kelly
- aren't you? Yes?

MA KELLY: Yes I'm Ma Kelly and I was on
the phone about a half hour ago about my
house burning down.

HENRY: When we were kids, why we used to
have such good old clean fun at your house.
(Sings MA KELLY)

ON MOTHER KELLY'S DOORSTEP
Sung: Slow and Nostalgic

f   l - s - m - d l_1 t_1
On Mother Kelly's doorstep
  m   d - r - m   *s*
Down Paradise Row
  d^1 l t s - s
We used to gather
  r - r   f m *d*
In the long ago
   s   l t d^1 d^1
We've wandered far now
  d - d - d   r m   *s*
But we wish we could go
  d^1 - d^1 l - l   t - t   s s
Back to Mother Kelly's doorstep
   r   f - f - m   *d*
Down Paradise Row

Little Boy Blue

On Mother Kelly's doorstep
Down Paradise Row
We used to gather
In the long ago
We've wandered far now
But we wish we could go
Back to Mother Kelly's doorstep
Down Paradise Row

Ma Kelly keeps interrupting his song with cries of "my house is burning down."

MA KELLY: *(stamping her feet)* How can you sing while my house burns to the ground? You're worse than the Firebug. You're as bad as big gubmint. You're driving me insane.

HENRY: Why, just forget it my dear lady, your house must be a goner by now. *(casually)* I'm sorry, you know, it's not my fault, it's just that we've so many psychological profiles and forms and reports to fill in, we get lost in the red tape. Really it's the government's fault. *(to audience)* Like everything else!

MA KELLY: Oh, but if Daisy didn't come here, *(walking up and down agitated)* where did she go? Oh, I'm so confused.

HENRY: Well, dear lady *(kindly)* next to the police *(stops)* ahem . . who likely wouldn't help much, the best thing to do about your daughter is to have a good worry about her.

MA KELLY: A what?

HENRY: WORRY, WORRY! If you worry hard enough about a thing, the scientific facts prove, the thing you worry about hardly ever happens. So let's have a good worry - just to head off the bad luck.

Henry frowns and walks up and down ostensibly worrying, moaning and groaning - Ma Kelly does likewise

MA KELLY: Oh, my poor little Daisy. I'm so worried. *(moans)* First her romance with that Italian rogue got broken up and then she goes missing. Maybe she got burned up in the house. Oh . . boo, hoo, hoo *(groans)* ohhh my. I'm so worried.

They walk up and down wringing their hands as they worry.

HENRY: *(on point of tears)* Yes, I'm so worried about your dear darling daughter. That she's been burnt up. I'm afraid your poor house has been burned down too and that's even worse. Dear, dear, to lose a daughter is bad enough but a whole house. Yes, I'm so worried.

MA KELLY: *(breaking into a loud wail)* Oh burnt out! Poor Daisy, oh, oh, oh. *(she weeps loudly and shakes her head at audience)* Oh I'm so worried! *(cries loudly, open-mouthed)* Poor Daisy gone forever!

Henry snivels.

HENRY: Oh, I worry so much about all that.

At this point Ma Kelly and Henry are standing somewhere in mid-stage, leaving the way clear for the next entrances.

Enter Antonio in similar fashion to his previous entrance, sailing across front-stage on his bike from right to left, grinning and raising his hat to audience, but this time he has in tow, a wheeled cage, hooked to the front or the back of his ice-cream box bike, containing a sullen Firebug. He is followed by Sergeant Sally, frowning and writing copiously in her notebook. Little Boy Blue blows his horn triumphantly and Daisy curtsies prettily to her mother and then embraces her. (Ma Kelly)

HENRY: *(cheerfully to Ma Kelly)* See, I told you that there's nothing works as well as a good WORRY. Why, the worst will never happen if only you worry about it hard enough. *(he dances up and down the stage smirking, seizing up his hand mirror and admiring himself)*

Oh, I'm Henry the Eighth, I am. *(one line only to Ma Kelly)* Worrying is the surest way to keep out of trouble. What you worry about almost never happens.

MA KELLY: *(to Daisy)* Isn't that Antonio, who left you? Oh, I'll kick his pants. *(she starts for Antonio)*

DAISY: *(restraining her)* Mother, I told you Tony and I just broke up - it was mutual. We're still friends, besides *(in stage whisper, looking at Little Boy Blue who is unaware of the conversation)* I've met another person who is <u>very</u> interesting *(in stage whisper)* shush . . it's Little Boy Blue, but he doesn't know how I feel. *(loudly)* You know it was Antonio who helped us catch Firebug, the same Firebug who set fire to Santa's bottom so that Santa would set fire to our house.

MA KELLY: Oh, that's very complicated - tell me it again, oh never mind. I can see Firebug's the culprit. I'll wring his neck.

DAISY: Relax mother, he's in a cage.

Ma Kelly approaches Firebug aggressively.

MA KELLY: So you it was who burnt my house down. Why I've a good mind to hand you over to the social worker.

FIREBUG: Oh, please Ma Kelly, don't do that, let me off with just handing me over to the police, please. I'm sorry I did it. Let me off with going to jail - say do you? *(holding out a cigarette)* Do you? Do you?

MA KELLY: Do I what?

FIREBUG: *(pathetically)* Do you have a light?

MA KELLY: Oh, you've a cheek! *(she aims to kick his cage)*

FIREBUG: All I want is a light, a match to feed my can't-help-it, tragic, lifelong, addiction to smoking.

MA KELLY: How dare you ask me for a light after you burnt down my house.

FIREBUG: *(weeping)* I can't help it. I was badly treated as a wee boy, a mere child . . .

MA KELLY: *(interrupting in mock, sarcastic sympathy)* Well, ain't that too bad. I do feel so sorry for you - but now you're going to be badly treated even worse, now that you've grown up into a real, life-size <u>firebug</u>. Take that. *(she kicks his cage, hurts her foot and hops around)*

FIREBUG: *(waving his cigarette around)* Has anyone got a light?

AUDIENCE: *(in unison, led by Little Boy Blue)* NO . . .

FIREBUG: *(to the audience - his hand shaking)* You don't want me to suffer from the shakes, do you? *(he trembles)*

AUDIENCE: *(in unison)* YES.

> *Firebug rattles his cage and yells.*
> *Little Boy Blue moves closer to Daisy and bows to her in background, center-stage. Henry looks at himself in mirror. Antonio gets off his bicycle and nods conversationally to Sergeant Sally who smiles at him and puts away her notebook.*
> ***Enter from left Jack and Jill,** who have lost their way from another pantomime.*

They are dressed as in the popular nursery rhyme books in 16th century English farm style clothes. Jack wears shirt, thick belt, pantaloons, socks and heavy boots. Jill wears long hair, a blouse, thick skirt to below the knee, socks and boots. Between them they hold a heavy wooden bucket filled with water. They approach Ma Kelly. The others watch in awe.

JACK AND JILL: *(in unison as one recognizing an acquaintance and smiling).* Hello, Ma Kelly.

MA KELLY: *(to audience)* Why it's Jack and Jill.

AUDIENCE: *(in unison)* HURRAY! HURRAY! HURRAY!

MA KELLY: *(suddenly concerned, to Jack and Jill)* But what are you doing here? This is the Little Boy Blue Show.

JACK AND JILL: We've come to play in the pantomime. Listen . .

JACK: Jack and Jill went up the hill.

JILL: To fetch a pail of water.

JACK: I fell down and hurt my crown.

JILL: And I came tumbling after.

MA KELLY: *(prancing up and down and still concerned, puzzled)* You should have been more careful up that hill. Look, what panto were you to appear in?

JACK AND JILL: Why, Jack and Jill, of course.

MA KELLY: *(unthinking)* Oh, of course. *(then suddenly jumping in the air)* What? Jack and Jill. Look. *(waves hand at Little Boy Blue)* This is Little Boy Blue. See?

JACK AND JILL: *(casually)* Oh, hi there Little Boy Blue.

MA KELLY: *(tearing her hair)* I'm not introducing him! Look, you two are in the wrong pantomime. See? This is the Little

Boy Blue pantomime. You should have gone to the Palladium - that's where you're supposed to be appearing, see? The Palladium *(stops in doubt)* or is it the Alambra. Here *(gives Jack money)* take this sixpence and here's thruppence for you Jill. Go get a taxi to the err . . Palladium - see, just tell the taxidriver - Jack and Jill Pantomime *(Jill begins to cry)*. What's the matter?

JILL: You gave him sixpence . . and just because I'm a girl. Oh, boo, hoo, hoo. I only got thruppence.

MA KELLY: *(at her wits end)* Oh, here's another thruppence for you, Jill. *(gives her money)* See, two thruppences *(two sets of three pennies)* make sixpence*, same as him.

JILL: But he got sixpence not two thruppences.

MA KELLY: *(giving Jill more money)* It's the same thing. All right here's sixpence. *(Jill brightens)*. Oh, you, you'll do well in the world.

* other currency equivalents include 4 x 25 cents = 1 dollar or 2 x 50 new pence = 1 pound.

All right. Cheerio, Jack and Jill, remember you're appearing at the Alambra or *(doubtful)* is it the Lyceum? *(suddenly changing her mind and thinking).* Here, lend me that a moment. *(takes bucket from Jack and Jill and approaches Firebug)* Firebug, this is real cold-as-ice mountain water straight out of a hilltop spring. See? Would you like a little drink - just a nice cool <u>little</u> drink.

FIREBUG: Oh no, please Ma Kelly.

MA KELLY: *(to Audience)* Should I?

AUDIENCE: *(in unison)* YES.

FIREBUG: *(to Audience)* You wouldn't let her do that to me, a poor old man in a cage would you?

AUDIENCE: *(in unison)* YES.

MA KELLY: *(to Audience, as in some doubt)* Perhaps I should let him off? After all, he did say he was sorry. Should I let him off?

AUDIENCE: *(in unison)* NO.

Ma Kelly quickly throws water over the Firebug (who cringes) quickly gives the pail back to Jack and Jill and smacks her hands together as a sign of work well done. Jack and Jill take their empty bucket back and leave the stage, waving goodbye to the Audience.

OTHERS ON STAGE: *(waving)* Bye, bye, Jack and Jill.

JACK AND JILL: *(leaving)* Cheerio, Little Boy Blue.

Little Boy Blue, who has been standing beside Daisy, steps forward to face Ma Kelly, resolutely. Antonio and Sergeant Sally move together to the one side to watch. They hold hands inconspicuously in anticipation of Little Boy Blue's remarks. Little Boy Blue proceeds to approach Ma Kelly.

LITTLE BOY BLUE: Ma Kelly. *(he looks at Daisy who drops her eyes)* With your permission there's a question I'd like to ask your daughter.

MA KELLY: *(pretending innocence to Audience)* Oh, I wonder what question that could be. *(with dissimulation, twiddling her thumbs and raising her eyebrows)* She's no good at sums or hard questions.

LITTLE BOY BLUE: Oh, but it's not a hard question . . .

MA KELLY: *(coyly and squirming around shyly)* Oh really. *(puts her index finger to her chin and turns away)* Oh, I wonder what question that could be!

> *Henry looks at himself in mirror and smirks. Antonio raises his eyebrows and hat to Audience, as before, and turns to smile at Sergeant Sally.*

LITTLE BOY BLUE: I'd like to ask her to marry me.

Others smile approvingly.

MA KELLY: *(still shyly)* Well, why don't you go ahead and just ask her. *(she smiles with the others, turns from side to side coyly, hand on chin, looking at the Audience, then turns, hands clasped to look at Little Boy Blue and Daisy).*

LITTLE BOY BLUE: *(approaching Daisy, taking her hand and kneeling down - Sings:)*

DAISY, DAISY
Sung: Cheerfully

s m *d* s₁
Daisy, Daisy
l₁ t₁ d l₁ d *s₁*
Give me your answer do
r s *m* d
I'm half crazy
l₁ t₁ d r m *r*
All for the love of you
m f m r s - m r - d
It won't be a stylish marriage
r m d - l₁ d l₁ s₁
I can't afford a carriage
s₁ d m *r*
But you'll look sweet
s₁ - d m *r*
Upon the seat
m f s - m - d r s₁ *d*
Of a bicycle built for two

Little Boy Blue

Daisy, Daisy
Give me your answer do
I'm half crazy
All for the love of you
It won't be a stylish marriage
I can't afford a carriage
But you'll look sweet
Upon the seat
Of a bicycle built for two

Others join in a second rendering as Little Boy Blue, about center-stage, stands up, takes Daisy's hand and all walk or dance about except for Firebug who still cringes and sulks in his cage.

Curtain

ACT THREE
AND HAVE FUN AT THE FIRESTATION
SCENE TWO: MA KELLY'S DOORSTEP

Same as in previous scene. As the curtain rises, the same characters are in much the same positions as at the previous closing curtain. This scene is the FINALE, which ties up a very few loose ends and brings together the whole cast for a last-minute song. Audience should join in. A leader to feed the spoken words, line by line, to the Audience (e.g., Little Boy Blue) and/or large printed cards, will be needed.

Enter the real Santa Claus, *as in Act One - Scene One, from left, running scared, looking over his shoulder. He sings:* **KELLY** (see p. 24)

Has anyone here seen Kelly?
K - E - Double L - Y
Has anybody here seen Kelly?
Kelly from the Isle of Man.

He dashes around looking for a place to hide and finally selects Fire Chief Henry's desk, which he crouches behind, looking out fearfully.

SANTA: Oh hide me. Don't tell. There's a homicidal maniac after me with a magnifying glass threatening to lock me up for life. Hushhhhh . . .

Enter Chief Constable Joshua.. He dashes into middle-stage, waving his glass around, peering at one and all, drawing back in his "double take" manner and then squinting forward myopically again.

JOSHUA: All right you collaborators - you accessories after the fact - now I've cornered the real, the true Santa, the villain *(to Ma Kelly)* don't hide him, don't shield him. He burnt down the house of a poor horrible old ugly half-witted woman.

MA KELLY: *(angry)* Oh the nit, hey that was my house! How dare you? *(kicks Joshua)* on the shin. *(he hops around)* You . . you poor man's Sherlock Holmes - you cheap plastic imitation of Inspector Maigret. The real Santa didn't burn down my house. *(pointing to Firebug)* He did! Arrest him.

Joshua does his usual squint-eyed doubletake and withdrawal at Firebug - who cowers scared in a corner of his cage. Joshua then runs off center-stage to just beside where Santa is hiding and gapes in fear, open-mouthed at Firebug. Joshua turns to Santa without recognizing him.

JOSHUA: *(to Santa)* What, what is that thing in that cage?

SANTA: *(coming out of hiding and holding out his hands together palms up to be handcuffed)* I don't know. All I know is, it isn't on my list of good children.

JOSHUA: *(squinting and recoiling at Santa's hands)* What do you want, a tip for evading me all over half the rooftops in town?

SANTA: You mean you're not going to arrest me?

JOSHUA: Of course not. *(gruffly)* Hasn't Ma Kelly just identified this critter there as the villain. *(points to Firebug and shudders).*

LITTLE BOY BLUE: *(flattering)* Oh thank you Joshua. We all knew you would find the true villain in the end and now all you have to do is arrest him.

Joshua trembles and approaches Firebug shortsightedly. Firebug, sensing a coward, snarls and Joshua retreats.

JOSHUA: *(to Audience)* You don't expect me to arrest him single-handed, do you?

AUDIENCE: *(in unison)* YES.

JOSHUA: Well I'll just *(gulps and hesitates)* arr . . arrest him then.

FIREBUG: *(nastily)* Oh no he won't.

AUDIENCE: *(in unison)* OH YES HE WILL.

FIREBUG: Oh no no he won't.

AUDIENCE: *(in unison)* OH YES HE WILL.

FIREBUG: When I get out I'll burn down the whole town.

AUDIENCE: *(in unison)* OH NO YOU WON'T.

FIREBUG: Oh yes I will.

AUDIENCE: *(in unison)* OH NO YOU WON'T.

Joshua plucks up his courage, opens the cage, hauls out Firebug and clamps the cufflinks on him. Firebug gives up without a struggle and stands by docily.

FIREBUG: I was only bluffing.

JOSHUA: Got you, Firebug. *(to Santa)* Now you're free of all suspicion Santa. I mean Father Christmas. I mean . . ah . . Saint Nick.

SANTA: Oh thank you, Joshua. *(then to Ma Kelly)* I'll get you a new house for next Christmas. Meanwhile you can stay at Santa Claus Factory and help look after my gnomes.

Ma Kelly embraces Santa and plants a big kiss on his side whiskers.

That way you'll have a place to live all year until I get your new house.

JOSHUA: *(sadly)* I'm sorry Ma Kelly. It's all my fault that there's probably nothing left of your poor house but the big stone doorstep.

MA KELLY: The big doorstep, now how did you know about that?

JOSHUA: *(remembers as one in a dream)* Yes, how did I? *(smacks his forehead)* Where was your house?

MA KELLY: Third from the corner . . .

JOSHUA: I mean what . . what was the address?

MA KELLY: *(to Audience, in disgust)* Now he asks me - now! Why you big nincompoop! It's too late to go now to poor old *(she snivels)* sob, sob, Paradise Row. It's all burnt down now. *(she thumps Joshua on the chest)* You brute of a rule-book maniac.

JOSHUA: I knew it. Paradise Row. Why, don't you remember me? I was one of the little kids who used to sit on your big stone doorstep - so long ago - you're Mother Kelly, oh we never called you Ma.

MA KELLY: *(pleased)* Oh well, kids today are less respectful. Yes, I'm Mother Kelly.

The rest begin to form a circle around Henry VIII and Ma Kelly in preparation for the final songs. Henry sings,

MOTHER KELLY'S DOORSTEP (see p. 74)
    On Mother Kelly's doorstep
    Down Paradise Row
    We used to gather
    In the long ago
    We've wandered far now
    But we wish we could go
    Back to Mother Kelly's doorstep
    Down Paradise Row

HENRY: *(eyes aglow with the excitement of remembering the happy days of his youth)* Yes, there were the big kids like me and Joshua and the younger ones like you Antonio and you Sally and why I do believe there was a tiny little toddler dressed all in blue.

Little Boy Blue and others bow and acknowledge his reference to them in turn.

Ah, but we all loved dear old Mother Kelly. You were so good to us. Mothers are so wonderful for children.

Ma Kelly smiles coyly and hides her face shyly. Others look curiously at Firebug and ruminate.

MA KELLY: *(motherly)* Oh, well, I wasn't really your mum. I was only a community . . I was a street mother. No child should ever be so neglected by the community, so rejected, so abandoned by humanity as to be brought up by its own mother. All nice children should rightfully be reared by *(mistily)* a jolly good street mum. Oh, I could have sailed the world instead of having that whole bunch of trouble dumped on my doorstep but I just loved you all so much.

HENRY: *(puzzled, amazed, scratches his head)* But I thought you were really our mum. I can't remember any other. We were street kids and you were our <u>adopted</u> mother. Oh, well, anyway and there used to be a little old toad there that we played with - I don't know if it ever grew up *(looks Firebug up and down)* no it's not him, the toad was a handsome little fellow. *(he shakes his head)* But O, Yes, there was good old Joshua.

> *All sing JOSHUA (see p. 60) as Joshua peers at them myopically through his magnifying glass, at all in turn.*
> Oh Joshua, Joshua
> Sweeter than lemon squash you are
> Eee, by gosh you are
> It's Joshu-osh-uah

> *All dance (or walk around in circular formation if no music is being used). After JOSHUA SONG, the Chief Constable smiles, pleased and releases Firebug from his cufflinks.*

JOSHUA: *(to Firebug)* On condition you behave!

FIREBUG: I'll never do bad things again. No more cold water for me. *(he shivers and joins in the finale, notably no longer menacing and even smiling and relaxed)*

HENRY: Then there was that little Italian kid - what was his name.

SALLY: Antonio - here he is.

All join in singing **ANTONIO** *(see p. 28) who gets back on his bike briefly and waves his hat at the Audience. He leaves stage right briefly.*
Ma Kelly (sings)

Oh, oh, Antonio
He's gone away
Left her alonio
All on her onio
I'd like to catch him with
His new sweetheart
Then up will go Antonio
And his ice-cream cart

JOSHUA: *(still in a daze of happy memories)* And Daisy was just a little kid, a mere toddler at the time but we loved to see her down at Mother Kellys. She was so pretty.

Antonio returns, enters stage right, pushing a tandem bicycle which he gives to Little Boy Blue and Daisy, who sail across front-stage on it as all sing **DAISY, DAISY** *(see p. 88) led by Little Boy Blue.*

Daisy, Daisy
Give me your answer do
I'm half crazy
All for the love of you
It won't be a stylish marriage
I can't afford a carriage
But you'll look sweet
Upon the seat
Of a bicycle built for two

HENRY: Of course, I was one of the regulars there at your front door Mother Kelly. I'll bet you never guessed I'd turn out as great a success as I did.

Ma Kelly rolls her eyes at the Audience and shrugs hopelessly.

Henry sings **HENRY VIII**: *(see p. 42)*
I'm Henry the Eighth I am
Henry the Eighth I am I am
I got married to the widow next door
She'd been married seven times before
Every one was an Henry
She wouldn't have a Willie or a Sam
So I'm her eighth old man named Henry
So it's Henry the Eighth I am

HENRY: Ah, yes, it's great to be a famous person. *(sighs)* It was great to have so many wonderful friends.

But you, Mother Kelly, *(he joins the others in a circle around Ma Kelly)* you were the best old mum of all. It was so good to be young and free of all the world's cares on those balmy evenings down there on . . .

Henry leads and sings: ON MOTHER KELLY'S DOORSTEP (p. 74)

The rest join in a repeat of the song and bow to Ma Kelly in the center of the circle.

On Mother Kelly's doorstep
Down Paradise Row
We used to gather
In the long ago
We've wandered far now
But we wish we could go
Back to Mother Kelly's doorstep
Down Paradise Row

<u>Final Curtain</u>

END OF PANTOMIME

Mother Goose

Short Story and Three-Act Pantomime
including well-known French and
English Popular Songs

The Story

Once upon a time Little Bo-Peep was out in the fields watching her sheep. Nearby was a large goose. A robin redbreast hopped around on a green tree under which was a dog, a cat and three field mice. Nearby, a large white egg lay in a nest. Apart from the flock of Bo-Peep, there were also three black sheep.

In the trees close by were larks, meadowlarks, skylarks and other songbirds singing. But lurking in the woods, sneaking around in the leafy small bushes, was a fox, a hungry, nasty, thieving, lamb-eating fox named Guyfox and also known by the nickname – Slyfox.

As Bo-Peep was sitting beside her sheep, the skylark flying above tried to warn her of the approaching danger by chirping and twittering. But Bo-Peep did not understand and sat on among her sheep eating a piece of the cheese that she had made from sheepmilk. Guyfox began to creep through the shrubbery and the birds flew up and around and flapped their wings.

Briefly, Bo-Peep stood up and peered at the bushes to see what was creating all the fluttering and fuss. At that moment the cat seized the cheese and began to eat it greedily. Bo-Peep turned around just in time to see the cat steal the cheese and try to run away. But before it ran off, Little Bo-

Peep gave the cat a good whack with her shepherd's crook.

Just then Guyfox and his band of baby foxes ran up, surrounded Bo-Peep and her flock, then drove them all off to Guyfox Castle. During this raid on the sheep, Brother Jackie the dog slunk away and fell asleep in a quiet place. What a cowardly pup! The cat was also paying no attention but rather was trying to answer riddles asked by Old Mother Goose – otherwise known as Mrs. Hubbard. The dog was intent on pleasing Mrs. Goose by praising and flattering her.

Meanwhile Squire Guyfox the Slyfox was sneaking around in old Mrs. Hubbard's garden, watching the cat hungrily. The cat was disgusted at the dog's flattery of Mrs. Hubbard.

The dog pleaded with Mrs. Hubbard, "Please give me a bone, Ma Goose."

So Ma Goose took the dog by the paw and led him over to her cupboard to get the dog a bone. But the cupboard was bare and while Ma Goose was looking hard and scrutinizing every corner to try to find a bone, crafty old Guyfox snuck over to the cat and grabbed it by the throat. The cat was too suffocated to scream for help.

The cunning Slyfox ran off with the cat towards Guyfox Castle, crying out to Ma Goose, "Bone appetite, my dears." Guyfox waved his wicked paw at Old Mother Goose and the dog.

Soon Ma Goose realized that her cat had been stolen. "What happened to the cat?" she asked the cowardly dog Brother Jackie.

Jackie replied, "Me no know, Ma."

"Well, you should have been looking out for her," cried Ma.

"I'm sorry about that," said Jackie the dog, trying hard to look sad.

Soon Squire Guyfox paid them a visit. "I have your cat as well as Little Bo-Peep and her sheep," he boasted. "They're all in Guyfox Castle. Now, I do want to be reasonable. I can't eat them all. So I'll sell you back your cat for a very small sum of money – just a few dollars – how's about that? It's a very fair deal. It's called extortion, kidnapping and blackmail, hee, hee, hee. I'm a reasonable criminal. Just wait until the rest of the neighbors get a load of me – hee, hee, hee."

Guyfox washed his hands in invisible water and chortled wickedly, "How's that grab you, Ma Goose? I mean old Mrs. Hubbard."

Mrs. Hubbard did not have any money but she did want to get her cat back. "Look, Squire Guyfox, you old Slyfox. I've no money or food left but if you will give me back my cat I'll give you the biggest hug and kiss that you've ever had."

Guyfox scoffed, "Not from you, you old hag. What do you take me for – a mug? I can't bank your kiss and hug."

Ma smiled sweetly and curtsied to the fox but it was no go.

"If I don't get the money from you Ma Goose – you stingy, ancient bag of bones – I'll get it from the gypsies. They'll think that your cat is a rabbit when I sell it to them, skinned and chopped for stew. Hee, hee, hee," Guyfox cried. "I'll give you a day to get the pay. Try the bank or a printing press, I say."

With that Squire Guyfox snuck off into the woods sniggering and washing his hands in thin air. "Ha, ha, ha, cats are a good investment," he chortled.

Just along about then, Cock Robin, the redbreast flew by. "Why are you crying, Ma Goose?" asked Robin.

"Guyfox has stolen Little Bo-Peep, her sheep and my poor cat. He'll sell them for stew or eat them himself if I can't find his set-them-free money."

"Never mind the money. Let's get together a rescue group, police and all. We'll go find Guyfox Castle and set the girls free. Then we'll throw the Slyfox into the Tower of London. Will you join me, Mrs. Hubbard and Brother Jackie, the dog?"

Ma was delighted, "O wonderful, Cock Robin," she agreed.

But the dog slunk away saying, "Bravery is for the upper classes. I'm content if I can get some food."

Ma asked the dog, "Are you a man or a mouse?"

Jackie scratched his head, "Why do you keep asking me all these hard questions?" he whined.

But Cock Robin flew up ahead, followed bravely by Ma Goose. Jackie the dog sighed, shook his head but followed furtively.

After a long trek through the woods they discovered a castle surrounded by trees and bushes. This was Guyfox Castle where the Slyfox reigned supreme and held his hostages – Bo-Peep, her sheep and Mrs. Hubbard's pet cat. The castle was surrounded by thick green bushes and shrubbery and there was a wide, deep moat all around it.

Mrs. Goose got her mobile phone out of her handbag and called for the police, telling them where to catch Guyfox and set free the hostages. Ma Goose looked sadly at the moat and asked Cock Robin and Brother Jackie if they could swim. Robin shook his head but offered to fly over the castle to reconnoiter.

This gave Jackie an idea, "Yes, I can do the dogpaddle. Watch me do it on dry land as I go back home!" He began to paddle the air as he ran away.

Ma brought him back and threatened to tie him down. "Wait for the police and army," she told the dog. "Try to think of a ruse to get Guyfox to open the gate of his castle," said Ma Goose.

"I can pretend to be collecting old bones," suggested Jackie.

"And then what?" asked Cock Robin.

"Then I grab the bone and run away," said Jackie but the others ignored him.

"I could pretend that I want to borrow a pen," Cock Robin said, "and then you, Ma and Jackie the dog could rush into the castle while the Slyfox is looking for a pen. You could untie the hostages and let them loose."

The dog was doubtful. "Guyfox might catch us and lock us in. Why don't I just run off and try to find the police – to show them the way," Jackie smiled eagerly.

"No need," Ma shook her head. "Here they come."

Sureinufski, along the forest road strutted Humpty Dumpty followed tamely by the three blind mice and the two black sheep.

Cock Robin was disappointed, "Where is the rest of your police force and your backup from the army?" he asked Humpty Dumpty who was so startled that one of his false legs fell off. The leg was instantly picked up and screwed back onto Humpty by one of the black sheep.

"Oh, you scared me with that sudden question," quivered Humpty.

"Well, where are they?" asked the dog, looking around fearfully.

"Where are who?" asked Humpty, peering around in a scared way.

"The rest of your men, you oaf, you dolt," shouted Mrs. Hubbard.

"How dare you call me a . . a loaf? Can't you see I'm an egg," Humpty outraged. "Well anyway, the rest of my forces have been taken off to the wars by my old Captain - Marlborough. Co-opted into the king's service, you see. Don't ask when they'll be back – fact is I don't know – maybe never if they get shot," Humpty replied sadly.

Then Ma Goose, Cock Robin and Jackie the dog were all devastated.

"Oh, well, we might as well just go home and forget the whole thing," the dog suggested quickly.

"Not so fast, I must get all of your names and addresses for my reports after we get back home," spoke up Humpty.

"I'm not going back anywhere without Bo-Peep and the sheep and the cat," promised Ma Goose.

"Look, Guyfox does not know that Captain Marlborough has taken away most of the law and order force. Let's bluff him. Tell him to open up and surrender or we'll invade and arrest him in the king's good name, eh?"

Humpty Dumpty was so scared that he immediately dropped off one of his false arms. This arm was dutifully screwed on again, at once, by the three blind mice. Humpty was smug, "Madam, I cannot tell a lie," he replied stiffly to Ma Goose.

"Then you're not a policeman," she replied. "Be yourself, constable, be a liar as usual."

"Less of the lip you creaky old door, you rusty, flaky, shaky old fence. I need to check up on you. I need to check your passport to make sure that you're here legally. I also need to see that your taxes are paid up so that you can use my police services or if I have to fine you for unlawful use of my time. How is your credit rating?

"Also, where is the proof that a crime has been committed? You can't just make any old accusations against the Squire, where's the proof? You too Jackie, where's your proof? How do I know that this isn't a conspiracy against Squire Guyfox?"

"Oh, sir, Sergeant Humpty Dumpty, I swear . . ." moaned the dog.

"Don't you dare swear at me, dog."

"I'm sorry," said Jackie, "but I swear it wasn't me what done it. It wasn't me. It was him – the little boy who lives down the lane. I saw him do it and then, and then he ran away. See, he's the guilty party."

Humpty Dumpty cried, "I knew it. There's been a party. Who held this party without police crowd-control permission?"

"Stop this rubbish," Mrs. Hubbard shouted, "Sergeant Humpty, stand still."

Old Mother Goose stepped up to the drawbridge of the castle. "Open up in the name of the king and his vast army. Come out, you Guyfox or we'll arrest you and throw you into the Tower of Babel or London or wherever. And set loose Little Bo-Peep and her sheep and my cat, you slinky old Slyfox."

Guyfox stepped out and threw open the door. He waved his hand innocently at the open door, "There must be some mistake here folks," he whined, "This is a legitimate guesthouse. No one is being held here against their will. I look after my guests so very well."

Turning to Humpty Dumpty he ushered out Bo-Peep and her sheep and the cat who joined Old Mother Goose and embraced her.

"See," said Humpty Dumpty, "you have been falsely accusing a distinguished philanthropist and his grateful guests."

"That's all right," smiled Guyfox, "Let's forgive and forget. No hard feelings. Everyone is invited to my big party. Thank goodness for our astute and hard working and conscientious police force."

Humpty Dumpty was so pleased that all his limbs fell off and bounced on the floor. Then everyone had a great big party and lived happily ever after.

END OF STORY

Contents of Pantomime

GENERAL STAGE INSTRUCTIONS

This script takes the form of a musical pantomime and includes some of the best-loved French and English nursery rhymes. The French songs have been presented in both the original language and in simple, singable and danceable English language versions so that either or both versions may be included in a production. The play itself, in English, tells how the sly Guyfox first steals the lambs, along with Little BoPeep and then kidnaps the cat of the Old Goose - Mother Hubbard. Other critter-characters are Cock Robin the Redbreast, Brother Jackie the Dog, Police Sergeant Humpty Dumpty and his constables - the Three Blind Mice and the Two Black Sheep. Even as the audience has a chance to cry Yes, No, Hiss or Boo, all the nursery rhyme characters come alive right before your very eyes.

Including both the prologue and the finale, there are essentially only two sets and the stage director may be creative with both of these scenes.

First, there is the scene - full stage and backdrop - representing pastoral joy and idealistic romance of the gardens, pools, orchards, birds and bees.

The second scene is mainly composed of the backdrop which is of Guyfox Castle and the hamlet of small nearby cottages where his tenants live.

This backdrop is downcast and somber for the satirical second set of the humorous scenes where Cock Robin and the Skylarks along with Old Mother Goose and her dog are pursuing the kidnapping fox to free the captive BoPeep, the lambs and the cat. This contrasts with the first sun and summer backdrop which was full of blues, reds, greens and browns of rushes and bushes and shrubbery alive with birds, beetles, streams and fountains, throwing up life and calmness like the joy of the plant that is reborn to life in the spring.

FAMOUS ENGLISH NURSERY RHYMES: *Old Mother Hubbard; Queen of Hearts; Pussy Cat, Pussy Cat; Death of Poor Cock Robin; Three Blind Mice; Baa, Baa, Black Sheep; Humpty Dumpty; Little BoPeep; Sing a Song of Sixpence; Remember, Remember.* (Plus the newly-written Mother Goose Song - based on traditional ideas)

FAMOUS FRENCH POPULAR SONGS: *Sur le Pont - On the Bridge; Aupres de ma Blonde - Home with a Good Companion; Alouette – Skylark; Il Etait une Bergere - It was a Little Shepherdess; Frere Jacques - Brother Jackie; Ah! Vous Dirai - je - Maman - Mother Let Me Tell You; Papa, les petits bateaux - Mama, the Little Boats; Le Mere Michel - Old Mother Hubbard Goose; Au Clair de la Lune - By the Moon's Clear Shining; Malbrough – Marlborough.*

All of the above are given in the original French as well as in English verse liberal (as opposed to literal) translations. The purpose is to introduce English speakers to French popular songs and vice versa.

CHARACTERS

The twelve actors - 6 male, 6 female and dancers and singers are all ethnic animals or birds.

OLD MOTHER GOOSE - an agitated, be-speckled goose, a schoolmarm, who teaches and tells stories - the Grand Dame. Her antics are the main comedy routines of the script and her married name is Mrs. Hubbard. She's bad tempered - really an old crow in disguise, usually played by a middle-aged male comedian.

COCK ROBIN REDBREAST - a brave, witty and humorous singing bird - a fine singer - the Principal Boy, usually played by a female.

LITTLE BOPEEP - energetic, lively and perky. This is the Principal Girl - really a sheep herself in human disguise.

BROTHER JACKIE THE DOG - a clown, a crawling sycophant as dumb as they come but still a lovable coward.

PUSSYCAT, PUSSYCAT - a clown - clever at riddles, a thief and a pickpocket.

GUYFOX THE SLYFOX - a lying, thieving, devious, treacherous Villain - truly a politician in training. Speaks with an English accent. Reward for capture.

HUMPTY DUMPTY - a big dumb egg - posing as a police sergeant on crutches.

THREE BLIND MICE - three policewomen - skittish and scared.

TWO BLACK SHEEP - two policemen - bleating numbskulls.

Dancers (female): At least three can-can dancers variously dressed as lambs or cats

Singers (male or female): At least three singers dressed as skylarks to sing or back up

Extras: Optional extras. Guyfox look-alikes, may man Guyfox Castle or help Guyfox round up the sheep.

A walk-on prompter may enter stage at right or left to hold up a card giving audience responses.

OUTLINE
SCENE BY SCENE

———

ACT ONE –
BOPEEP AND SHEEP ARE STOLEN
Scene One

The curtain opens on a pastoral scene with a wooden bridge occupying center stage. Left-stage there is a garden and orchard with bushes, bright flowers, thick foliage, birds and bees.

Right-stage there is a pool and winding riverbank covered with a green sheet of painted shrubs at present. Under this sheet is a room outline, i.e., frames only, of walls and doorway covered with a tablecloth of greenery. Within these walls there is a large cupboard, desk, seats, a broom. There is also a blackboard, three or four chairs set out in a neat schoolhouse arrangement beside the pool. A large white bowl and wooden spoon is secreted among the bushes. This all represents an informal outdoor schoolroom surrounded by leafy high bushes, to be uncovered for Act Two. To the left of the orchard, left-stage, just before the stage exit, is a sign showing the image of Guyfox and the words "To Guyfox Castle" and an arrow pointing offstage left.

On the backdrop there are large trees, bushes and flowers in the foreground of the picture. In the middle ground are stone field walls, some greenery, hedges and paths. In the background there are pastures of meadows beside a river and gently sloping hills with flocks of white and black sheep.

Painted on this backdrop, preferably in a supernaturalist style (e.g., humorous, humanist, angular, circular or geometrical), there are: a large goose, a robin redbreast, a large white sheep, a dog, a cat, a fox, a large egg in a nest, three field mice, two black sheep. These creatures represent the main persons in the play. On the distant hills the black and white sheep - who gambol and fool around - represent the dancers in the play.

On the right and left sides of this backdrop, scattered among the trees there are larks, meadowlarks, skylarks and similar songbirds who represent the singers of a chorus.

The producer will need to bring all these critter-characters alive - right before the very eyes of the audience by any chosen technology - but perhaps the simplest method would be to (1) brightly light up the entire backdrop, (2) black it all out, (3) have spotlights searching out and highlighting each of the 12 creature-characters in turn, as (4) the actor representing each persona walks on stage and bows.

This general introduction is followed by all characters leaving right.

Curtain

SCENE TWO

Scene Two: The curtain rises on the same set. **Enter Mother Goose** *with her pointer. As she speaks the narrative and sings the song she moves around the set pointing to the pictures on the backdrop of each character as it is mentioned.*
Old Mother Goose - (Mrs. Hubbard) - addresses the birds.

MOTHER GOOSE: *(narrating)*
O songbirds sing and sing and sing
There are all the songbirds, the larks, the robin redbreast
Here am I, Old Mother Goose -
My married name is Mrs. Hubbard -
Little BoPeep is a nice sister sheep
Watching her little lambs
Of course, there's always a dog and a cat and that old rogue
Guyfox is a Slyfox who
Often steals a lamb or a cat

For his dinner, but
Then that silly old goose egg -
Humpty Dumpty tries to keep
Law and order with the help of the King's
three soldiers - the 3 blind mice and the two
black sheep who have strayed away from the
army and have now joined the police.
So I, Mother Goose tell the stories.

Mother Goose now sings Verse One.

THE MOTHER GOOSE SONG

d r   m   r   m   r d
Mother Goose tells the stories
(she points to herself)
d^1d^1 d^1 r^1 d^1 l
As I teach in my school
l t d^1 s   t l   s m
Where ducklings and goslings
s   s l   s m   r
Swim around in a pool
s   f   m   r   m   r d
And the pup and the pussycat
d^1d^1 d^1 r^1 d^1 l
Sit down and are told
l t d^1 s t   l   s m
All the faraway fine fables
d   m   r   d   r   d
And the tall tales of old.

VERSE TWO
There's the tale of a garden
With lilacs and bees
Where the partridges and pigeons
Sleep deep in the trees.
There the doves and the lovebirds
And the fountain that springs
As the flowers of the forest
Spread their petals like wings.

VERSE THREE
Then the lambs skip and frolic;
The old fox, on the sly,
Steals a meal down in the meadow
Where the mice squeal and cry.
All around run the dance birds
While the larks fly up high
And the fearless Robin Redbreast
Sings a song of the sky.

Enter Little BoPeep, carrying her shepherd's crook - a long stick with a bent or curved end. She is followed by her lambs. This crook is used to rescue straying lambs by hooking it around their necks and pulling the lambs into line - which routine she enacts at times.

BoPeep and all her lambs are dressed to look like lamb-dancers in wooly headdress, long frilly white sleeves, white long lacy pantaloons and brightly colored, loose wide frocks (or skirts with white blouses) all suitable for lively dancing.

BoPeep sings ON THE BRIDGE as her flock dance with her.

ON THE BRIDGE SONG

VERSE

s   s   s
On the bridge
l   l   l
Near the town
t d^1 r^1 s
Folks go dancing
fe   s   l r
Folks go dancing
s   s   s
On the bridge
l   l l
Near the town
t d^1 r^1 s
Folks go dancing
l   fe   s
Round and round

VERSE AND REFRAIN
On the bridge near the town
Folks go dancing, folks go dancing
On the bridge near the town
Folks go dancing up and down

Sing the Verse then chant the following two lines at the end of each verse followed by the Refrain. The dancers do hand movements to represent each person.

VERSE ONE
The fine gentlemen do this *(bow)*
And then again like this *(bow)*

VERSE TWO
The fine ladies do this *(curtsy)*
And then again like this *(curtsy)*

VERSE THREE
The musicians do this *(play fiddle)*
And then again like this *(play fiddle)*

VERSE FOUR
The dressmakers do this *(sew)*
And then again like this *(sew)*

VERSE FIVE
The joiners do this *(hammer and saw)*
And then again like this *(hammer and saw)*

VERSE SIX
The soldiers do this *(present arms)*
And then again like this *(present arms)*

VERSE SEVEN
The washerwomen do this *(wring out clothes)*
And then again like this *(wring out clothes)*

FRENCH VERSION – SUR LE PONT

VERSE ONE
Sur le pont d'Avignon
l'on y danse, l'on y danse
Sur le pont d'Avignon
l'on y danse tout en rond
Les beaux messieurs font comme ça
Et puis encore comme ça

REFRAIN
Sur le pont d'Avignon
l'on y danse, l'on y danse
Sur le pont d'Avignon
l'on y danse tout en rond

VERSE TWO
Sur le pont d'Avignon
l'on y danse, l'on y danse
Sur le pont d'Avignon
l'on y danse tout en rond
Les belles dames font comme ça
Et puis encore comme ça

REFRAIN

VERSE THREE
Sur le pont d'Avignon
l'on y danse, l'on y danse
Sur le pont d'Avignon
l'on y danse tout en rond
Les musiciens font comme ça
Et puis encore comme ça

REFRAIN

VERSE FOUR
Sur le pont d'Avignon
l'on y danse, l'on y danse
Sur le pont d'Avignon
l'on y danse tout en rond
Les couturières font comme ça
Et puis encore comme ça

REFRAIN

VERSE FIVE
Sur le pont d'Avignon
l'on y danse, l'on y danse
Sur le pont d'Avignon
l'on y danse tout en rond
Les menuisiers font comme ça
Et puis encore comme ça

REFRAIN

VERSE SIX
Sur le pont d'Avignon
l'on y danse, l'on y danse
Sur le pont d'Avignon
l'on y danse tout en rond
Les militaires font comme ça
Et puis encore comme ça

REFRAIN

VERSE SEVEN
Sur le pont d'Avignon
l'on y danse, l'on y danse
Sur le pont d'Avignon
l'on y danse tout en rond
Les blanchisseuses font comme ça
Et puis encore comme ça

REFRAIN

Enter the Chorus and join in the singing. They are dressed as skylarks, i.e., similarly to the dancers but in more colorful dresses with headpieces that look like birds rather than lambs. They might also have floppy sleeves representing wings. As they dance over the bridge and all around the set, birds sing and bees hum. There is also the occasional sound of a dog barking, a cat meowing, a fox howling and geese or ducks quacking.

The overall atmosphere is that of spring or early summer - sun, new life, fun and dancing.

Enter the cat, who dances all over the stage. The female cat is wearing a snug woolen cap, whiskers, a cat-suit, gloves and dancing shoes.

*The chorus sing **SKYLARK** followed by **HOME WITH A GOOD COMPANION** as the dancers do the can-can, mainly consisting of high kicks and pirouettes. Mother Goose runs back and forth scolding them.*

MA GOOSE: *(intermittently)* Stop. Stop. Quack. Quack. Get back to school. This is a scandal, etc. Quack. Quack.

LITTLE SKYLARK SONG

VERSE ONE AND REFRAIN*

d r m m r d r m d s_1
Little Skylark pretty little Skylark
d r m m r d r m d
Little Skylark, I can see you fly
s_1 s_1 d r m f s
I can see you winging by
s s s f m r d
I can hear you singing high
s s s s s s
Winging by, singing high
s s s s s s *s*
Singing high, winging by, Ooo-hhh
d r m m r d r m d s_1
Little Skylark, pretty little Skylark
d r m m r d r m d
Little Skylark, I can see you fly.

During Verse One the Chorus steps back and forth and kick high.

*Refrain, not in original, added by the translator.

Verse Two
Little Skylark, pretty little Skylark
Little Skylark, I can see you fly
I can see your pretty neck
I can see your little head
Little head, pretty neck
Pretty neck, little head, Ohhh
Little Skylark, pretty little Skylark
Little Skylark, I can see you fly

During Verse Two, the Chorus move their necks and heads from side to side, while high kicking and holding their skirts.

Verse Three
Little Skylark, pretty little Skylark
Little Skylark, I can see you fly
I can see your pretty feet
I can see your little wings
Pretty feet, little wings
Little wings, pretty feet, Ohhh
Little Skylark, pretty little Skylark
Little Skylark, I can see you fly

During Verse Three, the dancers flap their arms like wings, kick their feet high up and then step up and down as they kick their legs. Then they hold one foot high in the air grasping it with one hand as they pirouette on the other foot.

VERSE FOUR

Little Skylark, pretty little Skylark
Little Skylark, I can see you fly
I can see your pretty tail
I can see your little back
Pretty tail, little back
Little back, pretty tail, Ohhh
Little Skylark, pretty little Skylark
Little Skylark, I can see you fly

During Verse Four the dancers first face downstage and then, skirts flopping, their backs to the audience, bow away from the audience. The dancers turn, re-face the audience, kick high, bow and curtsy or do the splits.

FRENCH VERSION - ALOUETTE

Alouette, gentille Alouette
Alouette je te plumerai
Alouette, gentille Alouette
Alouette je te plumerai
Je te plumerai la tête
Je te plumerai la tête
Et la tête, et la tête
Alouette, Alouette, O-o-o-o-oh

Alouette, gentille Alouette
Alouette je te plumerai

Alouette, gentille Alouette
Alouette je te plumerai
Alouette, gentille Alouette
Alouette je te plumerai
Je te plumerai le nez
Je te plumerai le nez
Et le nez, et le nez
Alouette, Alouette, O-o-o-o-oh
Alouette, gentille Alouette
Alouette je te plumerai

Alouette, gentille Alouette
Alouette je te plumerai
Alouette, gentille Alouette
Alouette je te plumerai
Je te plumerai les yeux
Je te plumerai les yeux
Et les yeux, et les yeux
Alouette, Alouette, O-o-o-o-oh
Alouette, gentille Alouette
Alouette je te plumerai

Alouette, gentille Alouette
Alouette je te plumerai
Alouette, gentille Alouette
Alouette je te plumerai
Je te plumerai le cou

Je te plumerai le cou
Et le cou, et le cou
Alouette, Alouette, O-o-o-o-oh
Alouette, gentille Alouette
Alouette je te plumerai

Alouette, gentille Alouette
Alouette je te plumerai
Alouette, gentille Alouette
Alouette je te plumerai
Je te plumerai les ailes
Je te plumerai les ailes
Et les ailes, et les ailes
Alouette, Alouette, O-o-o-o-oh
Alouette, gentille Alouette
Alouette je te plumerai

Alouette, gentille Alouette
Alouette je te plumerai
Alouette, gentille Alouette
Alouette je te plumerai
Je te plumerai le dos
Je te plumerai le dos
Et le dos, et le dos
Alouette, Alouette, O-o-o-o-oh
Alouette, gentille Alouette
Alouette je te plumerai

Alouette, gentille Alouette
Alouette je te plumerai
Alouette, gentille Alouette
Alouette je te plumerai
Je te plumerai les pattes
Je te plumerai les pattes
Et les pattes, et les pattes
Alouette, Alouette, O-o-o-o-oh
Alouette, gentille Alouette
Alouette je te plumerai

Alouette, gentille Alouette
Alouette je te plumerai
Alouette, gentille Alouette
Alouette je te plumerai
Je te plumerai la queue
Je te plumerai la queue
Et la queue, et la queue
Alouette, Alouette, O-o-o-o-oh
Alouette, gentille Alouette
Alouette je te plumerai

Little BoPeep leads her sheep in dancing the can-can to both SKYLARK and the following song, orchestrating them with her crook, which she uses like a baton.

BOPEEP: *(to audience)* I'd like you to meet my sheep.

The sheep smile, curtsy and bow to the audience. Chorus and BoPeep sing:

AT HOME WITH A
GOOD COMPANION SONG

VERSE ONE
d   m m   m r   d d
Down in my father's garden
m   s s   l   l   s
The blossoms bloom their best
d   m m   m r   d d
Down in my father's garden
m   s s   l   l   s
The blossoms bloom their best
s   l l   l m   f f   f
And all the birds of all the world
f   s   s   s   r m   s
Go there to make their nest - at

REFRAIN
d   d d   r   f m s
Home with a good companion
r   f   m r   d l_1 s_1
That's the happy place I see
d   d d   r   f m s
Home with a good companion
r   f   f   m   r d
That's where I want to be

VERSE TWO
The partridge and the pigeon,
The quail and small white dove
The partridge and the pigeon,
The quail and small white dove
Are singing all the day long
And all the night, for love - at

REFRAIN:

VERSE THREE
The fountain in my garden
Is a clear and pretty stream
The fountain in my garden
Is a clear and pretty stream
Beside my happy lovebirds
But I'd give it all to be - at

REFRAIN:

VERSE FOUR
I sing for all the good girls
Who do not have a friend
I sing for all the good girls
Who do not have a friend
I sing that one fine morning
Our solitude will end - at

REFRAIN:

FRENCH VERSION - AUPRES DE MA BLONDE

Au jardin de mon père, les lauriers sont fleuris
Au jardin de mon père, les lauriers sont fleuris
Tous les oiseaux du monde vont y faire leur nid.

REFRAIN:
Auprès de ma blonde,
Qu'il fait bon, fait bon, fait bon,
Auprès de ma blonde,
Qu'il fait bon dormir.

La caille, la tourtelle et la jolie perdrix
La caille, la tourtelle et la jolie perdrix
Et la blanche colombe qui chantent jour et nuit.

REFRAIN:

Elles chantent pour les filles qui n'ont pas de mari.
Elles chantent pour les filles qui n'ont pas de mari.
Elles ne chantent pas pour moi car j'en ai t'un joli.

REFRAIN:

Il n'est pas dans la danse il est bien loin d'ici
Il n'est pas dans la danse il est bien loin d'ici
Il est dans la Hollande, les Hollandais l'ont pris.

REFRAIN:

Mother Goose

Que donneriez-vous belle pour qu'on vous le rendit?
Que donneriez-vous belle pour qu'on vous le rendit?
Je donnerais Versailles, Paris et Saint-Denis.

REFRAIN:

Et la claire fontaine de mon jardin joli,
Et la claire fontaine de mon jardin joli,
Et ma jolie colombe pour avoir mon mari.

REFRAIN:

The dancers are followed by the cat, in cat-suit, who dances all around. After this joyous round of three dances. Mother Goose tries to imitate the dancers and falls flat on her face. The set becomes quiet and relaxed as the young sheep-dancers and the skylark-singers range around the periphery of the set and sing **SHEPHERDESS.**

BoPeep brings out the hidden bowl and spoon, sits center and mimes the stirring of cheese, as cat watches her and then steals the bowl. Chorus of skylark-singers sing (perhaps with some help from others).

SHEPHERDESS SONG

VERSE ONE

m l   t   de^{1}t   l l m
It was a little shepherdess
  m m   fe fe   m m   fe fe   fe m
With a rightfoot, rightfoot, little BoPeep

  m l   t   de^1 t   l l m
It was a little shepherdess
  m^1 de^1 l   t m   l   l l
Who guarded all her sheep, BoPeep
  m^1 de^1 l   t m   l
Who guarded all her sheep.

VERSE TWO

She mixed a dish of white cheese
With a leftfoot, leftfoot, little BoPeep
She mixed a dish of white cheese
Of milk from all her sheep, BoPeep
Of milk from all her sheep.

VERSE THREE

The cat is watching slyly
With a rightfoot, rightfoot, little BoPeep
The cat is watching slyly
With a naughty little peep, BoPeep
A naughty little peep.

VERSE FOUR
Don't you dare put your paw in
With a leftfoot, leftfoot, little BoPeep
Don't you dare put your paw in
Or you'll get whacks from me, BoPeep
Or you'll get whacks from me.

VERSE FIVE
It didn't put its paw in
With a rightfoot, rightfoot, little BoPeep
It didn't put its paw in
But the cat drank long and deep, BoPeep
But the cat drank long and deep.

VERSE SIX
The shepherdess was angry
With a leftfoot, leftfoot, little BoPeep
The shepherdess was angry
And whacked the small cat-thief, BoPeep
And whacked the small cat-thief.

FRENCH VERSION - IL ETAIT UNE BERGERE
Il était une bergère,
Et ron, ron, ron, petit patapon,
Il était une bergère
Qui gardait ses moutons, ron, ron
Qui gardait ses moutons.

Elle fit un fromage,
Et ron, ron, ron, petit patapon,
Elle fit un fromage
Du lait de ses moutons, ron, ron,
Du lait de ses moutons.

Le chat qui la regarde,
Et ron, ron, ron, petit patapon,
Le chat qui la regarde
A un petit air fripon, ron, ron
A un petit air fripon.

Si tu y mets la patte,
Et ron, ron, ron, petit patapon,
Si tu y mets la patte
Tu auras du bâton, ron, ron,
Tu auras du bâton.

Il n'y mit pas la patte,
Et ron, ron, ron, petit patapon,
Il n'y mit pas la patte,
Il y mit le menton, ron, ron,
Il y mit le menton.

La bergère en colère,
Et ron, ron, ron, petit patapon,
La bergère en colère,
Frappa son petit chaton, ron, ron,
Frappa son petit chaton.

BoPeep rises and dances around center-stage as the cat acts out its cheese theft. Little BoPeep plays the part described in the song and wildly chases offstage the cat who has stolen the cheese bowl. The cat still holds the cheese bowl as it escapes.

The cat with the stolen (and part-eaten) cheese runs offstage right and Little BoPeep shakes her crook at the departing cat. She then follows the cat offstage right, followed by Mother Goose, still shouting and scolding. While they are offstage, Guyfox enters left-stage with or without one or two helpers dressed like himself. He half hides behind the bushes, watching the sheep wickedly. He, too, carries a crook. He wears a high-brimmed hat with some straw hanging down around his face. He looks like a fox, has pointed ears and his thin-nosed face has long gray whiskers and beard. He has a long, curved bushy tail which he holds up from time to time. His hands wear furry gloves or mittens. He looks around furtively and suddenly sees the audience. He is startled and addresses the audience. He speaks with an English accent.

GUYFOX: *(sneeringly)* Ah, what an idyllic, pastoral scene. The birds, the bees, the flowers, the trees - and oh, the little darling lambs. I know what I could do with them. *(he laughs, smacks his lips and rubs his stomach)* Yum, Yum, Yum, what a meal deal. Add water, dressing and salt and pepper and you'll have enough stew to feed a hungry fox for years and years. Hee, Hee. Just wait till they get a load of *(points to himself)* old Guyfox. Hee, Hee. I'll just blow them away. Up, up and away. He mimes plunging an explosion.

*Guyfox emits a fierce burst of weird horrendous laughter. Guyfox creeps out of the bushes, brandishing his shepherd's crook and begins to drive the dancers (lambs) offstage left, past the sign **TO GUYFOX CASTLE**.*

The frightened skylarks, too, run offstage right at the same time as the lambs. Guyfox, with or without extras as his henchmen dressed like himself, shouts and yells as he hooks the lambs by the neck with his crook to ensure that they leave the set quickly. The lambs, bleating occasionally, leave the stage left as the skylarks leave right.

GUYFOX: Get back there to my lair, you little lambs, I'll take care, good care, of you all there - hee, hee, hee.

Guyfox remains on stage, left, crouched among bushes chortling and rubbing his hands with glee.
***Enter BoPeep,** from right, running.*

BOPEEP: O help. Help me. Where are my sheep? What has become of them? *(to audience)* Where are they? Have they been stolen away?

AUDIENCE: *(in unison)* YES.

GUYFOX: *(sarcastically)*
Little BoPeep has lost her sheep
And doesn't know where to find them
(he bows to BoPeep and waves his left hand towards exit left)

Leave them alone and they'll come home
A-wagging their tails behind them.

> *He wiggles his bottom to wag his tail and
> walks towards his lair beckoning Little
> BoPeep to follow him, which she does
> tentatively, looking ahead for her sheep.*

BOPEEP: But where are they Squire Guyfox?

GUYFOX: Just a little further along, BoPeep.
That's where they are, BoPeep, down along
there in little old Guyfox's Lair. Hurry along,
my dear, or you'll be late for tea (and hee,
hee, hee - did I say tea for me with nice lamb
chops, hee, hee, hee).

> *Still shading her eyes with one hand as she
> looks ahead, Little BoPeep leaves stage left
> by the sign pointing to Guyfox Lair.*

GUYFOX: *(hiding in the bushes, left, and looking
to center-stage)* Who is this I hear coming?
(putting a hand to his ear) It sounds like a little
Robin Redbreast. Tweet, Tweet, Tweet,
Tweet. Hmm. I hope it's not the dreaded

Cock Robin - that fierce and furious rescuer of ladies in distress. *(trembling)* I'd better lie low.

Enter from right Robin Redbreast. Usually, but not necessarily, acted by a gentle girl. He is dressed in blue, somewhat like Robin Hood except that the front of his tunic is red. He wears a cocked hat and light tunic covered with feathers. His yellow pants are also feathery and his sandals or shoes are like bird's feet.

ROBIN: *(with arms widespread to the audience)* I heard a cry for help. Has BoPeep been here with her sheep?

AUDIENCE: *(in unison)* YES.

ROBIN: Are they all safe and well?

AUDIENCE: *(in unison)* NO.

ROBIN: Will I need help to find them and rescue them?

AUDIENCE: *(in unison)* YES.

Robin retreats towards the bridge, crosses it, looking around as though for possible help or to find the sheep. Robin exits downstage among the bushes or rocks. Guyfox re-emerges from bushes left and walks to center upstage, draws his cloak over his chin in a conspiratorial gesture and addresses the audience (or camera).

GUYFOX: Ha, Ha, Ha. So that's the great Cock Robin, is it eh?

AUDIENCE: *(in unison)* YES.

GUYFOX: Oh, really! He'll be no match for me! Why *(sneeringly)* he's little more than a lad - he's run off already. To get help. Ahah - yes he'll need it - to get help indeed - I've heard that one before somewhere. I know what I'll do with that little bird. *(he gloats and draws his hand across his throat in a cutthroat gesture - then to audience)* Little Cock Robin. He's no match for me, is he?

AUDIENCE: *(in unison)* YES.

GUYFOX: He'll never catch up with me, will he?

AUDIENCE: *(slowly, in unison)*
OH YES HE WILL.

GUYFOX: *(slowly and formally)* O - no - he - won't.

AUDIENCE: *(in unison)* OH YES HE WILL.

GUYFOX: *(laughing, sneering and walking up and down as he sings)*

COCK ROBIN SONG

d   d   f   f   f   f
All the birds of the air
f   m   r   r   r
Fell a sighing and a sobbing
r   r   s   s   s   s
When they heard of the death of
f   m   r d
Poor Cock Robin
d   d   l   f   m r taw
When they heard of the death of
s   f m   f f
Poor Cock Robin.

He's as good as a goner, ain't he?

Again he draws his index finger across his throat.

AUDIENCE: *(in unison)* NO.

GUYFOX: *(furiously shaking his fist)* YES, YES, YES!!!

AUDIENCE: *(in unison, with enthusiasm)* NO, NO, NO!!!

GUYFOX: We'll see about that, when I get them all together in my lair. He'll not be so cocky then when I blow them all up. *(shaking his fist in the air)* Yes, Cock Robin, bring all your friends back with you to help you rescue BoPeep and her sheep. I'll love it. I'll love it. I'll get them all in my lair and . . and . . and *(laughing fiendishly)* I'll blow them all up - so I will. Yes I will. Skyhigh Guy that's me. I'll blast them all skyhigh with my long-treasured store of gunpowder and dynamite. Hee, Hee, Hee.

Remember.
Remember the fifth of November.
The day of the gunpowder plot.

He kneels on one knee and, as before, mimes plunging off explosives and laughs again hysterically. The stage is darkened. There is the sound of an explosion(s), followed by red or blue light flooding the stage.

GUYFOX: *(to audience)* Just call me "the Plunger." Wait till they get a load of Guyfox!

He mimes again plunging off an explosion.

GUYFOX: *(fiendishly)* Ha, Ha, Ha.

AUDIENCE: *(in unison)*
BOO, BOO, BOO, HISS, HISS, HISS, as

Curtain
End of Act One

ACT TWO
PUSSYCAT IS STOLEN
SCENE ONE

The same. The school area right is now to be seen and is no longer covered with greenery. At left-stage among the trees in the orchard, the dog is sleeping on the shrubbery with his hands behind his neck, his head supported by a log or branch. The dog is wearing a doggy-eared headdress, a hairy jacket, pants and shoes, mittens like dog's paws, brown makeup on face. He is snoring loudly and making deep guttural noises, his mouth opening and closing rapidly. **Enter from right Old Mother Goose - Mrs. Hubbard.** *She carries her teacher's pointer. She looks all around and calls out loudly.*

MA GOOSE: Jackie, Where are you? Jackie. Be a good dog now and come home. It's time for school. I don't allow you to stay out all night. Jackie come here at once.

Ma Goose sees the dog asleep among the trees and pokes at him with her pointer. He stirs, turns over but continues to sleep and snore and roar.

MA GOOSE: It's school time and you need a bite of breakfast too. *Sings BROTHER JACKIE.*

BROTHER JACKIE SONG

f s   l f
Brother Jackie
f s   l f
Brother Jackie
l taw d^1
Sleeping still?
l taw d^1
Sleeping still?
d^1 r^1 d^1 taw   l f
Wake-up bells are ringing
d^1 r^1 d^1 taw   l f
Wake-up bells are ringing
f   d   f
Ring, ding, ding
f   d   f
Ring, ding, ding

FRENCH VERSION – FRERE JACQUES

Frère Jacques,
Frère Jacques,
Dormez vous?
Dormez vous?
Sonnez les matines,
Sonnez les matines,
Din, din, don!
Din, din don!

Come on now, Jackie Dog, follow me. I'll get you your breakfast and help you to start off school.

DOG: O, Ma Goose - I mean *(more respectfully)* Dear Mrs. Hubbard, the keeper of the cupboard. I do love you so much dear Ma but I just hate school.

MA GOOSE: *(jumping up and down)* What an outrage! You hate my poor school. *(she begins to cry and sob)* O, I do do my best for to teach you'all. Now I don't know what I'll do. Alas, I suppose I must retire and just sit in my old armchair and rock and rock until I fade away. Boo-hoo.

DOG: *(with sympathy)* O, No - Ma Goose, I'll come to school and do my best. I promise. I promise. It's just that, well to tell you the truth - I don't understand all the hard sums and difficult questions and besides PussyCat, PussyCat is so much smarter than me - I feel so bad and sad about it.

Sings
MAMA, LET ME TELL YOU TRUE SONG

<pre>
d d   s   s   l   l   s
Mammy, let me tell you true,
  f   f   m m   r   r d
What is making me so blue!
  s s   f   f   m   m   r
Daddy wants me to think through
  s   s   f   f   m m   r
Hard sums just like grownups do.
  d   d s l   l   s
As for me, I say: Sweet food
  f   f   m   m   r   r   d
Helps me more than hard sums could.
</pre>

FRENCH VERSION –
AH! VOUS DIRAI-JE MAMAN

Ah! Vous dirai je, Maman,
Ce qui cause mon tourment!
Papa veut que je raisonne
Comme une grande personne,
Moi, je dis que les bonbons
Valent mieux que la raison.

Ma Goose gives dog some candies, which he begins to eat and stick in his pocket.

MA GOOSE: That's a good dog. Have some sweets. Later I'll get you a good meal.

Dog nods, fawns, sticks out his tongue and crawls after Ma as they head towards the previously hidden schoolroom.

Curtain

SCENE TWO

The curtain opens on the same set where the school subsection is uncovered and which now has Mother Goose (otherwise, Mrs. Hubbard) standing by her blackboard holding her pointer. There is the desk, the old cupboard and the other props listed in the second paragraph in Act One, Scene One. In the seats in front of her are PussyCat, PussyCat and Brother Jackie the Dog. The cat is dressed as before. The cat and the dog are looking at the little blackboard as Ma Goose lectures them. They yawn. Ma Goose stamps her feet in anger.

MA GOOSE: *(furious)* How dare you yawn in my class? Am I boring you? *(to cat)* Am I?

CAT: *(yawns)* Oh, no, certainly not, Ma Goose. I'm just tired after my journey.

MA GOOSE: *(to dog)* Well, what have you to say for yourself?

DOG: *(scratching his head)* Ahhh . . let me see?

MA GOOSE: *(sternly raising her pointer)* Well?

DOG: *(puzzled)* Ah, Ma, What was the question again?

Ma Goose slaps her pointer down on the desk, furiously. PussyCat takes advantage of the distraction to pickpocket some of the dog's sweets and eats them.

MA GOOSE: Please pay attention.

DOG AND CAT: *(nodding)* Oh, yes, Ma. *(they sing)*

PUSSYCAT SONG

r^1 r^1 t r^1 t t s
So PussyCat, PussyCat,
  l t d^1 l r^1 t s
Where have you been?
  r^1 t r^1 t s
I've been to London
  l   t d^1 l r^1 t s
To visit the queen.
  l l fe   l fe r
PussyCat, PussyCat,
  m fe s   m   l   r
What did you do there?
  l   l fe   l r m   fe   s m   l   r
I frightened a little mouse under a chair.

MA GOOSE: *(to cat)* So you're just tired after your journey? So PussyCat, PussyCat, Where have you been?

CAT: I've been to London to visit the queen.

MA GOOSE: PussyCat, PussyCat, What did you do there?

CAT: I frightened a little mouse under a chair.

DOG: Ain't you the genius. So you really saw the Queen - there's lots of queens - which one did you see? *(aside)* As if I believed her story. *(pointing to the cat)*

CAT: *(recites or sings primly)*

QUEEN OF HEARTS SONG

```
  d    d m    r      f
The Queen of Hearts
  m    s    m     d
She made some tarts
  d d   m r f m      d
All on a summer's day.
  d    d m   r     f
The Knave of Hearts
  m    s    m    d
He saw those tarts
  s    s    r    f    m d
And stole them all  away.
```

See, us girls are creative and productive. *(to dog)* You young fellahs are always fighting, stealing and telling lies. Let me give you another example.

SING A SONG OF SIXPENCE SONG

d^1 d^1 t   l   s $d^1 d^1$ m
The King was in his counting house
m s   l   s   m s
Counting out his money
d^1 d^1 t   l   s d^1 m
The queen was in the parlor.
r l   l   l   l
Eating bread and honey.
l   s d^1 d^1 d^1 $d^1 d^1$
The maid was in the garden.
l r^1 r^1 r^1 r^1
Hanging out the clothes.
r^1 $m^1 r^1$ d^1 t d^1 t l
When down came a blackbird
s   l d^1 t r^1 d^1
And pecked off her nose.

Sing a song of sixpence
A pocket full of rye
Four and twenty blackbirds
Baked in a pie
When the pie was opened
The birds began to sing
Now wasn't that a dainty dish
To set before the king

MA GOOSE: The grasping old money-grabber.

CAT: See, the nice queen was in the parlor.
Eating bread and honey.

MA GOOSE: What a sweet old dear.

DOG: Greedy overfed foodstuffer.

CAT: The maid was in the garden.
Hanging out the clothes.

MA GOOSE: So hardworking and dedicated to her job.

DOG: Scared of being fired. Would do anything for a few pennies.

CAT: When down came a blackbird (a vile little boy)
And pecked off her nose.

MA GOOSE: Oh what a nasty horrible bird. If I catch that blackbird, I'll hang it out to dry with the clothes. *(she grabs up the broom and begins to run back and forth hitting invisible birds with the broom)* Take that you nasty nose-eater, you little cannibal! I'll get you.

I'm an old crow in a white dress you know *(swipes the air)* you bad bird.

DOG: *(resentfully)* I never did anything bad like stealing a nose or tarts or bread and honey or *(looks at cat)* cheese *(feels his pockets)* or sweets, eh? *(cat shrugs)*

MA GOOSE: *(shaking her head)* It's the old story. The dog was good and stayed at home and so he got a bone. The bad cat used to stray and steal and so she rarely got a meal. *(to cat, suspiciously)* Are you sure you weren't out stealing cheese again or pick-pocketing sweets from Brother Jackie?

DOG: *(to cat)* Yes, that's why you're always so guilty looking. You're a pickpocket.

CAT: *(cringing subversively and covering face with paw)* I never steal anything - hardly ever nowadays. How dare you accuse me of being a thief. *(to audience)* I didn't steal anything, did I? *(shakes her head negatively as a clue to the answer)* Sure I didn't?

AUDIENCE: *(in unison)* OH YES YOU DID.

CAT: *(subdued)* O no I didn't.

AUDIENCE: *(in unison)* OH YES YOU DID.

CAT: *(brightly as having an idea)* I know - let's have some riddles. You <u>would</u> like that wouldn't you, boys and girls?

AUDIENCE: *(in unison)* YES.

CAT: All right - the first riddle is . . .

MA GOOSE: *(breaking in)* Just a minute, I'm the teacher - <u>I'll</u> ask the riddles. *(thinks)* Hmm. Let me see now . . . What has four legs, two heads and eats cookies?

CAT: *(smugly)* I know - a four-legged, two-headed cookie-eater.

MA GOOSE: Rubbish, there's no such thing. *(primly)* The real answer is - a cookie-eating competition team of two small boys.

CAT: *(counting on fingers, suspiciously)* Two heads, four legs . . hmm . . .

MA GOOSE: *(pleased with herself)* What is green, grows and has wheels?

> *Cat shakes her head at a loss . . . Dog brightens and jumps up.*

DOG: Grows and is green and wheels - I know - grass, grass - I got it - the first time in my life I ever got the right answer - Grass - isn't that right Ma? The Grass!!

CAT: You imbecile, since when has grass got wheels?

DOG: *(excitedly)* Grass, grass, grass - I got it.

MA GOOSE: *(soothingly)* Quite right, Jackie, good dog - that's the right answer - Grass. *(nodding approval)*

CAT: But, Ma, grass hasn't got wheels.

MA GOOSE: Eh?

CAT: Grass has NOT got wheels!

MA GOOSE: So what? I was lying about the wheels. Good dog, Jackie.

Cat is open-mouthed in astonishment.

CAT: That's not fair.

DOG: Riddles are never fair. They're meant to catch you out, see? *(proudly)* But it didn't catch me out - I was right wasn't I, Ma?

Cat screws up her nose. Ma beams on dog.

MA GOOSE: All right. Answer this. *(with a schoolmarmish air)* How would you catch a polar bear?

DOG: I got it, I got it - by the tail.

CAT: Then it would just turn around and bite your head off and serve you right you silly-Billy old parasite.

Dog is dumbstruck and openmouthed. Scratches his head in wonder.

MA GOOSE: All right, what's the answer, Miss PussyCat?

CAT: Dig a big hole in the ice. All around the top of the hole, place a row of green garden peas - See?

DOG: How does that catch the polar bear?

CAT: *(smiling smugly)* That's easy - it's the peas that does it - Polar Bears just love peas. See? Then, when the Polar Bear comes up to take a pea - you kick him in the hole.

Cat looks up at the sky, innocently blinking her eyelids.

MA GOOSE: Stop it. I won't allow such bad language. Quack. Quack.

Ma flaps her arms and runs up and down in an agitated burst of utter outrage.

CAT: But Ma, I only said . . .

MA GOOSE: Quiet! Don't dare repeat it - I heard you the first time. Don't you dare. Quack. Quack.

Ma wags her finger at cat. Cat shrugs innocently.

MA GOOSE: All right now, back to law and order. Now I'll let <u>you</u> ask sensible questions. I'm the teacher.

Dog sings the first verse of

MAMA, THE LITTLE BOATS THAT FLOAT

m m   m   r r   d
Mama, the little boats
m   m   m r   r d
That float upon the sea.
s   d^1 d^1 t l t   d^1 s s
Do they have legs to walk upon
m   r   d   m   r   d
Just like me Just like me

MA GOOSE (singing)

m m   m r   r d
Silly, of course they do
m m   m r   r d
Have legs just like you
  s d^1 d^1 t l t d^1 s s
How else could they float and go their way
  s d^1 d^1 t l t d^1 s s s
How else could they bounce up and down and play
  s d^1 d^1 t l t d^1 s s
How else could they bob and swim away
  m m r d m m r d
The way they do The way they do
  s d^1 d^1 t l t d^1 s s
So the little boats must have legs like you
  m r d
Just like you

FRENCH VERSION –
PAPA, LES PETITS BATEAUX

Papa, les petits bateaux
Qui vont sur l'eau
Ont ils des jambes?
Mais oui, petit bêta,
S'ils n'en avaient pas
Ils ne marcheraient pas!

DOG: *(reciting primly)*
Mama, the little boats
That float upon the sea.
Do they have legs to walk upon
Just like me
Just like me

Ma Goose recites the second verse of
LITTLE BOATS.

MA GOOSE:
Silly, of course they do
Have legs just like you
How else could they float and go their way
How else could they bounce up and down
and play
How else could they bob and swim away
The way they do
The way they do
So the little boats must have legs like you
Just like you

*Cat swoons in despair as Ma gives her
answer.*

Curtain

SCENE THREE

Scene Three: The Same. Ma, cat and dog are still at blackboard. Guyfox slinks out of bushes unseen by the three others on stage.

CAT: *(rhetorically)* Get me outa here!

GUYFOX: *(aside)* Certainly PussyCat. I'll be glad to help you move to a better location - better for me that is. Heee!

MA GOOSE: *(running up and down and peering left stage)* Did I hear a noise out there like a fox howling? Get away you bad blackbirds *(swinging her broom at invisible birds)* let me get at that wicked rascal of a fox instead.

Ma looks suspiciously in the direction of Guyfox who lies low in bushes and sneers.

DOG: There's nobody out there, Ma. *(respectfully)* I mean Mrs. Hubbard, O please Ma, don't get upset and run away after the foxes. All this talk about bread and honey and tarts is making me so hungry. I love you so much, Ma. *(rubbing his tummy)* I'm so good, I'm such a good dog and you're such a good teacher, Ma. Please give me a bone, Ma.

MA GOOSE: *(beaming on dog and patting his head)* Yes, good dog - good dog. You deserve a bone for being so smart and giving me all those good answers.

Cat rolls her eyes and shrugs, spreading her hands helplessly.

CAT: *(to audience)* Here we go again with the sycophantic cringing and crawling.

Dog smiles, fawns, rolls over, puts his legs and arms up in the air, rolls back onto his feet, sticks out his tongue and pants and smiles at Ma.

MA GOOSE: Yes, come to the cupboard and I'll give you a nice big juicy bone.

The cupboard should be some few feet or yards away from Ma and the dog. Ma leads the dog over to the cupboard as the cat leans back in her chair, puts her hands behind her neck and recites or sings.

OLD MOTHER HUBBARD SONG

VERSE ONE

f   f f   f f m   r   d taw_1 l_1
Old mother Hubbard has lost her cat
d   d   f f   s m   f
At the window, leaning through
   f   f   f   f m r   d taw_1 l_1
She cries - Will somebody bring it back
   d   f   f   s   m   f
Oh search for it, boo, hoo!
   f f   s   l taw d^1 l   f
Guyfox then answers – Weep and moan!
   s   l   l   l   s   f   s
You do go on you do!
    l   s   f   f   f   m r d taw_1 l_1
Your cat's not lost and could come home
    d   f f   s   m   f
Oh mother, that's so true.

REFRAIN:

With . . a cry of - Everyone brighten up
To the air of sad and blue.
With a song of - All cheer up, cheer up.
To the tune of boo - hoo - hoo.

VERSE TWO
Old Mother Hubbard began to cry
You say (boo hoo, boo hoo)
My dear little cat is just nearby?
Are you the person who
Has found my little cat, the pet?
Guyfox replied, It's true
If you pay out you'll get your cat
I'll bring it back to you.

REFRAIN:
With . . a cry of - Everyone brighten up
To the air of sad and blue.
With a song of - All cheer up, cheer up.
To the tune of boo - hoo - hoo.

VERSE THREE
The old mother cries, It is no lie,
My mind's made up for sure.
If you bring back my cat then I
Will give a kiss to you!
But Guyfox says I don't like that
I want no kissing from you.
So I'll sell your cat as a rabbit that
They'll make into a stew.

REFRAIN:
With . . a cry of - Everyone brighten up
To the air of sad and blue.
With a song of - All cheer up, cheer up.
To the tune of boo - hoo - hoo.

FRENCH VERSION - LA MERE MICHEL
VERSE ONE
C'est la mère Michel qui a perdu son chat.
Elle crie par la fenêtre qui le lui rendra.
C'est le compère Lustucru qui lui a répondu:
Allez, la mère Michel, votre chat n'est pas perdu.

REFRAIN:
Sur l'air du tra la la la la,
Sur l'air du tra la la la la,
Sur l'air du tra déridéra,
Sur l'air du tra la la.

VERSE TWO
C'est la mère Michel qui lui a demandé:
Mon chat n'est pas perdu! Vous l'avez donc trouvé?
Et le compère Lustucru qui lui a répondu:
Donnez une récompense, il vous sera rendu.
Refrain:

VERSE THREE
Et la mère Michel lui dit: C'est décidé,
Si vous rendez mon chat, vous aurez un baiser.
Le compère Lustucru, qui n'en a pas voulu,
Lui dit: Pour un lapin votre chat est vendu!

REFRAIN:

CAT: *(aside - This is Ma Goose, but her married name is Old Mother Hubbard)*
(recites, pointing to Ma)
Old Mother Hubbard
Went to the cupboard
To get the wee doggie a bone
But when she got there
The cupboard was bare
And so the poor doggie got none.

Ma and dog begin to ransack every shelf and drawer and door in the cupboard - peering closely at the contents - just a few empty boxes. As they are so preoccupied, the fox creeps up behind the cat, holds one hand over her mouth and hauls the cat back towards his lair, exiting with her – left-stage. The cat struggles only a little and is barely able to make a noise.

GUYFOX: *(to Ma Goose and Dog as he leaves stage left)* Bone appetite, my dears. Bone appetite. *(he waves his paw)*

Ma shakes her head in disappointment. The dog hangs his head and drops his jaw.

MA GOOSE: I'm sorry, there isn't anything there at all. Maybe the bad old Guyfox has been stealing again. I'm sure my dear PussyCat would never steal your bone, Jackie. She's not really a bad cat, just a bit of a smart-aleck. Isn't that so, Pussy? *(she does a double-take and sees that PussyCat is gone)* Where are you, Puss? Come out. *(she leans down)* Push, Wush, Push, Wush. Come out. Now you know I was only teasing you. *(in desperation to dog)* Where is she?

DOG: *(scratching his head stupidly)* Me no know, Ma.

MA GOOSE: You dopey dog. You should have been watching out for her. Now where is she? I thought you were a watchdog.

DOG: I am, Ma. I'm a good watchdog. *(tongue out)* I watch out for good food all the time.

Enter Guyfox, from left, slinks across stage and then confronts Ma and dog.

GUYFOX: I have just pounced on PussyCat and sent her - along with my men - away off to my lair, where she will be well hidden along with Little BoPeep and all her sheep. Now I don't want to be unreasonable. I don't need them all. You can have your cat back if you wish, for a small sum - a mere trifle. You see, I'm trying to earn a little *(his hands make the money gesture rubbing his thumb across the other fingers . .)* ah . . goodwill. *(he bows to Ma)*

Ma looks through the window of her open-frame schoolhouse and begins to wail.

MA GOOSE: Ohhh. Ohhh.

GUYFOX: *(to audience)* She should pay up, yes?

AUDIENCE: *(in unison)* NO.

GUYFOX: Yes.

AUDIENCE: *(in unison)* NO.

GUYFOX: O yes she should.

AUDIENCE: *(in unison)*
OH NO SHE SHOULDN'T.

Guyfox snarls away and shakes fist.

MA GOOSE: Oh my poor cat, my pet. I'm so sorry for all the silly things I said to her. Oh Squire Guyfox you're so kind. If you bring her back, I'll give you a big, big kiss. I've no money or any food or bones left but I'll give you the biggest kiss you ever had. I'll be so grateful. *(blinking her eyes flirtatiously)*

GUYFOX: *(turns down his hands and thumbs, looking disgusted. Pauses)*
No thanks, Grandma, O no, not from you!
Get some fast money or I'll sell Puss for a stew.
Hear me - for a stew!
They'll think she's a rabbit *(hee, hee)*
When I've skinned her too.
Ho, Ho, Ho. Better get some dough, Mother,
Or I'll never set her free.
(to audience) See! See! See!

AUDIENCE: *(in unison)* HISS, HISS, HISS, BOO, BOO, BOO.

GUYFOX: *(to audience)* Better give me money or I'll skin you too. For a stew.

Guyfox defiantly exits left shaking his fist. Ma is distraught and runs around in circles waving her arms and howling and crying. The dog puts his head in his hands, kneels and howls and sobs.

Curtain

SCENE FOUR

Scene Four: The same. Dog and Ma are as before. **Enter Robin Redbreast** *from right and flaps his arms as though they were wings.*

ROBIN: Old Mother Goose and Brother Jackie Dog I heard all your weeping and wailing when I was flying around - even up in the trees. I have come to help you if I can. What has happened?

Ma and dog stop crying for a while.

MA GOOSE: Guyfox the sly fox has stolen my dear little PussyCat who was so cheeky and nice, I mean clever and nice, to me. Please help me get her back.

ROBIN: That scoundrel - Guyfox the sly fox - only this morning he kidnapped Little BoPeep and all her sheep. I've been flying around all day trying to spy out where he has taken them. So far I can't find him. *(he points offstage left)* Deep in the black forest, over there somewhere, he disappears but I'll wheedle him out with some help from you and other friends. Will you help me, Ma Goose and Brother Jackie Dog?

MA GOOSE: Oh yes, Cock Robin, I will gladly.

Dog is sullen and silent and evasive, looks away.

ROBIN: What about you, Jackie Dog?

DOG: *(subversively)* Well, I dunno . . . I'm a bit afraid of that nasty fox. It's all right for you

Robin. You can fly up high to get away and Ma has her big broom for self-defense but I'm only a poor little peanut. *(crouching down and covering his head)* I leave courage to the superior classes. Bravery is good but food is better.

ROBIN: Come on Jackie. Are you a man or a mouse?

DOG: *(scratching his head)* Why do you all keep asking me such hard questions? Man or Mouse? You got me there! *(to audience)* Man or Mouse? - What am I?

AUDIENCE: *(in unison)* A DOG.
The dog brightens up and begins to growl and snarl.
DOG: Oh yes, why yes, I'm a dog, a terrier. *(pounding his chest)* Grr . . I'll tear him apart. *(pausing)* Who did you say we were after?

MA GOOSE: Who are we after? Guyfox, of course, you imbecile! I'm beginning to have second thoughts about you! We're chasing Guyfox! Don't you get it ?

DOG: *(cowering a little)* Oh yes, Guyfox. I'll get <u>him</u> all right. You lead the way, Cock Robin. I'm right behind you. Grr. *(double-take)* Did you all say Guyfox - you mean <u>THE</u> GUYFOX? *(with open mouth and eyes)* Oh, *(trembling)* no, what am I doing?

> *Looking a little dubious, dog follows Robin and Ma as they begin to walk around the stage.*
> **Enter the dancers**, *all in catsuits, catmasks and catmakeup, somewhat like PussyCat. All dance around, can-can style.*
> **Enter the Chorus**, *still as Skylarks, and sing:* **OLD MOTHER HUBBARD** *(see p. 170) led by Robin.*

(see p. 170)

VERSE ONE
Old mother Hubbard has lost her cat
At the window, leaning through
She cries - Will somebody bring it back
Oh search for it, boo, hoo!
Guyfox then answers – Weep and moan!
You do go on you do!
Your cat's not lost and could come home
Oh mother, that's so true.

REFRAIN:
With . . a cry of - Everyone brighten up
To the air of sad and blue.
With a song of - All cheer up, cheer up.
To the tune of boo - hoo - hoo.

*During the refrain the company look cheerful
or sad in time with the words.*

VERSE TWO
Old Mother Hubbard began to cry
You say (boo hoo, boo hoo)
My dear little cat is just nearby?
Are you the person who
Has found my little cat, the pet?
Guyfox replied, It's true
If you pay out you'll get your cat
I'll bring it back to you.

REFRAIN:

VERSE THREE
The old mother cries, It is no lie,
My mind's made up for sure.
If you bring back my cat then I
Will give a kiss to you!
But Guyfox says I don't like that
I want no kissing from you.
So I'll sell your cat as a rabbit that
They'll make into a stew.

REFRAIN:
With . . a cry of - Everyone brighten up
To the air of sad and blue.
With a song of - All cheer up, cheer up.
To the tune of boo - hoo - hoo.

MA GOOSE: Stop it. Stop. Quack. Quack.
Get back to school. What an outrage. Quack.
Quack.

Ma runs around waving her pointer or broom, scolding them and chasing them. Finally, she falls down after trying to do the can-can, herself, much as before.

DANCERS AND SINGERS: *(shouting)* Old spoil sport.

Ma gets up and shakes her stick at all. Then as the dancers follow Ma, dog and Robin lead the way with an upbeat air of hope and enthusiasm and some high kicks and pirouettes in the can-can style.

MA GOOSE: *(to audience)* Let's get Guyfox.
Let's rescue BoPeep and my poor PussyCat.

She leads the way offstage left, waving a come-on to the others, as Robin and finally the dog leave stage left behind her - followed by dancers and singers all waving to the audience.

<u>Curtain</u>

End of Act Two

ACT THREE - COCK ROBIN
PURSUES GUYFOX

SCENE ONE

<u>Scene One:</u> *It is night, the full moon and stars shine, the backdrop, down-stage, represents a picture of the Guyfox Castle. Outlines of soldiers can be seen at some of the castle windows. At each side of the backdrop there are one or two small cottages. At the center of the castle is a large door or gate which can be opened or closed. Close beside it there is a window which can likewise be opened or closed.*

In front of the gate extending upstage, towards the audience, is a bridge, now camouflaged with dark hangings of plants and ivy. Below the bridge and surrounding the castle is a moat. Thus, the castle and the open end of the bridge now face the audience, occupying the down-stage and part of the center-stage area.

The rest of the stage, center and upstage is the approach to the castle with a road surrounded by trees and bushes giving the impression that the castle is set far away in the forests of the fox kingdom. Here Guyfox reigns supreme and his captives - BoPeep, her sheep and the pet PussyCat of Old Mother Goose (Mrs. Hubbard) are all held in captivity at this Guyfox stronghold surrounded as it is by the great moat and wall and the greenery of forests.

Enter from right Cock Robin, Ma and Dog, *walking along the road towards the bridge leading to the castle. Screams, moans and cries for mercy fill the air.*

MA GOOSE: Halt! I can hear the sounds of villainy. *(she cocks her ear and declares loudly)* There is the bridge leading to the Guyfox Castle, we could walk over the bridge and knock but then they would be expecting us. *(scratches her head at a loss)* As for climbing in some other way, the castle walls are protected by a moat. Robin, I can swim, can you, Robin? Can you swim, Brother Jackie?

ROBIN: I can fly up high and spy.

DOG: Yes, I can do the dogpaddle. Watch me do it as I run away.

The dog begins to dogpaddle his way - moving his arms in a circle as he runs to stage right entrance.

MA GOOSE: Come back here, Jackie, or I'll tie you down. I swear it - this is war on terrier. Now behave. I have sent for the police and the army. They'll be here soon.

Dog returns, head low, scared and sulky.

ROBIN: There's no point in going up to the door. Guyfox's men will be waiting for us with swords and spears. We need to wait for the army and police to help us break in and set free BoPeep, sheep and cat. This is a remote castle and village. It may be a long time before the army or police get here. Let's try a ruse of some kind.

DOG: What's that?

MA GOOSE: Use our brains, think of a trick to get Guyfox to open up the gate, then push him aside. I'll put my hands round his throat. I'll jump on him and pin him down while you, Jackie, groan and pretend to be a tough dog while Robin guides out the sheep and PussyCat and Little BoPeep. See the plan?

ROBIN: Well, what excuse, what trick would work?

MA GOOSE: Think! *(screwing up her face and walking up and down with her hands behind her back)*

DOG: Think? What's that? Think? Oh yes, I get it. I get it: use my brain if I could find it.

All march up and down scratching their chins and thinking and frowning.

DOG: I got it, I got it. Why don't I say I'm collecting old bones for the dog's home, then when he opens up ah . . dah. Lemony think *(brightening)* - I take the bone and run, see?

MA GOOSE: *(slowly and sternly)* Try to grasp it, Jackie, we're here to get BoPeep and the cat and the little lambs - not old bones. Understand?

ROBIN: *(patiently to dog)* See . . . We're trying to trick Guyfox so that we can seize him, Brother Jackie. He's suspicious. He would not believe you.

DOG: *(offended)* Why not?

MA GOOSE: You dimwit, you dope: Nobody goes around the neighborhood to collect bones in the middle of the night.

DOG: *(dumbstruck, open-mouthed)* I do.

Robin goes back to a thinking stance.

MA GOOSE: Brother Jackie, I mean nobody normal. I mean no sane person. Now. *(walks up and down frowning)* Now, let me think - what do people do in the middle of the night. Who sits up late? Ah, I know . . students burning the midnight oil - that's it. We'll say we've come to borrow a pen then when he opens up, you grab him by the throat, Jackie. O.K?

DOG: I grab who?

MA GOOSE: Guyfox, of course.

DOG: You've got to be kidding - not me. Grab Guyfox by the throat - you're joking. Besides, it's past my bedtime. I'm going back to bed.

MA GOOSE: Quiet, you cowardly cur. I'll grab him if you just help Robin guide out the girls, O.K?

The dog stares open-mouthed at the moon, howls and begins to tremble.

ROBIN: Shushh . . let me try. *(approaching the castle door)*

*Robin sings first verse of **BY THE MOON'S CLEAR SHINING.** Ma joins in the singing as Dog howls in the background. A castle window opens and Guyfox appears suspiciously in a nightcap and nightgown with a candle in hand and sings Verse Two of **BY THE MOON'S.** Guy then closes the window with a sly sneer.*

BY THE MOON'S CLEAR SHINING SONG

VERSE ONE

s   s   s   l   t l

By the moon's clear shining

s   t   l l   s

My dear fellow, please

s   s   s   l   t l

Let me do some writing,

s   t   l   l   s

Lend your pen to me.

l   l   l   l   m m

All my lights are failing,

l   s   fe m   r

Hear my honest plea,

s   s   s   l   t l

I have no more heating,

s t   l   l   s

Open up for me.

Guyfox shakes his head suspiciously and sings.

VERSE TWO

By the moon's clear shining,
Hi my good old friend,
I have just been sleeping,
I've no pen to lend.
Try our neighbor's home, now
She's in there, I know
For in her living-room now,
There's a fire aglow.

Guyfox closes the window and Robin retreats back to join Ma and Dog.

FRENCH VERSION – AU CLAIR DE LA LUNE
  VERSE ONE
    Au clair de la lune,
    Mon ami Pierrot,
    Prête moi ta plume,
    Pour écrire un mot;
    Ma chandelle est morte,
    Je n'ai plus de feu;
    Ouvre moi ta porte,
    Pour l'amour de Dieu.

  VERSE TWO
    Au clair de la lune,
    Pierrot répondit;
    Je n'ai pas de plume,
    Je suis dans mon lit.
    Va chez la voisine,
    Je crois qu'elle y est;
    Car dans sa cuisine,
    On bat le briquet.

MA GOOSE: Bah.

ROBIN: Foiled again. He's too sly and cunning. We'd better just wait for help.

DOG: So what about the bone?

MA GOOSE: What bone? *(looks up at the moon as if for help and holds out her arms in despair)* What, WHAT on earth bone? Tell it to me!

DOG: *(meekly)* The bone I was going to collect: at the door, don't you remember?

Ma and Robin spread out their hands in despair and shake their heads. A loud gong rings out. **Enter from right Humpty Dumpty** - *proudly, even arrogantly, strutting, staff in hand ahead of the three blind mice and two black sheep who wear hoods and gowns shaped to look like mice and sheep.*

Humpty has a rotund egg-shaped, artificial, body enclosing his real arms, which nevertheless come thru slits at times. His visible arms are screw-on fakes that fall off every so often, to be attentively re-attached by one of the black sheep. The slits in his egg body should be large enough for his real hands to do their work now and then. The black sheep and mice carry bags of custard fudge cakes as supplies of war.

LOUD VOICE OF A CHILD IN THE AUDIENCE:
Look, it's Humpty Dumpty!

All remain still.

Curtain

SCENE TWO

Scene Two: *The same, everyone as before.*

HUMPTY: *(in an English accent, halting at attention, face to face with Robin)* I'm Sgt. Humpty Dumpty - here at your request, Cock Robin, to help you rescue Little BoPeep with all her sheep, as well as PussyCat, PussyCat. At your service, Cock. *(he bows)*

Humpty tries to salute but his arm falls off, only to be put back on by one of the black sheep. Humpty recovers his composure and shuffles back into a dignified position.

MA GOOSE: But, Humpty, where is your army and the police force?

HUMPTY: *(smugly)* All present and correct, Madam. Here they are - the two black sheep and the three blind mice. This is the entire police force and army - all that is left to us - now that all the best men are out in the fields of war - here are all that we can get.

Dog barks suspiciously at black sheep and blind mice.

ROBIN: Oh dear!

MA GOOSE: What a miserable apology for the usual police riffraff. What leftovers. What a bunch of rotting apples to fight against Guyfox! The real and original Guyfox. Still, half a mob is better than no rabble at all. *(shaking her head sadly)*
(to mice) Can you walk?

They shuffle up and down the stage stiltedly and bump into each other.

Ma Goose sings THREE BLIND MICE

    m   r   d
Three blind mice
    m   r   d
Three blind mice
   s   f   f   m
See how they run
   s   f   f   m
See how they run
  s d^1 d^1 t l t d^1s   s
They all ran after the farmer's wife
  s d^1 d^1 t l t d^1 s s s
She said she cut off their tails with a knife
  s d^1 d^1 t l t d^1 s s s
Did ever you see such a thing in your life.
  f   m   r   d
As three blind mice

MA GOOSE: *(to Humpty, in a surprised tone)* They're blind Humpty - don't you see?

HUMPTY: O, I see, Mother Goose, but they don't.

MA GOOSE: But . . how can they arrest people?

HUMPTY: *(thoughtfully)* Well, they can grab someone - anyone!

MA GOOSE: *(outraged)* But it might be the wrong person!

HUMPTY: *(stiffly)* Madam - so - how does that make them any different from ordinary police? Police most always arrest someone, guilty or not, in order to please and appease the general population and prove that crime does not pay. Besides I am not permitted to discriminate against the visually impaired, Ma'am. Also blind mice have a compensatory strong ability to think and to smell out the facts - like ah . . cheese, for instance. See?

MA GOOSE: Well I do - but they don't. See?

HUMPTY: I do but they don't - O stop it - look here!

MA GOOSE: *(interrupting)* Well I can, but they can't.

HUMPTY: Stop this. I'd have you to know that these fine upstanding three blind mice can think - yes think, Madam - better than I. Would you believe that?

ROBIN: O I really can - I can believe that Humpty.

MA GOOSE: *(shaking her head again)* Me, too.

HUMPTY: *(pleased)* Yes indeed. That's why we're such a great team. *(proudly)* I can <u>see</u> and the three blind mice can <u>think</u> and the two black sheep they can stray away and get lost so I don't need to pay them or feed them much when they're not here a lot of the time - it represents a great budgetary saving - you know.

ROBIN: What good is that? You don't have the benefit of their services.

HUMPTY: So what? Their services are completely useless anyway. Their being away is a pure budgetary saving, I can assure you.

MA GOOSE: That doesn't sound like you're going to be able to rescue my little pet cat, and BoPeep and her sheep! I doubt if you're up to the task, Humpty. Don't you realize they've been kidnapped by Guyfox?

HUMPTY: *(soothingly)* Of course, of course, Ma'am. That reminds me, can I have a description of the stolen property - just for identification purposes you understand.

MA GOOSE: *(clutching her hands together and raising her head beseechingly)* I do NOT understand. I'm here to rescue my cat, Little BoPeep and all her sheep - they were all so witty, so cute, so friendly, so kind and they wear such brightly colored dresses and they're so nimble and sweet at dancing. They're like little sisters to me and so pretty and nice.

HUMPTY: O, in that case . . it is no wonder they were stolen!

MA GOOSE: Now you can't justify stealing away good girls.

HUMPTY: *(gruffly and quickly)* NO, NO, NO of course not, Madam. I didn't mean that, Madam.

MA GOOSE: Don't you dare Madam me, Humpty - I'm only their teacher but I <u>must</u> get them back - they're so dear to my heart. They're such good little girls. *(she weeps)* BOO, HOO, HOO. *(clutches her heart and throws wide her arms)*

HUMPTY: *(with an embarrassed rough cough)* Hghm . . . Right, Mother Goose, let's get down to business. *(to one of the black sheep who shuffles about with paper and pen)* Write this down, Officer. *(to Ma)* Description of missing person? Your authorization for the use of this police force? Are your taxes paid up to date? To whom should we send the bill? Who are the witnesses that this is a case of kidnapping? How do I know that you didn't bump them off for the insurance money, eh? Full name and age and address of complainant? That's you Madam.

MA GOOSE: ME. You're calling me a complainant - the cheek of it! How dare you - you bad egg - you! Quack. Quack.

Ma runs up and down and flops in despair.

MA GOOSE: This is Rubbish: While you're taking all these statements, Guyfox will have time to escape and take all my little ones with him. Don't you realize that, while you waste time, my friends are being . . .

HUMPTY: *(matter of factly)* I know, I know, kidnapped and all that - held against their will - of course, of course, Ma'am. But don't worry, *(soothingly)* maybe little Old Mr. Guyfox will return them all for a reward - then we wouldn't need to fight over them - settle it all out of court amicably. There's two sides to every story you know. Right? Guyfox is a big taxpayer. I need to know his point of view: fair is fair.

MA GOOSE: *(pointing her finger at Humpty)* You're afraid of Guyfox, you're afraid to march in and rescue by force, Little BoPeep and . . .

HUMPTY: *(yawning)* and your little pet, PussyCat. I know, I know - but it doesn't matter if I'm scared or not, I'm not even authorized to use force, I'm only a sergeant. Only the captain himself - Captain Marlborough can give the word to invade, or charge or bust in or seize by force - and *(shrugging and yawning)* the captain is miles and miles away.

ROBIN: But why isn't the captain <u>here</u> doing his job?

HUMPTY: *(laughing)* O bless you sir - corblimey - stone - the - crows, why sir, Captain Marlborough IS doing his job lorlovee. Ho, Ho, Ho. Why he was called up to serve the King - the gallant captain is at the wars, on the battlefield miles away.

The dog listens in wide-mouthed and wide-eyed astonishment and fear.

MA GOOSE: But when will the captain be back to give you leave to seize Guyfox?

HUMPTY: *(stuffily and stiffly)* Ma'am, how could I possibly know that? He might never come back - wars can last for years and years. *(he yawns)* We might as well make camp here and watch whatever takes place. It should be interesting to see what happens.

Enter the singers right, still as skylarks. Humpty sings MARLBOROUGH and is joined by the rest of the company. They totter and stumble and march from left to right stage and return center.

THE MARLBOROUGH SONG

d l   l   l   s l   taw taw l
Marlborough has gone to the battlefield
s s s   s s s   s f l f
Mironton, mironton, mirontaine
d l   l   l   s l   taw taw l
Marlborough has gone to the battlefield
r^1 l   f   s   s   f
Don't know when he'll come back
d^1 d^1 l r^1 r^1 d^1
Don't know when he'll come back
d^1 d^1 l r^1 r^1 d^1
Don't know when he'll come back

REFRAIN:

d l   l   l   s   l   taw taw l

Marlborough has gone to the battlefield

r¹   l   f   s   s   f

Don't know when he'll come back

We thought he'd come home for Eastertime
Mironton, mironton, mirontaine
We thought he'd come home for Eastertime
Or the Sunday after that
Or the Sunday after that
Or the Sunday after that

REFRAIN:

Now Trinity Sunday is past and gone
Mironton, mironton, mirontaine
Now Trinity Sunday is past and gone
And Marlborough never came back
And Marlborough never came back
And Marlborough never came back

REFRAIN:

FRENCH VERSION - MALBROUGH
Malbrough s'en va t'en guerre
Mironton, mironton, mirontaine
Malbrough s'en va t'en guerre
Ne sait quand reviendra

Ne sait quand reviendra
Ne sait quand reviendra

Il reviendra à Pâcques
Mironton, mironton, mirontaine
Il reviendra à Pâcques
Ou à la Trinité
Ou à la Trinité
Ou à la Trinité

La Trinité se passe
Mironton, mironton, mirontaine
La Trinité se passe
Malbrough ne revient pas
Malbrough ne revient pas
Malbrough ne revient pas

(to audience) It's all absolute confusion but it'll be worth watching, won't it?

AUDIENCE: *(in unison)* YES.

The skylarks leave stage right.

MA GOOSE: *(in desperation to Humpty)* Please, please Humpty - What are you here for - if not to set the girls free?

HUMPTY: Madam, I am here to investigate whether a crime has been committed. I see no signs of a crime. *(to Robin)*

Dumbstruck and at great length, they all examine the ground.

You there, Cock, err. I mean . . sir. Robin Redbreast. Do you see any signs of a crime? Lookee around and show me the signs? *(to Ma)* Show me the evidence, hmm? *(to dog)* Where is the proof that a crime has been committed, eh?

DOG: *(trembling)* A what? What's that Humpty?

HUMPTY: *(scrutinizing the dog suspiciously and loudly)* A crime, a crime - show me the crime, Brother Jackie. Come on, where's the evidence of a crime?

DOG: *(in horror and panic)* A crime?

HUMPTY: *(aggressively)* Yes, Jackie, a crime!

DOG: *(shaking)* I didn't do it. Honest, Humpty. Ask your own men, ask them there

black sheep about it. Don't ask me. They
know more than I do.

ROBIN: Doesn't everyone? *(then sings)*

BA BA BLACK SHEEP SONG

d d s   s
Ba Ba Black Sheep
l   t   d^{1}l s
Have you any wool
f f m m
Yes sir, yes sir,
r   r   d
Three bags full
s   s s   f f
One for my master
m   m   m   m   r
And one for my dame
d   s s   s   f s l
And one for the little boy
f   m   r r   d
That lives down the lane

HUMPTY: *(to the black sheep)*
Baa, Baa, Black Sheep.
Have you any wool?

BLACK SHEEP: *(in unison)*
Yes sir, yes sir, Three bags full
One for my master *(they bow to Humpty)*

And one for my dame *(they bow to Ma Goose,
Mrs. Hubbard)*
And one for the little boy
That lives down the lane

DOG: *(in fear and desperation)* Yes, that's him -
that done it for sure - that nasty little boy
who lives down the dirty, mucky, muddy,
slippery lane - he done it. I saw him. It was
him. I wasn't even there at the time. I was
miles away. *(running about in distraction)* It
was the little boy who lives down the lane.
Him, Him, Him. *(hysterically)* Listen Robin!
Ma! Mr. Sergeant Humpty! You must
believe me. I'll take a lie detector test - that
proves I'm innocent doesn't it? *(breaking
down, kneeling and weeping)* I cannot tell a lie -
it wasn't me - it wasn't me - it was him - the
little boy . . him not me . . him who . . .
   All are in stunned silence.

HUMPTY: *(breaking in, casually)* Who lives
down the lane. Yes, I see. *(suspiciously)* I
must have a word with that little boy. Lives
down the lane, does he? Give me *(to the black*

sheep) the little boy's address later and I'll see that we investigate the matter.

DOG: *(in grateful tears)* Yes, sir. Yes, sir. Thank you, sir, Humpty. O thank you for your integrity and kindness and honor, sir.

HUMPTY: *(pleased)* Well, that's just little old me.

MA GOOSE: *(to Humpty with vigor)* Just a minute. *(to Dog)* You shut up, you dope. *(to Humpty)* Sergeant Dumpty. Exactly what - what matter are you going to investigate? *(slowly and meanly)* I thought you were investigating - Where is Little BoPeep, all her sheep and my poor little pet PussyCat, eh? Eh? What about Mr. Guyfox, the sly fox? How's about him? *(poking Humpty with her pointer)* You Little Old Sergeant Policeman you? Eh?

HUMPTY: *(a little confused)* O yes, Guyfox. Him? Absolutely. Well, I'd sure make short work of him except that I don't have Captain Marlborough's sayso. I need that sayso to proceed with force, Ma'am, and Captain Marlborough . . as I told you . . Marlborough . . .

They all sing the first two lines of Marlborough,

> Marlborough has gone to the battlefield
> Mironton, mironton, mirontaine

then stop suddenly as Ma screams.

MA GOOSE: *(loudly)* STOP, STOP, you singing imbeciles. If you don't storm Guyfox and seize him, I'll do it myself and then throttle everyone of you and let the girls out. *(to the door of the castle)* I call upon you to set the prisoners free.

> *Robin and dog and black sheep and the three blind mice all raise their hands and cheer.*

ALL (EXCEPT HUMPTY): Hurray! Hurray, Hurray.

HUMPTY: *(now shaky)* Now don't Ma, don't take the law into your own hands.

MA GOOSE: Well, it's not in your hands anyway.

HUMPTY: Relax! I'll think of something, some way to proceed in good law and order. Calm down, Ma. Be calm. Don't worry - things you worry about never happen. *(after a pause, brightly)* That's it. Let's all have a good worry about PussyCat, BoPeep and her sheep and lambs <u>never</u> being set free <u>never</u>. Let's all worry about them. Worrying always works - that way they will soon be set free. See?

They all walk up and down, with faces screwed up and shaking their heads.

ALL: Worry, Worry, Worry.

HUMPTY: That's it - worry about the worst that could happen and then it won't.

DOG: O yes, I see. The things that you worry about never happen. So let's all worry and then the bad things we worry about will never happen. I get it. Ah hum.

MA GOOSE: *(after a good walkabout worry)* Stop it. This is getting us nowhere. *(to Humpty)* You say - Don't take the law into my hands - but whose hands is it in? Answer me that, you fat egg.

HUMPTY: What do you mean? Why, how dare you suggest that I'm not competent. *(pointing to dog)* Are you putting me in the same despicable pit as that cowardly cur? The law is in my hands, right here, Ma'am.

> *He stomps his staff on the stage and one of his arms falls off, to be affixed back on by an obsequious black sheep, as the three mice squeal in support of their leader.*

MA GOOSE: *(to Humpty innocently)* Oh, so you're in charge, are you?

HUMPTY: *(indignantly)* Certainly, Madam!

MA GOOSE: Oh, you're acting captain *(sweetly)* are you dear Sgt. Dumpty, in the absence of Captain Marlborough.

HUMPTY: *(pleased and proud)* That's me - yes, Hmm . . I'm acting captain. I'm important enough to get a job but not to get myself suspended on full pay. *(dreamily)* I just wish that I could get myself suspended on full pay but I don't have quite the political clout to achieve that at present but yes meanwhile I'm acting captain, Yes, Ma'am. *(he preens himself)* Certainly Ma'am.

MA GOOSE: *(loudly and aggressively)* Oh, you're not quite able to get yourself suspended on full pay, eh? Well I'll get you suspended from a tree on no pay if you don't help us. The point is you're acting captain and so you don't need anyone else's permission - so get in there and rescue those little girls or I'll do it myself. Understand?

ALL (EXCEPT HUMPTY): Hooray, Hooray, Hooray.

Humpty walks around uncertainly and drops another limb which is instantly screwed on again by a black sheep.

HUMPTY: *(to audience, meekly)* I can't very well just march in the dead of night right up to the dark Castle of Guyfox and demand the release of the girls, can I?

AUDIENCE: *(in unison)* O YES YOU CAN.

HUMPTY: O no I can't.

AUDIENCE: *(in unison)* O YES YOU CAN.

Humpty hesitates, addressing the audience.

HUMPTY: *(querulously)* O yes I can?

AUDIENCE: *(in unison)* O YES YOU CAN.

HUMPTY: But what about Guyfox?

AUDIENCE: *(in unison)* BOO, BOO, BOO, HISS, HISS, HISS.

HUMPTY: You think I have the authority, the cheek, the gall, the temerity, the courage to face up to Guyfox?

AUDIENCE: *(in unison)* YES, YES, YES.

HUMPTY: *(stomping his staff)* I'll do it then, if you all believe in me!

AUDIENCE: *(in unison)* YES, YES, YES.

HUMPTY: Very well then *(to Ma)* but I must follow the strict protocol of the King - so that everything I do will be according to law and order, Madam.

Ma rolls her eyes.

MA GOOSE: *(sighing in resignation)* Oh, all right, Humpty but hurry. My cat and little BoPeep and her sheep are being . . .

HUMPTY: I know, imprisoned and all. *(abstractedly)* Let me see, now. You Robin, fly around, take a look and see what is going on.

Robin flaps his arms, runs up to the castle door, looks around, then turns back and nods an O.K.

ROBIN: It's all quiet and still, Humpty.

HUMPTY: *(to Ma and the three mice)* You get ready to raise a big yell and howl when I knock the door.   Pretend like you're the King's army, not a mere rabbely police mob, O.K? *(they nod in agreement)*

And *(to the audience)* you all out there can shout out too.

(to the black sheep) Meanwhile, you write down this proclamation from the King.

As Humpty mutters something inaudible, the black sheep fuss around with paper and pens and hand a blank sheet of paper to Humpty. The atmosphere is conspiratorial.

HUMPTY: *(approaching the castle gate, holding out the paper and shouting loudly to Guyfox)* In the name of the King, I, Humpty Dumpty who, as all the world knows, commands the full army and horses of the King, I call upon Squire Guyfox, the sly fox and thief of Chicken, Cat and Lamb Counties, to release BoPeep, all her sheep and PussyCat.   Ah, ahem.   Remembering that I . . as reported worldwide.

HUMPTY DUMPTY SONG

d m   r f   m s   m d
Humpty Dumpty sat on a wall
d   d m   r f   m   d l_1 t_1
And Humpty Dumpty had a great fall
d   r   m   f   s f   m
Then all the King's horses and
m   f   s   l
All the King's men
$d^1 d^1$ l $r^1 r^1$
Couldn't put Humpty
d^1 t l   t d^1
Together again.

So therefore, calling once again upon all the King's horses and all the King's men *(he signals with an upraised hand to the company and the audience to be ready)* all here assembled, present and correct and ready to invade, I hereby formally read this the Riot Act to the said Squire Guyfox and call upon him to restore law and order to the King's domain and set the aforesaid prisoners free or suffer *(he still holds up his hand)* or suffer the wrath of the King's army, men and horses, all here assembled. NOW. *(he lowers his hand as a signal and the cast and audience roar)*

CAST AND AUDIENCE:
OPEN UP. OPEN UP. OPEN UP.

Guyfox appears meekly at the door and surrenders. He is handcuffed by the two black sheep. BoPeep and PussyCat emerge and embrace the rescuers.

GUYFOX: *(innocently)* There must be some mistake, here, folks. This is a legitimate hotel. No one is being held here against their will. I look after my guests so very well. Why, I was just expecting the bakersmen to arrive with a very special breakfast.

ROBIN: *(embracing BoPeep while PussyCat hugs Ma)* Wonderful, the bakersmen have arrived. That's us. *(waving a hand at the black sheep and the three blind mice)* Give Squire Guyfox some of those nice cakes for breakfast.

Humpty's followers produce their custard and fudge cakes and throw them all over Guyfox and the dog who stagger weakly with knobbly knees under the onslaught. Some little cake naturally also falls on Humpty Dumpty and even a little on

PussyCat, Robin and BoPeep. The lambs now enter the stage from the castle interior, mid stage, once again dressed like dancer-lambs as in Act One, Scene One, followed from right stage by the singers as the skylarks. All shuffle around to take their place for the finale . . .

Curtain

SCENE THREE - Finale

Scene Three: The Same. At left-stage, in some shadow, as a scene within a scene, Guyfox is tied to a stake and surrounded by brush and branches and firewood. No one is paying any attention to Guy except the dog who stands by with a red flare, or box of matches, ready to set fire to the pile.

Robin and BoPeep stand hand in hand at center upstage bowing to each other. To right of Robin and BoPeep, Ma pats PussyCat on the head. Right-stage Humpty Dumpty is being fitted with new limbs by his followers. The mice squeal and the black sheep "baa" in support of Humpty. Downstage left stands the chorus as skylarks and downstage right the lambs are gathered as dancers still dressed as in Act One, Scene One. While this festival of finale and success occupies most of the cast, they are unaware of Guyfox fooling the dog and making his escape. Lights focus briefly on Guyfox.

GUYFOX: *(to dog)* Come here, Brother Jackie.

The dog approaches Guy, mouth open and nodding vacantly.

GUYFOX: Sergeant Humpty Dumpty is just waving to you and shouting something to you.

Dog looks around, wide-eyed and open-mouthed but sees nothing.

DOG: What is it, Squire Guyfox?

GUYFOX: I can't quite hear for all the noise but I think Cock Robin is saying that you should free me and drag and manhandle and haul me over to him and his police force. Hmm. I suppose he wants to interrogate me. *(to audience)* Isn't this true?

AUDIENCE: *(in unison)* NO. NO. NO.

GUYFOX: *(to dog)* Go ahead, Brother Jackie. I don't mind. Like he says, take me over to the sergeant. He wants to torture me. Ain't it only natural. Ain't it so folks? *(to audience)*

AUDIENCE: *(in unison)* NO. NO. NO.

Dog unties and frees Guy who pushes dog down and runs toward offstage left.

GUYFOX: *(to audience)* Ha, Ha, some army Humpty Dumpty has - I don't think. *(shakes his fist at the audience)* You fooled me this time but I'll soon round up my soldiers again. I'm the Squire, Guyfox. You can't stop me. I come back every year and I'll be back - I'll get you all - next year for sure!! I'm the plunger into darkness - Skyhigh Guy!

He mimes plunging off an explosion as before. He slinks offstage, still shaking his fist defiantly at the company and the audience.

DOG: *(to stage company)* Guyfox has escaped.

They stop their formation.

ROBIN: Oh never mind. Everyone is free and safe and happy. Guy and his men have run away and we've taken over his castle. We'll just have to forgive him, this time. Come and join in the songs, Brother Jackie.

> *Dog joins the main company center.*
>
> *The entire company, including Guyfox who rejoins and bows to audience, all take part in the singing and dancing of the various numbers following much the same format and style as before. If there is time, all of each song can be sung and danced. If there is not sufficient time, selected verses and refrains should be presented. PussyCat and Mother Goose dance together as does Dog and Humpty. Robin and BoPeep dance at the center of attention.*
>
> *Generally the songs may be sung in any order but **SKYLARK** (see p. 128) should be the last song but one and the very last song should be **HOME WITH A GOOD COMPANION** (see p. 134) featuring Robin*

and BoPeep as the central figures around whom the rest dance and sing. Finally, BoPeep and Robin join hands center stage and all bow to the audience.

Final Curtain

END OF PANTOMIME

Old Working Dog

Short Story and Three-Act Pantomime

The Story

One day there were two pickup trucks driving along the road. One truck was driven by a security officer and the other was driven by a crook. In the back of the security officer's truck was Barkie, a large German Shepherd, who helped his owner as a guard dog. Sometimes Barkie was loaned out to people who needed their premises guarded, perhaps because of a threat or an outbreak of burglaries in the district.

In the other truck was Sniffie who belonged to a crook. Sniffie's job was to sniff out contraband. His master was in the habit of selling forged money and the like to the general public and then Sniffie would smell around and locate the contraband so that his master could steal it back and, of course, offer it for sale again. Sniffie was a cheerful black and tan beagle.

The two dogs looked at each other from their respective trucks and seemed to take a liking to each other. It was a stormy, wet and misty day so that neither the crook nor the security officer had a clear view of their surroundings.

As the two trucks approached a fork in the road, they came quite close together. Sniffie and Barkie both jumped at each other. Each dog wanted to join the other but both ended up in the opposite truck. They stared at each other in a friendly way though both were in a strange truck. Before they had even a chance to bark, each truck was driven at top speed along the two different roads that lead from the fork.

When they arrived home, the crook and his pal were astonished to find a strange dog in their truck. Likewise, the security officer was surprised to end up with Sniffie, a dog that he had never seen before. The crook and his pal soon discovered that Barkie was not much good at sniffing out contraband. But they decided to keep him as a guard dog to prowl around their old scrapyard. This yard was filled with stolen parts and sometimes attracted curiosity seekers who had to be reminded to pay for the parts if they wanted them.

In the meantime, the security officer advertised on the local radio and in the newspaper that he had found Sniffie the beagle and asked for the return of Barkie the German Shepherd. For some strange reason Sniffie was never retrieved by the crooks. Clearly they did not want to get too close to the law. So Sniffie remained with the security officer.

Meanwhile, the crooks who now owned Barkie had counterfeited a large pile of paper money. They passed the word out among all their acquaintances that their very well printed paper notes were on sale at twenty percent of their nominal value. This meant that anyone who bought the counterfeits for real money could travel around and buy cheap items from stores, markets or fairgrounds and collect real notes in their change. Even allowing for the small cost of the items bought, they would still be able to double or treble their money in a couple of weeks.

One day an undercover private eye phoned up to make an appointment with the crooks. She told them that she wanted to buy ten thousand counterfeit bills for two thousand in real genuine money. This seemed like a good deal to the crooks so they invited her to visit them. When she arrived at their scrapyard, Barkie jumped up in a friendly way. This was hardly surprising as the visitor who wanted to buy the counterfeits was none other than a friend of his former owner. After handing over two thousand for the ten thousand counterfeits she pressed the alarm button on her mobile phone. Soon her friend, the security officer, arrived and arrested the two crooks. The crooks were crestfallen when it was explained to them that their mistake had been not to collect their former dog Sniffie from the security officer's house. This had given the clue to the security officer that Barkie's new owner had something to hide. The authorities had already been investigating the fact that some bad money was being passed in that general area. After that, they began asking around if anyone had seen or heard of a new guard dog in the district. This resulted in the crooks getting arrested and convicted of forging money.

The security officer and his friend, the private investigator, now owned two dogs. For the crooks had been sent to jail. Both dogs were taken by their new owners to the school of dog professions. Barkie did a course in crowd control and another as household guard to improve his skills. Sniffie was also able to learn more about being a seeing-eye dog and a hunter. Both dogs were able to graduate with a certificate in their professional doggie skills.

Sniffie and Barkie became the best of friends. After all, this had been their original intention when they had changed places by jumping into each other's truckbeds on that wet and stormy day.

END OF STORY

Contents of Pantomime

PRODUCTION SPECIFICATIONS

SETS   There are two scenes – the junkyard and the police station.

STAGE TIME   60-90 minutes depending on the treatment of the songs.

ACTORS   Six or Seven

MUSIC   There are four catchy songs: *Old Working Dog; Drink your Tea; What a Good Dog I Will Be; I'm Just an Old True Blue.*

CHARACTERS

BARKIEDOG: (Principal Boy)

SNIFFIEDOG: (Principal Girl)

SAMMY: Original owner of Barkiedog.

PADDY: SniffieDog's original owner.

A likeable but shady junkyard part-owner.

SHIFTYBOY: The Villain – Paddy's partner.

POLICE SERGEANT: A full-time police officer.

POLICEMEN (one or two)

DAME CATCHACROOK: Grand Dame

OUTLINE

ACT ONE – WHERE HAS MY DOGGIE GONE?

Scene One: Grand Dame tells a Story

Scene Two: At the Police Mad House

ACT TWO - IN THE OLD JUNKYARD

Scene One: BarkieDog finds a Home

Old Working Dog

Scene Two: Time for a Teabreak
ACT THREE - FUN AND GAMES FROM GRAND DAME
Scene One: Dame Catchacrook and the Villain
Scene Two: BarkieDog and SniffieDog

ACT ONE
WHERE HAS MY DOGGIE GONE?
SCENE ONE: GRAND DAME TELLS A STORY

Enter the Grand Dame dressed like a cleaner and carrying her broom. She sweeps up and down the stage then stops and points the broom at the audience.

DAME CATCHACROOK: *(in a gossipy tone, to the audience)* Have I got a story for you. Look, two pickup trucks just stopped at a fork in the road over there. *(she points her broom offstage)* You'll never guess what happened then. *(leaning on her broom)* Each truck had a dog in the back and those two dogs jumped at each other and each one landed up in the other's truckbed. They must have taken a liking to each other. *(flashes of thunder and lightning are heard)*

Anyhow, each pickup went in a different direction at the fork. Imagine when those guys get home. Each one will have a strange dog in his truck. Now .. they'll never find out till they get home. It's difficult enough to see the road ahead of you in a storm - never mind keeping track of what's behind you ... I'd like to see their faces ...

Hey, have you ever thought what it would be like to change places with another person just like those two dogs?

Well . . . We'll have the parts of the dogs played by persons – Principal Boy and Principal Girl – just to make the whole thing vivid for you.

I'm heading up to the old lunatic asylum police station to find out what's going on there.

She hobbles offstage, still swinging her broom.

Curtain

ACT ONE
WHERE HAS MY DOGGIE GONE?
SCENE TWO: AT THE POLICE MAD HOUSE
The scene is set in the local police station. In the background, several policemen are engaged in jumping around, shooting water pistols at each other and arresting each other, doing cartwheels, blowing police whistles, twisting arms behind backs. In general there is chaos. These scenes of mayhem can be acted out or painted on a backdrop – whichever is preferred.

Enter Sammy the security officer with his new-found dog, SniffieDog (Principal Girl), dressed in light outfit for dancing. She has a doggie headdress and a bushy tail. Sammy approaches the desk sergeant.

SAMMY: Hello officer. When I got home after that storm I found this dog. I call her SniffieDog because she sniffs quite a lot. She was sitting in the back of my truck. There was no sign of my own dog, old BarkieDog.

The sergeant blinks and stares hard at Sammy while he continues his story.

You see? . . . This old dog here showed up in my pickup truck after the storm just a couple of days ago. It looks like my own dog, BarkieDog, must have jumped out and this girl here jumped in.

It's strange but we sent out a radio announcement describing her *(he looks at SniffieDog in admiration)* and asking her real owner to claim her. *(shakes his head and shrugs)* Well we're going to carry on with more announcements but so far - absolutely no reply. I wonder why?

SERGEANT: You're under arrest. *(he begins to thumb through wanted posters, then holds up the poster of a big, fat, bearded wanted outlaw)* No, I don't think you're him or you must have grown a great beard.

Sammy looking bored, blinks in astonishment

SERGEANT: So, why are you here if not to give yourself up? And who is this dog that you've brought into our nice, clean police station? So you say you found her in your pickup truck and at the same time you lost your own dog? A likely story. You didn't steal her, I suppose? Sounds very suspicious to me.

Enter a police constable.

POLICE CONSTABLE: All the police are on mutiny, Sergeant.

SERGEANT: Why?

POLICE CONSTABLE: They haven't had a mutiny in years, sir. They're about overdue for a revolt, aren't they?

SERGEANT: Oh, gee whizz! Shoot them all . . especially the ring leader.

*Enter **Dame Catchacrook** with her broom. She puts the soft end of the broom under her right armpit and points the other end at all in turn.*

DAME CATCHACROOK: Rat-a-tat-tat.   Lie down. You're all dead.

SERGEANT: *(ignoring her and addressing the police constable)* Who is the ring leader of this mutiny?

POLICE CONSTABLE: You are, Sergeant.

SERGEANT: *(astonished and almost speechless)* But I know nothing about all this rioting.

POLICE CONSTABLE: *(saluting respectfully)* Why should <u>we</u> not have elected you, sir, as our leader? We greatly respect you, sir.

Sergeant is a little mollified by this flattery

POLICE CONSTABLE: Ignorance is not an excuse for crime, sir. But don't worry . . I'll shoot you anyway with my trusty water pistol.

He takes his water pistol out of his belt and squirts water at the sergeant, who splutters and fumes

SERGEANT: How dare you! You halfwit.

DAME CATCHACROOK: *(again pretends to shoot all and sundry)* Rat-a-tat-tat. Lie down. You're all dead.

SAMMY: Is this is a mad house?

DAME CATCHACROOK: O no, not a mad house! No never, never, since the patients took over.

SAMMY: *(ignoring her remarks)* See . . I don't know what this dog can do. I don't know what to do with her. I used to use my other dog for my security work. But for all I know this dog is no good to me. Can she go on guard duty? Can she scare off the burglars? For all I know I might not be able to afford her high-class meals or her pedicures and grooming.

DAME CATCHACROOK: *(looks Sammy up and down)* Ah, I see you are a security officer. I just stopped by at the right moment. I can catch anyone, anywhere. *(she seizes Sammy by* *the shoulder)* I can solve all your mysteries. I'm a private eye. Ain't that right, Sergeant?

SERGEANT: How would I know? I only deal with legitimate cops.

SAMMY: *(shaking himself free from her grip)* The only mystery I've got at the moment is - who is this dog? Where has my dog gone? And what can this dog do for a living to earn her keep?

SERGEANT: *(to Grand Dame)* Where's your private investigators certificate and badge?

DAME CATCHACROOK: Here they are Sergeant. *(she produces them out of her shoulderbag)* I know they're genuine. I bought them through an advertisement in the children's favorite comic – that sterling paper, the Beano or was it the Dandy?

SERGEANT: Hmm . . . that's what I was afraid of. *(shakes his head sadly and rolls his eyes)*

One of the policemen approaches and salutes the sergeant respectfully

SERGEANT: Oh, another clean-shaven one. You're under arrest.

POLICEMAN: But Sergeant, I belong to this police station. I want to make a helpful suggestion.

Sammy turns to Grand Dame and shakes his head

SAMMY: Is this a police station or the monkey house in the zoo?

DAME CATCHACROOK: You misunderstand. This place is no monkey house. I've already checked it out. It used to be a mad house, a raving lunatic asylum but the inmates took over and have never yet been kicked out.

SAMMY: But surely the government had them removed and the . . err . . hospital reinstated?

DAME CATCHACROOK: Well, normally they would but this time they said they had no money for the changeover. So they just left it as a police station to humor the inmates and save some money. That's why its still in this state.

(to audience) This nice police station isn't a mad house, is it?

AUDIENCE: *(in unison, with deliberate emphasis)* OH YES, IT IS.

DAME CATCHACROOK: Oh not, it isn't.

AUDIENCE: *(in unison)* OH YES, IT IS.

SAMMY: *(to audience)* Surely a police station cannot be a mad house?

AUDIENCE: *(in unison)* OH YES, IT IS.

SERGEANT: *(to audience)* What an insult to me.

AUDIENCE: *(in unison)* BOO. HISS.

POLICEMAN: *(still saluting the sergeant, continues his speech)* My idea was . . if you want to find out about this dog, why don't you ask her?

The sergeant beams on the policeman

SERGEANT: That's a great idea.

Sammy shrugs and addresses the dog

SAMMY: What can you do to earn a living? Will I be able to afford your special tastes?

They all sing Verse One of **OLD WORKING DOG**. *The Principal Girl, SniffieDog, sings the Refrain.*

OLD WORKING DOG
Sung: Lively

VERSE ONE

m   s   l   s   m   d   d - d   t₁   l₁   l₁   l₁

There are all kinds of dogs in this wide world, we know

d - d   t₁   l₁   l₁   s₁   l₁ - s₁   m

There are dogs that can jump over sticks

m   s   l   s   m   d   d - d   t₁ - l₁   l₁   r

There are dogs that can bark off the burglars, and bite

r - r   f   r   t₁   s₁   l₁ - t₁   d

And bright dogs that do clever tricks

m   s   l   s   m   d   d - d   t₁   l₁   l₁   l₁

There are bad dogs and good dogs and old dogs and all

d - d   t₁   l₁   l₁   s₁ - l₁   s₁   m

And dogs that can tumble and jog

m - s   l   s   m   d   d - d   t₁   l₁   l₁   r

But I'll bark and run till my day's work is done

r - r   f   r   t₁   s₁   l₁ - t₁   d

For I'm just an old working dog. *(woof, woof)*

REFRAIN:

m   s   l   s   m   d - d   d   t₁ - l₁   l₁   l₁

There are dogs that are pampered and pretty and proud

d - d   t₁   l₁   l₁   s₁   l₁   s₁   m

There are dogs that live high on the hog *(woof, woof)*

m - s   l   s   m   d   d - d   t₁   l₁ - l₁   r

But I'll earn my pay any hard-working way

r - r   f   r   t₁   s₁   l₁ - t₁   d

For I'm just an old working dog *(woof, woof)*

Old Working Dog

VERSE ONE
There are all kinds of dogs in this wide world we know
There are dogs that can jump over sticks
There are dogs that can bark off the burglars and bite
And bright dogs that do clever tricks
There are bad dogs and good dogs and old dogs and all
And dogs that can tumble and jog
But I'll bark and run till my day's work is done
For I'm just an old working dog. *(woof, woof)*

REFRAIN: *(sung by SniffieDog)*
There are dogs that are pampered and pretty and proud
There are dogs that live high on the hog *(woof, woof)*
But I'll earn my pay any hard-working way
For I'm just an old working dog *(woof, woof)*.

End of Song and
Curtain

END OF ACT ONE

ACT TWO
IN THE OLD JUNKYARD
SCENE ONE: BARKIEDOG FINDS A HOME

Set in an old junkyard. Mostly derelict cars but some household appliances are strewn here and there. The junkyard is surrounded by a wooden fence, right and left. The backdrop is that of continuing wooden fences meeting up with the back porch of an old house.

Enter left ShiftyBoy and Paddy, *two colorfully dressed, be-suited, slick crooks, owners of the junkyard. Shiftyboy sports a large black moustache. Paddy is leading in BarkieDog (Principal Boy) who is dressed lightly for dancing with a doggie headdress and a bushy tail. Paddy looks at her in astonishment, shakes his head, shrugs his shoulders at ShiftyBoy.*

PADDY: ShiftyBoy, I swear I don't know how it happened!

SHIFTYBOY: *(incredulously)* You're telling me you didn't swap this dog? You don't know where you got her? Now Paddy, what are you trying to give me?

PADDY: ShiftyBoy. It's true *(laughing)* I didn't see a thing. There was snow and light blackouts and sleet. Somebody musta taken advantage of me at a traffic light and switched dogs on me. Gee, the world is full of crooks. *(shakes his head)* Takes our nice SniffieDog and puts in her place this old critter who does nothing but bark. I didn't suspect a thing until we were home and I saw that SniffieDog was gone.

SHIFTYBOY: Why didn't you tie SniffieDog down?

PADDY: Oh come on ShiftyBoy. You know you shouldn't tie a dog down when the road is slippery. Why if we'd slid or had a wreck she'd a bin trapped . . . Why . . .

SHIFTYBOY: *(interrupting)* Oh, the storm . . O.K. O.K. *(spreads his hands quizzically)* Well, what are we going to do with this big gal?

As long as she's here we'll have to get her something to do.

He pats BarkieDog on the head and back

SHIFTYBOY: Is she a good dog or a bad dog, do you think?

PADDY: Oh, she's a good dog, I'm sure.

SHIFTYBOY: How do you know?

PADDY: I can tell by her face and her demeanor - her general conduct and looks - see . . .

SHIFTYBOY: *(interrupting)* Now just a minute. You're going by her looks and manner?

PADDY: *(nods)* Sure.

SHIFTYBOY: Well, how do you know she's not just a mean, bad dog who's a good actor? Some dogs are real cunning hypocrites you know.

PADDY: *(laughing and patting BarkieDog)* You can see she's a sincere dog - look at those big cheerful Irish eyes. Right girl, you're honest aren't you? If you're a bad dog bark once and if you're a good dog bark twice.

BARKIEDOG: Woof, Woof.

PADDY: There, I told you she was a good dog and she has just barked twice.

SHIFTYBOY: *(continuing and pointing to BarkieDog)* If that dog is honest as you say – she'll be no good to us. She'll inform on us to the cops.

PADDY: Let's ask her more directly. *(addressing BarkieDog)* Will you behave yourself? Will you be good and do what you are told?

BarkieDog leads the singing of **O WHAT A GOOD DOG I WILL BE.** *While both ShiftyBoy and Paddy are cavorting and throwing stage money in the air.*

WHAT A GOOD DOG I WILL BE
Sung: Cheerful and Rollicking

VERSE ONE

d   r   m   m   m - m   r   d   m   s   s - s
Now the bad dogs today just won't do as we say
l   s   m   d - d   r   m   l₁
But still they expect to get food
d   m   m   m - m   r   d   m   s   s - s
Why should they get fed and why should they get bed
l - l   s   m   d   r   m - r   d
When their manners are not very good.

REFRAIN:

m - m   s   s   s   s   l   t d^1 - d^1 l - d^1
I will sit up and beg and then hold up a leg
l   s   m   d - d   r   m - l₁   m   l₁
I'll stick out my tongue and agree (you'll see)
d   m   m   m   m   r   d   m s   s   s
O please let me do all you're asking me to
l   s   m   d   r   m   r   d   r   d
O what a good dog I will be (you'll see)

ShiftyBoy sings as he walks up and down and looks with aloof aspersion at BarkieDog. Paddy acts the part of a dog along with BarkieDog, getting down on all fours and miming the responses and promising to be good.

SHIFTYBOY: *(looking down on BarkieDog)*
Now the bad dogs today just won't do as we say
But still they expect to get food
Why should they get fed and why should they
get bed
When their manners are not very good.

BARKIEDOG: *(crouching on all fours)*
I'll run round in a loop or I'll jump through a hoop
I'll crawl on the ground and lie low
I'll cover my face and pretend to say Yes
I'll bring back whatever you throw.

> *They throw more stage money in the air
> and dance around.*

SHIFTYBOY: *(strutting up and down and looking
at BarkieDog with evident distaste)*
Still it's quite an affront when they can't do a stunt
Like cringe away down and play dead
If they can't earn their pay in some groveling way
I don't think they ought to get paid.

PADDY: *(acting out the parts of the verse, on his
hands and knees)*

REFRAIN:
I will sit up and beg and then hold up a leg
I'll stick out my tongue and agree (you'll see)
(he puts out his tongue and nods)

O please let me do all you're asking me to
O what a good dog I will be (you'll see)
(Paddy holds his hands before him like begging paws)

Curtain

ACT TWO
IN THE OLD JUNKYARD
SCENE TWO: TIME FOR A TEABREAK
Same scene: The old junkyard. The two crooks are inspecting their hoards of counterfeit money and stolen car parts.

SHIFTYBOY: *(to Paddy)* I'm glad to know that BarkieDog is going to tag along with all our enterprises.

PADDY: Yes. I think everything is going to turn out just fine.

SHIFTYBOY: Let's just all relax now and get on with our thieving and counterfeiting as usual.

PADDY: Right. That sounds like a good time to have a teabreak.

They all sing DRINK YOUR TEA.

DRINK YOUR TEA
Sung: Jolly

VERSE ONE:

d   d   d   d l_1 - d
Don't get scared or skittish
f   f f   r - f
Fight to the finish
d   d   d   d   r - d
Be proud to be British
d l_1 s_1
Drink your tea
d   d   d   d l_1 - d
No matter how you suffer
f f f   f   r - f
Keep a true stiff upper
f f f   f   m - m
Eat a good fish supper
f   s   f
Drink your tea

PADDY:
Don't get scared or skittish
Fight to the finish
Be proud to be British
Drink your tea

SHIFTYBOY:
No matter how you suffer
Keep a true stiff upper
Eat a good <u>fish supper</u>
Drink your tea

BARKIEDOG:
Don't let worries hook you
Don't let life rebuke you
Let's all go cuckoo
Drinking tea, drinking tea

PADDY:
Let's not get flappie
Let's not be snappy
Let's all be happy
Drink your tea.

BARKIEDOG: Drink your tea, everybody.

SHIFTYBOY: That's fine everybody. You BarkieDog, have now got a new home and a new job. We're going to keep you on as a guard dog for all our little stolen treasures. Anytime anyone comes snooping around here without our sayso . . give a good loud bark and we'll soon come running.

BARKIEDOG: Woof, Woof.

SHIFTYBOY: *(to audience)* BarkieDog will be happy to join us. Won't she?

AUDIENCE: *(in unison)* OH NO, SHE WON'T.

SHIFTYBOY AND HIS SIDEKICK (PADDY): Oh yes, she will.

AUDIENCE: *(in unison)* OH NO, SHE WON'T.

SHIFTYBOY: *(to audience)* She's going to join our gang whether she likes it or not. *(sneering at audience)* See!

AUDIENCE: *(in unison)* BOO. HISS.

The spotlight remains on all three as:.

Curtain
END OF ACT TWO

ACT THREE
FUN AND GAMES FROM GRAND DAME
SCENE ONE: DAME CATCHACROOK
AND THE VILLAIN

The scene opens on the junkyard and, much as before, a few minor rearrangements of props being possible to indicate the passage of a few days or weeks. BarkieDog is walking about quietly in a corner. It is dusk and lighting is low but all props and action should be visible. The house in the background is lit in the windows.

Enter from right ShiftyBoy and Paddy *both carrying bags of counterfeit money. These may be made up of bundles of plain paper cut the same size as regular currency notes with stage money on top. They sit down center stage and examine the counterfeit money in admiration and pleasure, holding it up and whistling and laughing.*

PADDY: *(holding up a counterfeit bill)* This is my answer to inflation - make your own money. Money ain't worth what it used to be - so make a little more of it.

SHIFTYBOY: Pity we can't spend it ourselves. I guess we're too well known but at least we can help others share our good fortune. For a fair price, of course. I'm expecting a good buyer along later tonight.

PADDY: *(chortling)* O we'll soon be back in clover again, ShiftyBoy, me boy. With the real money piling in for this phony stuff, why - before you can say Jack Robinson, we'll be living the life of Riley up on Easy Street.

They laugh.

SHIFTYBOY: That sounds like the title of one of those books on Get Rich Quick.

PADDY: That's the name of the book all right, me boyoh - Get Rich Quick.

They pull out of their bags a couple of bottles or cans of drinks.

SHIFTYBOY: I'll drink to that.

They drink a toast to each other.

PADDY: To all this counterfeit money.

SHIFTYBOY: We'll soon have enough real money to buy back the good old days.

PADDY: Yes, here's to the good old days before the war.

SHIFTYBOY: Which war?

PADDY: Oh, any old war. Wars are run like fashion shows - for the rich. Wars only make life worse for poor boys like us.

SHIFTYBOY: Do you know that's the truth Paddy. Things weren't so bad before the war, indeed. And that's why we have to be so hard-working to make it in life.

They laugh hugely and slap each other in mirth. Then they pause as there is the sound of knocking on wood offstage, left.

SHIFTYBOY: Hshh. There's someone at the gates.

PADDY: Probably our customer. I'll go and check.

Paddy leaves stage left and reenters with Dame Catchacrook, dressed as before and carrying a shoulderstrap handbag.

PADDY: *(to ShiftyBoy)* Allow me to introduce the investor we were expecting. This is Miss Willowby.
(to Dame Catchacrook) Meet my esteemed partner . . ah . . Billy McGowan. Now, Miss Willowby I understand *(Paddy raises his eyebrows)* that you are interested in investing in bank notes. One official one for five unofficial. Yes?

DAME CATCHACROOK: Let's speak plainly – I'll buy. I have the money here, *(she taps her handbag)* forged money at one fifth its nominal value. I'll give you one good note for every five phony ones. O.K?

SHIFTYBOY: We understand each other perfectly. But I hope that R ... Ralph here has told you, that this is wholesale only. We'll only sell a minimum of 5,000, as you like to say, forged for 1,000 at a time, all right.

DAME CATCHACROOK: (naively) You'll only sell 5,000 worth? Gee, that's a problem. (Paddy and ShiftyBoy look shocked) I wanted 10,000 worth for 2,000 real money. Maybe I should try elsewhere . . .

SHIFTYBOY AND PADDY: (relieved) Oh, no, Miss Willowby.

PADDY: Oh, that's not a problem. That's fine.

SHIFTYBOY: (smiling calmly) Not to worry. I said a minimum of 5,000 - that means at least that. Of course you can have as many phony bills as you want.

PADDY: (eagerly) No, No, there's no maximum - only a minimum.

DAME CATCHACROOK: (pleased) Oh yes. (to ShiftyBoy) You did say a minimum. How silly of me. Well . . can I have 10,000 worth for this *(she produces a roll of bills)* <u>real</u> 2,000 notes?

Paddy and ShiftyBoy cheerfully rubbing their hands together, nodding and winking to each other, begin to count out 10,000 in stage money.

While they are engaged in this activity, Dame Catchacrook looks around the yard suspiciously. She then looks at her watch surreptitiously by holding it up to the faint light and giving the impression of being anxious. She produces the pre-counted 2,000 from her bag and hands it to ShiftyBoy as Paddy gives her the larger packet of 10,000 phony money.

PADDY: Now this is a lot of hot money, 10,000. Do you know not to try to pass more than one 20 bill at a time, making sure there is a lot of real money in change and only in crowded places where checkout clerks are in a terrific hurry? For example, fast food stands, fairgrounds, bookies, busy cafes and the like?

DAME CATCHACROOK: *(interrupting)* I know how to pass them off. Here is your 2,000 <u>real</u> money for these 10,000 phony notes. *(putting the phony money in her bag)*

SHIFTYBOY: *(smiling)* Now when you put it like that, you make us sound like positive crooks. But look, you'll end up with about 7,000 or 8,000 in real money. That's a lot better than <u>anyone</u> could do in legitimate dealing. Why that's 400 percent profit in just a few months of passing off phony bills in bits and pieces *(he laughs)* of course, that is, if you're not caught . .

DAME CATCHACROOK: Me caught? No. But you two are. I'm Dame Catchacrook, I'm a private investigator. You're both under arrest for selling phony money. Get back - over there. Put your hands up.

Paddy and ShiftyBoy move back stunned and surprised, hands in air. Then suddenly ShiftyBoy produces his water pistol.

SHIFTYBOY: *(to audience)* She's just a dirty doublecrossing spy, isn't she?

AUDIENCE: *(in unison)* OH NO, SHE ISN'T.

PADDY: *(to audience)* Private Eye? Rubbish – she's an informer and a squealer, isn't she?

AUDIENCE: *(in unison)* OH NO, SHE ISN'T.

Dame Catchacrook looks nervously again at her watch. She then produces a much larger water pistol from her bag and points it at ShiftyBoy and Paddy. ShiftyBoy and Dame Catchacrook both squirt water from their water pistols all over each other.

DAME CATCHACROOK: Yes, I'm a spy and an informer. Now you have a right to remain silent but anything you say may be used against you.

Dame Catchacrook takes a whistle out of her bag and blows it. She is clearly afraid and looks left stage to the gate in concern that no relief is coming. Seeing her concern,

ShiftyBoy and Paddy begin to recover their self-confidence and cheerfulness. They begin to move towards Dame Catchacrook, their hands in the air but becoming clearly menacing and threatening.

PADDY: *(in a soft and charming tone)* Och, now, you can't shoot us for selling phony money. Now if we were just to run for it, you wouldn't shoot us in the back, now, would you?
(to audience) She wouldn't soak our backs with that big water pistol, would she?

AUDIENCE:*(in unison)* OH YES SHE WOULD.

Paddy and ShiftyBoy advance tentatively towards Dame Catchacrook, who backs away to left stage.

DAME CATCHACROOK: You're both under arrest. If you come closer I'm authorized to shoot the entire contents of this water pistol at you in self defense. *(edgily as she retreats)* Get back.

Dame Catchacrook blows her police whistle again but Paddy and ShiftyBoy, hands held high, advance towards her slowly but with increasing confidence. She suddenly lowers her water pistol and runs behind BarkieDog. ShiftyBoy and Paddy draw back in fear as BarkieDog stands between them and Dame Catchacrook.

DAME CATCHACROOK: *(to BarkieDog and pointing towards Paddy and ShiftyBoy)* Don't let them get me, BarkieDog.

BARKIEDOG: Woof, Woof.

SHIFTYBOY: Look here, we're not trying to get you. We're just leaving. Don't panic. We're not going to outstay our welcome. Are we Paddy?

PADDY: No, of course not. Let's go.

SHIFTYBOY: *(to audience)* We're going to make a run for it. We'll get away with it. Won't we?

AUDIENCE: *(in unison)*
OH NO YOU WON'T.

SHIFTYBOY: Oh yes, we will. *(twirling his moustache)* We have it all worked out.

AUDIENCE: *(in unison)* BOO. HISS.

They turn and dash towards right stage as:

<u>Curtain</u>

ACT THREE
FUN AND GAMES FROM GRAND DAME
SCENE TWO: BARKIEDOG
AND SNIFFIEDOG

Scene: The same junkyard. **Enter right stage Sammy with SniffieDog.** *Sammy bumps into ShiftyBoy and Paddy trying to make their escape. Sammy grapples briefly with Paddy and ShiftyBoy, stands them against a wall, with hands raised and frisks them, then handcuffs them.*

PADDY: *(to Sniffiedog)* SniffieDog! It's me, yo'll pal. How can you do this - help to arrest me? Don't you know your old friend - Paddy?

SNIFFIEDOG: Woof. Woof.

SAMMY: *(to Paddy)* This used to be your dog. But now, as far as she's concerned you're just like any other crook that needs rounding up.

PADDY: Well I can see it from my old pal's point of view. *(he pats BarkieDog on the head)* Yes, ShiftyBoy and I are just like sheep who need to get back into the flock - after a few weeks I hope I come back home here, eh?

SHIFTYBOY: *(looks sadly at BarkieDog and SniffieDog)* Goodbye BarkieDog. Goodbye SniffieDog. See you in a few weeks if you haven't starved or been put down by the Dog Pound.

SAMMY: No chance of that while I'm here . . .

SHIFTYBOY: *(surprised)* Oh, really. Well, in that case you can have a gift of BarkieDog there. That's O.K. with you, Paddy isn't it?

PADDY: Sure. You take both of them, sir, if you like'em. They're both good dogs, you know, in their different ways. But can I ask you just one question.

DAME CATCHACROOK: Yes. But make it quick.

SHIFTYBOY: *(breaking in)* I'll ask it. How did you find us?

Paddy nods as much as to say yes that's the question.

SAMMY: A witness saw the dogs exchange places and called in to the local radio station. We broadcast an appeal to the new owner to get in touch but no one did. That gave us the clue that maybe the new owner of BarkieDog didn't like the police.

PADDY: Well, who does?

DAME CATCHACROOK: Then some of your neighbors noticed that you had a new guard dog and reported it to us. Anyway, I'm getting too old for helping out like this. No more Private Eye for me *(thinks)* at least unless I have BarkieDog here to help me. She was loyal and devoted and brave. A real true blue.

Old Working Dog

Enter Sergeant and Policemen from Act One, Scene Two. They join the others in singing:
I'M JUST AN OLD TRUE BLUE, *followed by* **OLD WORKING DOG** *(see p. 240),*
DRINK YOUR TEA *(see p. 249) and*
WHAT A GOOD DOG I WILL BE *(see p. 246)*
All four songs to be accompanied by the appropriate actions, cavorting, rolling, mining, etc.

I'M JUST AN OLD TRUE BLUE
Sung: Lively

VERSE ONE

s - f   m m   d r m   f t₁   d
There are a thousand colors that

d   r - m   r   d   d   d
Can light up a dog's highway

m   s   s   s - l - t   d¹   m   f
Pups have their auburns, pinks and blonds

s   l   l   t   l   s
Old dogs their iron and gray

m   s   s - s   s - l   t   d¹   m   f
Now once   I   was keen to fight and chase

s   l - l - l   t   l   s
Down many a path I flew

s - f   m   m   d - r   m   f   t₁   d
In those young days my flag was red

d   r   m   r   d   d   d
Now I'm just an old true blue

VERSE ONE
There are a thousand colors that
Can light up a dog's highway
Pups have their auburns, pinks and blonds
Old dogs their iron and gray
Now once I was keen to fight and chase
Down many a path I flew
In those young days my flag was red
Now I'm just an old true blue.

REFRAIN: *(sung by BarkieDog)*
When I was young and fond of fight
I hunted around all night
If long dark city streets were brown
The city lights were white
But time has torn my red flag down
And slowly changed its hue
I'm a good old boy, I'm the real McCoy
For I'm just an old true blue. *(woof, woof)*

VERSE TWO
The golden sun that sets at dusk
Keeps going down too soon
Then I howl at all the silver stars
To scare the yellow moon
For the purple planets pass on by
And don't care what I do
But I'll go bow wow at the black clouds now
For I'm just an old true blue.

Old Working Dog

REFRAIN: *(sung by SniffieDog)*
When I was young and fond of fight
I hunted around all night
If long dark city streets were brown
The city lights were white
But time has torn my red flag down
And slowly changed its hue
I'm a good old boy, I'm the real McCoy
For I'm just an old true blue. *(woof, woof)*

All the cast remain on stage and bow to audience as BarkieDog and SniffieDog (Principal Boy and Principal Girl) dance together center stage and give their last woof, woof, bow, wow.

Curtain

END OF PANTOMIME

Santa and the Nursery Rimers

Short Story and Three-Act Pantomime

The Story

Once upon a time Father Christmas was riding in his sleigh above a large snowy forest in Merry Old England. Cold winds were blowing fiercely and blew Santa off his sleigh, which traveled on without him. Santa fell through the snow and landed high up on the thick limb of a large gnarled evergreen tree which was leafy and snow covered.

Santa sprawled awkwardly on the large limb where he had just been accidentally jettisoned from his sleigh. Then he sat back more comfortably on a fork of the tree. All around, the trees were covered in snow. Underneath Santa was a stony path worn more or less clear of snow by frequent passers-by. It wound in and out far into the distance beyond.

Santa shouted and pointed up at his sleigh, "Come back and get me. I've fallen out." None of the reindeer heard him above the howling wind and soon the sleigh disappeared into the distance, shaking from side to side, to spill out the presents to lucky children underneath.

Santa was too high up in the tree to climb down, so he looked around for some help.

Sure enough, along the road, one by one there came quite a few well-known nursery rhyme persons. First of all came Dick Whittington and his

Cat. They promised to help Santa by fetching a ladder sometime soon.

Likewise, many of the other characters promised to fetch help in the near future. There was Jack and Jill who were too busy getting water from the nearby well.

Simple Simon, who was always hungry, was too busy looking for a free freshly-baked pie.

Little Jack Horner was also far too busy looking for a pie.

The Little Girl with the Little Curl right in the middle of her forehead had a fit of temper and stomped off in a huff.

The Old Woman who Lived in a Shoe had so many children that she didn't know what to do. She too didn't know how to get Santa down from the tree. She promised to return later when she had put all her children to bed.

There was an Old Soldier who wouldn't die but was only fading away.

Dr. Foster who went to Gloucester, was so unsure footed that he couldn't help Santa.

By the time these characters had all passed by, Father Christmas was nearly frozen when at long last Dick Whittington's Cat approached.

The Cat squatted on the path underneath Santa and washed its face. "See, Santa . . Old King Cole came back here with me to help you."

The Cat pointed to a small fat figure in the distance.

Santa peered into the distant snow, shook his head and told the Cat, "Well, I can't see him."

The Cat replied, "There's many a thing one can't see that's there after all. I know that Dick thinks that I'm a fibber but I'm really a good truthful cat . . ahem, meow . . most of the time. I never, never, never tell a lie . . hardly ever nowadays. Look, here comes Old King Cole now."

Surenuffski, along came Old King Cole cheerfully puffing, panting and carrying a ladder. He was very fat and dressed as a medieval king in robes and with a chain around his neck, tartan trews, heavy boots and, of course, a crown on his head.

Puffing and blowing, he addressed the cat, "Cat, you're so fast, I couldn't keep up with you. Where's Santa? Oh, yes there you are Santa. Hang on and we'll have you down in a jiffy."

Santa became quite afraid and placed his hand on his heart, "Oh, I'm afraid of jiffies. What are they anyway?"

Old King Cole raised his hand to calm down Father Christmas, "I just mean . . in a minute, you'll be back down on terra firma."

Santa was relieved and began to cheer up, "Great! Oh, I'm so pleased you came - Old King Cole. What can I get you for Christmas?"

Old King Cole began to shiver and rub his hands, "I could use a nice hot pie right now," he said to Santa.

The Cat began to lope about happily meowing and licking his paws and a-washing of his face in circular fashion.

Suddenly, out of the nearby bushes came Simple Simon, dazed, blinking open-mouthed and looking all around hopefully. He cried out, "Did somebody say "Pie"?"

Old King Cole shook his head, "Sorry, that was a mistake, Simon. No pie."

Simon was disappointed and muttered, "I do deserve a pie don't I?"

Then out of the woods ran Little Jack Horner, jumping and stomping his feet in a bad temper. "No, No, No. No pie for Simple Simon. You don't deserve a pie?"

At these words, Simple Simon turned away disappointed and disappeared into the woods again, followed by Little Jack Horner.

Old King Cole placed the ladder against the tree branch and beckoned Santa to descend. But Santa remained stiff and timorous.

He pleaded with Old King Cole, "I'm stiff and afraid of falling, come up and help me down."

Old King Cole replied, "Of course, of course, no problem."

Old King Cole climbed the ladder and sat on the same stout limb as Santa, leading him to the ladder. The Cat held the ladder firm as Old King Cole sat on the tree to the left of the ladder, puffing and panting with great merriment. Santa climbed down the ladder joyfully.

Gratefully he thanked the Cat and Old King Cole, "Oh, thank you Cat and Old King Cole - now I'll be able to get all these presents out on time. Quick, there's no time to lose, Cat."

The Cat and Santa dashed off, along the pathway, carrying the ladder between them and waved to Old King Cole, who was still up the tree.

Father Christmas shouted out, "Thanks a whole bunch, Old King Cole. Cheerio."

Old King Cole shouted back, "Cheerio Santa. Cheerio Cat. Give my regards to Dick Whittington, Cat."

Then the Cat nodded, meowed and waved as they disappeared into the snowy woods.

Old King Cole, still sitting on the limb of the tree, appeared to be relieved, "Hee, hee, hee. It was so nice of me to help out."

Then he looked down and gasped, "Hey, what about me? Help. Come back. Now it's me who's up a tree. Cat, come here - bring back that ladder."

The last that anyone saw of Old King Cole, he was still sitting on his snowy throne, high up in the tree. Perhaps we should stop by and visit him some day.

END OF STORY

Contents of Pantomime

PRODUCTION SPECIFICATIONS
One Set: Two Scenes
Thirteen Actors: Male or Female. Plus one or more extras as children.
Stage Time: 70-100 minutes.
Age: Mainly pre-teen audience. Actors of all ages.
Music: Some traditional nursery rhymes, arranged by the author, with new verses added.

CHARACTERS
Santa Claus a.k.a. Father Christmas
Dick Whittington's Cat
Dick Whittington
JackFrost (the Villain)
Dr. Foster
Little Jack Horner
Simple Simon
Jack (Principal Boy)
Jill (Principal Girl)
Little Girl with a Curl
Dame Liveinashoe (Grand Dame)
Old King Cole
Jolly Old Soldier
One or more Children as Extras

OUTLINE
ACT ONE - JACKFROST STRIKES
Scene One: Meet the Villain, JackFrost

ACT ONE
JACKFROST STRIKES
SCENE ONE: MEET THE VILLAIN - JACKFROST

A snowy forest in the Merry Old England of Nursery Rhyme.   In center stage is a large gnarled evergreen tree with a leafy and snow covered huge limb jutting out of the side (secured by concealed wire).   There are no large branches near this limb which is really a small narrow platform.   The backdrop shows more snow covered trees and a patch of wintry sky where the sleigh of Santa Claus, drawn by four reindeer, is just visible.   The sleigh, laden with parcels but minus Santa himself, is just disappearing upward into the distance near the clouds.

Enter JackFrost (the Villain). He is dressed in a white costume covered in icicles and he wears a white top hat dripping with snow and ice. His face is white and wintry. He has a long, sharp-pointed nose. His ears, nose and fingers are lean and sharp. His wide, handlebar moustache and his neat goatee beard appear to be stiff and frozen.

JACKFROST: My name is JackFrost. I am the winter villain who has blown in on the north wind. I'm going to make sure that Santa does not deliver any toys at Christmas. I will send a cold blast to knock him out of his sleigh.

I will blow Santa from his sleigh
And send his reindeers far away
I will make sure that girls and boys
Will not get their Christmas toys (ha, ha)

He twirls his wide moustache and gives the audience an evil sneer.

All you girls and boys have far too many toys anyway. You don't need any more. Do you?

AUDIENCE: *(in unison)* OH YES, WE DO.

JACKFROST: Oh no, you don't. You don't need any more presents.

AUDIENCE: *(in unison)* OH YES, WE DO.

JACKFROST: Well, I'll see to it that you don't get any. So there! You don't like Santa Claus anyway.

AUDIENCE: *(in unison)* OH YES, WE DO.

JACKFROST: Oh no you don't.

AUDIENCE: *(in unison)* OH YES, WE DO.

JACKFROST: Well, that's just too bad.

He slinks off the stage, giving a last sneer to the audience before disappearing through the trees. As he leaves, he cries out to the audience.

JACKFROST: *(shaking his fist at the audience)* I am JackFrost – remember me. I'll be back.

AUDIENCE: *(in unison)* BOO. HISS.

Curtain

ACT ONE
JACKFROST STRIKES
SCENE TWO: JACKFROST CAPTURES JILL

Santa Claus, sometimes known as Father Christmas, is sprawled awkwardly on the large limb where he has just been accidentally jettisoned from his sleigh. He sits back more comfortably on a fork of the tree. All around are trees covered in snow. Underneath Santa is a stony path worn more or less clear of snow by frequent passers-by. It winds in and out, from front left to back right.

SANTA: *(shouting and pointing at sleigh)* Come back and get me. I've fallen out.

*Enter Jill (**Principal Girl**) carrying a pail of water. Jill wears a skirt and apron, knitted jacket, bonnet and walking shoes.*

SANTA: Hello Jill. Where's Jack?

JILL:
Jack and Jill went up the hill
To fetch a pail of water
Jack fell down and broke his crown
And Jill came tumbling after
Up they got and home did trot
As fast as they could caper
Jack went to bed to mend his head
With vinegar and brown paper

Sorry I can't stop but I'm in a hurry Santa.

SANTA: Cheerio Jill. If you see anyone with a ladder, tell them to come and help down from here.

> *Jill pulls the pail of water across to left-stage, moaning and groaning as she goes.* **Enter JackFrost.**

JACKFROST: What are you up to Jill?

JILL: I must take this water to Jack all by myself. He's not allowed to climb. He's in bed with a sore head and I need to make him some tea.

JACKFROST: Well, I'm Sheriff JackFrost. Where is your written permission to take water from that well? If you don't have such a paper, I'll have to arrest you.

JackFrost handcuffs Jill to his left wrist.

JACKFROST: *(to the audience)* You do elect me sheriff, don't you? You do want me to keep law and order, don't you?

AUDIENCE: *(in unison)* OH NO, WE DON'T.

JACKFROST: You do want me to arrest this criminal, don't you?

AUDIENCE: *(in unison)* OH NO, WE DON'T.

JACKFROST: Well, I'm going to arrest her anyway. So there.

AUDIENCE: *(in unison)* BOO. HISS.

Curtain

ACT ONE
JACKFROST STRIKES
SCENE THREE: JACKFROST MEETS
DAME LIVEINASHOE

Enter Dame Liveinashoe. She is elderly and wearing a large cape, long skirt, a large bonnet and walking shoes. She carries a broom and a large shoe-shaped carpetbag apparently full of clothes. She is followed by a number of children, large and small. (dancers) She berates JackFrost with her broom and demands the release of Jill. Then, putting aside the broom, she thumbs her nose at JackFrost and shakes her fist and dances around.

DAME LIVEINASHOE: Come on, stand up and fight like a man or I'll knock the living daylights out of ye. Come out fighting now. Didn't I hear you say you've arrested Jill? But there's no police anywhere.

JACKFROST: I know, that's how I get away with this. Give me £100 for her release on police bail.

DAME LIVEINASHOE: But she hasn't done anything wrong. She hasn't committed any crime.

JACKFROST: So what. The jails are filled with people who haven't committed any crimes.

DAME LIVEINASHOE: No, but they sure make up for it when they get out.

JACKFROST: Yes, the jails are filled with people who have been reprimanded in custard.

DAME LIVEINASHOE: Don't you mean remanded in custody?

JACKFROST: That's certainly true but its none of my business. All I want is my money, see?

DAME LIVEINASHOE: You have no right to appoint yourself as a policeman.

JACKFROST: You admitted there were no official policemen around here. What right have you got to suppress the spirit of private enterprise. I'll let her go if anyone can pay the £100 fine.

JackFrost dashes off stage left, pulling Jill along with him. Shouts and jeers at the audience as he goes.

DAME LIVEINASHOE: *(to children)* Look children, see Santa up in that tree. Say hello to Santa. Hi Santa.

The children wave to Santa.

SANTA: *(laughing and happy again)* Howdy folks. Hey, can you help me down from here.

DAME LIVEINASHOE: *(scratching her head)* I wish I could think of some way. Let me see - they could all climb up on my shoulders and we could stand under you and you could climb down us like a human ladder.

Santa shakes his head doubtfully. She hesitates.

DAME LIVEINASHOE: *(reconsidering)* Well, maybe not. I could get a piece of thread, tie it to a piece of string, tie that to a piece of thick cord, tie that to a rope, then get a bird to fly up with the thread. You could take the thread off the bird, pull up the rope and tie the rope to the branch and climb down.

Santa does not look too happy with that idea either.

SANTA: It might take a while to do all that and train a bird, maybe years.

The children are chattering away and playing around.

DAME LIVEINASHOE: Now children, behave yourselves. Be good. I'm trying to think. I know. Suppose I piled up logs and you climbed down the pile.

SANTA: *(unhappily)* I'd get buried alive.

DAME LIVEINASHOE: Now children be quiet. I'm trying to work out a plan. Oh, I can't even hear myself thinking, Santa. I'll just have to go and get these kiddies back home to my old shoe. Then I'll come back and try to work it out for you Santa. Come children, let's go. We'll look for a ladder to help Santa get down from that tree.

They leave by the path right.

SANTA: *(to audience)*
That was the old woman who lived in a shoe
She'd so many children
She didn't know what to do . . .
(spreading his hands helplessly)
And neither do I . . .

<u>Curtain</u>

ACT TWO
SANTA IN THE TREE
SCENE ONE: THE PASSERS-BY

Enter Dr. Foster, from right, carrying a large black umbrella and a small black bag, dressed in short cape and boots. He has dark hair brushed back, a black moustache and neatly trimmed sharp pointed beard.

SANTA: Hi there, Dr Foster, help me down out of this tree.

DR FOSTER: Oh, good morning Santa. I'm pleased to see that you're getting exercise - very good for the heart, I'm sure. Keep up the good work.

SANTA: Help me out of here.

DR FOSTER: I'm sorry I can't see you now. Make an appointment with my secretary. Besides if I went off this track I'd fall into a snowdrift or hole. *(looks at ground)* I make a habit of it, you know. Can't take a chance on it, old chap, I'm so unsure footed.
(to audience)
> I'm Dr Foster
> Who went to Gloucester
> In a shower of rain
> I stepped in a puddle
> Up to my middle
> And never went there again

It begins to rain and Dr. Foster puts up his umbrella.

AUDIENCE*: (in unison chant)* Quack, Quack, Quack.

Dr Foster waves to Santa and the audience as he leaves left.

SANTA: *(waving his fist in anger)* You silly goat.   Why can't you look where you're going?

DR FOSTER: *(turning back and sticking just his shoulders and head back on stage for a moment)* Why don't <u>you</u> watch where <u>you're</u> going, Santa? Then you wouldn't be stuck up there.

Dr Foster leaves again, left.   Santa waves his fists in the air and moans and groans.

Enter Little Jack Horner *from right, skipping along.   He is short, fat, wearing pantaloons and a short tunic. He is laughing.*

SANTA: Hello there, Little Jack Horner. Help me get out of here.

JACK HORNER:
I'm little Jack Horner
Who sat in the corner
Eating my pudding and pie
I stuck in my thumb
And pulled out a plum
And said "What a Good Boy am I"

I have to dash on, Santa - there's another big pie waiting for me at home. Hee, hee, hee. *(he waves his hand)* Santa, bye, bye. Hello, pie. Besides helping would be work. I'm not allowed too much of that. All work and no pie makes Jack a dull boy.

SANTA: *(to audience)* Oh, let me get him. *(to Jack)* I mean let me get you something for Christmas.

Enter from left Simple Simon, dressed in knee britches held up by suspenders (braces), a rough heavy wool shirt or jersey, long country boy boots, hair sticking up in the air. His demeanor is stiff and naive like that of a simple country yokel but there is a sly look in his eye that belies the simplicity.

SIMPLE SIMON: *(with an air of phony innocence)* Oh, who mentioned a pie? I was just wanting to try a pie.

JACK HORNER: *(scowling and jealous)* You can't have my pie, you overfed gorb. My ma won't give it to you. Don't be greedy.

SANTA: Greedy! This is the pot calling the kettle black if ever I heard it.

SIMPLE SIMON:
Simon is just a simple country boy
(points to his own chest)
Simple Simon
Met a pieman
Going to the fair
Said Simple Simon to the pieman
Let me taste your fare
Said the pieman to Simple Simon
Show me first your penny
Said Simple Simon to the pieman
Sir I have not any
(points again to his chest)

Simple Simon is just a poor country boy. No money, no food. Kind lady back there, gave me a pie. Said her little boy wasn't home on time. So Simple Simon ate pie. Where's this new pie?

JACK HORNER: *(suspiciously and on the verge of tears)* Was she a red haired lady with a pink and white spotted apron?

SIMPLE SIMON: *(smiling)* Yes. How did you know? You're clever. *(points to self)* Simple Simon is not smart - just a poor country boy. *(he spreads his hands innocently and opens his mouth and blinks)*

Jack Horner clenches his fists and beats on Simple Simon's chest, then begins to cry. He rushes off stage left.

JACK HORNER: You stole my pie.

SIMPLE SIMON: Oh no I didn't. *(to audience)* Did I?

JACK HORNER: Oh yes he did, didn't he.

AUDIENCE: *(in unison)* OH NO HE DIDN'T.

JACK HORNER: *(leaving)* Ma, Ma, where's my pie?

SANTA: Now Simon, help me down from here.

SIMPLE SIMON: *(pointing to his stomach)* Simple Simon is just a poor boy.   He wouldn't know what to do to get you down.
Simple Simon begins to leave right, in a daze, mouth open and arms apart.   He turns around at the last second and waves to audience.

SANTA: *(shouting after him)* You're not so simple when it comes to getting free pies.

Simple Simon leaves, right, along the pathway, still walking stiffly, blinking his eyes and with open mouth, as one in a daze.

SANTA: *(sighing resignedly)* Oh well, I wish they hadn't been so clumsy, then they could have got me free to get their presents.   As it is

I'm stuck here. But wait, here comes the little girl who has the little curl right in the middle of her forehead.

> *Enter Girl with Curl, from stage left, along the path. She is wearing a long party dress, neat shoes, and a short jacket or woolen cardigan. She has many golden curls all over her face and forehead. For comic effect this part may be acted by an older, fat male actor.*

GIRL WITH CURL: *(smiling sweetly, curtseying with one index finger pointing under her chin)* Oh, Santa, I love you Santa. You're so cute and cuddly. So round and plump and loveable. Your cheeks are so red and your eyes are so blue. I think you're so pretty *(shyly)* and so kissable too.

> *Girl with Curl curtsies again, sweetly.*

SANTA: What a sweet little girl.

GIRL WITH CURL: Oh, I hope you'll visit us on Christmas Eve. I'll leave out some pie for you. *(coyly)* I was hoping for a talking doll. *(she swivels from side to side, shyly, finger still under chin)*

SANTA: Of course, why you're just a little talking doll yourself. I'll be so pleased to get you one but first you need to help me get out of this tree.

GIRL WITH CURL: But why?

SANTA: See. I'm stuck here.

GIRL WITH CURL: *(stamping her foot in a sudden change of mood)* Now, how can I help you? I don't know anyone around here. Why should I lose my nice Christmas talking doll just because you're so silly you got stuck in a tree. I didn't put you there *(boo - hoo - hoo she weeps and wails)* why should I have to get you out? Oh my poor doll. *(boo hoo)* You stupid old, freaky old miser. Keep your horrible doll. If you had any decency you'd never have ended up there. I hate you, you old rolly poley fatso. *(stamps her foot again)*

GIRL WITH CURL: *(to audience)* It's all his fault, isn't it? Say yes, yes, yes.

AUDIENCE: *(in unison)* NO, NO, NO.

GIRL WITH CURL: *(to audience)* You don't want me to help Santa down do you?
(stage whisper) Say no.

AUDIENCE: *(in unison)* OH YES, WE DO.

GIRL WITH CURL: *(doubtfully)* Oh no, you don't.

AUDIENCE: *(in unison)* OH YES, WE DO.

GIRL WITH CURL: Oh no, you don't.

AUDIENCE: *(in unison)* OH YES, WE DO.

GIRL WITH CURL: Did someone dare to say boo?

AUDIENCE: *(in unison)* BOO.

*Girl with Curl stamps her foot and puts her head in air and **leaves** stage right by way of the woodland path.*

AUDIENCE: *(in unison)* BOO. HISS.

SANTA: *(sadly)*
That was the little girl
Who had a little curl
Right in the middle of her forehead
And when she was good
She was very very good
But when she was bad she was horrid

Curtain

ACT TWO
SANTA IN THE TREE
SCENE TWO: ALONG COMES A
JOLLY OLD SOLDIER

*Enter Jolly Old Soldier dressed in full uniform of WWI and swinging between two crutches. **Enter JackFrost**. He speaks quietly and confidentially to the Old Soldier.*

JACKFROST: Hey, Old Soldier. Before you go any further, you'll probably meet an old crackpot who thinks he's Santa Claus. Pay no heed to him. He's quite harmless. Just humor him.

OLD SOLIDER: Okay, JackFrost. You're sure he haint really, Santer Claws? I wouldn't want to miss out on 'elping him with his Christmas presents for the girls and boys.

JACKFROST: Oh, no, I wouldn't want to stop Santa delivering all those lovely toys.
(to audience and winks) I wouldn't want that, would I?

AUDIENCE: *(in unison)*
OH YES, YOU WOULD.

JACKFROST: Oh No, I wouldn't. Hee, Hee, Hee.

AUDIENCE: *(in unison)*
OH YES, YOU WOULD.

JACKFROST: Well, that's just too bad, isn't it!

AUDIENCE: *(in unison)* BOO. HISS.

Exit JackFrost, leftstage.

As the Old Soldier continues towards Santa Claus he sings: **BLIGHTY**

BLIGHTY
Sung: Rollicking

fe - fe   fe   fe   fe   *s* fe
Carry me 'ome to Blighty
m - m - m   m - m - m   *fe* m
Tiddelly   Idelley   Itey
fe - r   d   r   *fe*   l   *s*
Blighty is the place to be

Carry me 'ome to Blighty
Tiddelly Idelley Itey
Blighty is the place to be, etc

He pauses and looks up at Santa, bows, holds out his cap as a begging sign:

You owe me five farthings
Said the Bells of St. Martins, etc.

OLD SOLDIER: Corr luvee, squire, spare us just a few bob, for an ole sojer. Just home from Flanders Fields. Blew an 'old in me big toe I did, just to get out of the mud like and get me home to Hold Hengland.

SANTA: Hold what?

OLD SOLDIER: Hold Hengland. I suffer from unrequired love.

SANTA: You mean unrequited.

OLD SOLDIER: No, she doesn't require me no more, see.

SANTA: I can't 'elp you, I mean help you till you help <u>me</u>. But if you do help me, I'll give you anything for Christmas see. I'm Father Christmas - you can 'ave, I mean have anything you want. O.K?

OLD SOLDIER: O, so you're Farver Chrismis eh, gov? *(aside, tapping his head)* O, ee thinks he's Farver Chrismis does he? *(to Santa)* Oh, govner, just throw us down a copper or two *(looks around)* just a cupla bob and I'll not tell 'em where to find you. I swear it and I never,

never, <u>never</u> tell lies - *(aside)* hardly ever nowadays.

SANTA: I'm not hiding. I'm not mad. I'm really Father Christmas.

OLD SOLDIER: *(scratching his head, still holding his cap)* Come on, just a few pennies, squire, I mean, err, Farver Chrismis, just to help me get over to Tipperary. *Sings:*

IT'S A LONG WAY TO TIPPERARY
Sung: With a Rousing and Marching Beat

t_1 d   r - r   r m - fe - s t
It's a long way to Tipperary
t   l   s   m   s r
It's a long way to go
t_1 d   r - r   r m - fe - s t
It's a long way to Tipperary
fe   s   l - m   fe   s l
To the sweetest girl I know
r - r   m - fe - s t
Goodbye Piccadilly
d^1 - m   s - l t
Farewell Leicester Square
s   l   t   t   s   l - s - m r
It's a long way to   Tipperary
s   t   s   l s
But my heart lies there

It's a long way to Tipperary
It's a long way to go
It's a long way to Tipperary
To the sweetest girl I know
Goodbye Piccadilly
Farewell Leicester Square
It's a long way to Tipperary
But my heart lies there

SANTA: Make up your mind where you're going. First it was Blighty, now it's Tipperary. Are you English or Irish? Tell any story to make a buck, eh. You're just a panhandler, a phony. You're on the make, that's it. Keep the home fires burning. Yes but not for highway robbers.

OLD SOLDIER: Oh no, boss. I'm a Henglishman. You got me all wrong. It's my 'art and the sweetest girl I knew wot lives there in Tipperary - not me. See, yer 'Onor. They shipped me out of Flanders to Dover, carried me 'ome to Blighty, then I went to Lundin, see, Squire? Just like I said, then to Leicester Square and Old Pickalilly. That's where I met my girl, okay Mate? She's Welsh but she lives with her Scotch mum what's married to a Hirishman in Tipperary, see?

SANTA: But you said you lived in Tipperary didn't you?

OLD SOLDIER: O no I didn't.

SANTA: O yes you did.
(to audience) Didn't he?

AUDIENCE: *(in unison)* O NO, HE DIDN'T.

OLD SOLDIER: *(scratching his head)* I didn't did I?

AUDIENCE: *(in unison)* O NO, YOU DIDN'T.

SANTA: *(eagerly)* O yes he did. Didn't he?

AUDIENCE: *(in unison)* O NO, HE DIDN'T.

> *Santa squirms and looks confused, tries to work it out on his fingers but fails.*

SANTA: *(flicking thumb and fingers)* Blighty - where's that? Leicester, Scotland, Wales . . Oh, I give up. *(to Old Soldier)* Well, anyway, blowing up your toe to get out of fighting for your country, that doesn't show much love of country, does it, Old Soldier?

OLD SOLDIER: Who me? No love of country? Corr - lovee, Guv course I love my country, yer old nitwit. I'm cowardly yes, mean and deceitful absolutely. *(slaps his leg)* But certainly all was done for love of old Hengland. See? Nuffin shows more love of country, Squire, than a visit to the home countries of Old Hengland - the North Country, the West Country, the Midlands or London Town - eh?

SANTA: Oh, I'm sorry to question your love of country, but lookee at me 'ere and just get me down please.

OLD SOLDIER: Oh, 'oo me? Oh I'd be afeerd to setee loose - that I would, Captain. Yer think you're Santer Claws don't yer? *(aside, to* *audience)* 'Ee ain't Santer is he? *(tapping the side of his head and nodding slyly)*

AUDIENCE: *(in unison)* OH YES, HE IS.

OLD SOLDIER: Oh no he haint.

AUDIENCE: *(in unison)* OH YES, HE IS.

OLD SOLDIER: Oh no he haint.

Old Soldier shakes his head and begins to ***leave stage right*** *on his crutches, singing, Carry me home to Blighty. He tutt tutts and shakes his crutch at the naughtiness of Santa.*

OLD SOLDIER: *(to Santa)* Cheerio, General. *(in a stage whisper)* Yer mean, barmy old 'arfwit.
(aside) Poor old geezer. Thinks he's Farver Chrismis.
(to Santa) But if yer behaves yerself I'll never tell 'em where to find yer.

SANTA: *(aside)*
That was Jolly Old Soldier
Old Soldiers never die, never die

Old Soldiers never die - they only fade away

I just wish he'd fade away - somewhere else. Thinks I'm mad, does he? Wouldn't help me down either. I know what I think of 'im. I mean him - he's got me hat it. I mean at it. O heckedy heck. What do you say to 'im, hold Sojer . . What?

AUDIENCE: *(in unison)* BOO. HISS

SANTA: *(cupping his ear)* I can't hear you, did you say who? I mean old soldier. What do you think of him, eh?

AUDIENCE: *(louder, in unison)* BOO. HISS.

SANTA: *(pleased)* O yes, I agree. Let me join you in one big BOO . . .

AUDIENCE AND SANTA: BOO and HISS.

Curtain

ACT TWO
SANTA IN THE TREE
SCENE THREE: SANTA AND THE CAT

Enter right stage loping along, an actor wearing a cat suit, complete with long tail, pokey, perky ears and whiskers. The human face is clearly seen but looks like a cat, with painted whiskers and fur.

CAT: *(meowing loudly, stops to look at Santa)* Hello Santa. Please bring me a whole bunch of mice for Christmas. *(it jumps past Santa to continue on its way)* Cheerio, Santa.

SANTA: Here, just a moment, Cat.

CAT: Yes, Santa.
Cat sits down and washes its face with its paws.

SANTA: Whose cat are you?

CAT: *(paws his face and ears)* Dick Whittington's. *(meow)*

SANTA: Well, tell Dick to come here and rescue me. I'm stuck here.

Cat shakes its head and meows.

CAT: *(rubbing its face)* Why don't you just stick your claws in the wood and climb down.

SANTA: I haven't got any.

CAT: *(scratching its ear)* What no wood? Don't be a sillybilly, the whole tree's covered with it.

SANTA: *(holding out and flicking the fingers of one hand)* No, no, no. I mean no claws. I'm not a cat you know.

CAT: *(meowing and scratching behind its ears)* Oh, I see. How dopey of me. You've no claws. *(puzzled)* Then how did you climb out on that limb?

SANTA: I didn't. I fell off my sleigh by accident and came tumbling out of the sky. If this tree hadn't been covered with leaves and snow, I'd have broken my neck.

CAT: *(scratching its tummy)* Well my master *(meow)* Dick is away, far away, in London on business. I'm just on holiday here. But I'll see if I can find *(meow)* either Dick or someone else to rescue you. *(meow)*

SANTA: Thanks, but I can hardly hold on so hurry. It's cold here.

CAT: *(meow)* *(stroking its tail)* Hey, that's funny, you've no fur either - that's just an old *(meow)* red and white suit you're wearing. Oh, hee, hee *(meow)* it's so funny. *(meow)*
  He lopes around and giggles and purrs and meows.
No fur, no claws and climbing around in trees. But you've certainly got a tail, ha, ha, a tale to tell, hee, hee *(meow)*. He fell out of his sleigh, out of the sky! What a story!
  Meow. The cat jumps up and down on all fours.

The audience may join in as the cat recites or sings with meows and purrs inserted at random

I SAW AN OLD MAN

Sung: Fast and Jolly

VERSE ONE

d d - d - d - d   m-m
I saw an old man in
s   m - m   d
The crabapple tree
r - r - r - r
The crabapple tree
t_1 l_1 - l_1 - s_1
The crabapple tree
d d - d - d - d   m-m
I saw an old man in
s   m - m   d
The crabapple tree
d - d   r   r s_1 l_1 t_1 d - d
On a snowy and shivery morning

VERSE TWO

d   d   m   s   m   d
Guess who the old man was
d   r   r   r
The old man was
d t_1 l_1 s_1
The old man   was
d   d   m   s   m   d
Guess who the old man was
d - d   r   r s_1 l_1 t_1 d - d
On a   snowy and shivery morning

VERSE ONE
I saw an old man in
The crabapple tree
The crabapple tree
The crabapple tree
I saw an old man in
The crabapple tree
On a snowy and shivery morning.

VERSE TWO
Guess who the old man was
The old man was
The old man was
Guess who the old man was
On a snowy and shivery morning.

VERSE THREE (same tune as Verse Two)
Old Santa Claus* the old man was
The old man was
The old man was
Old Santa Claus* the old man was
On a snowy and shivery morning.
* Or Old Father Christmas

SANTA: Oh stop *(reciting or singing)* verses about my plight and go find someone to help.

CAT: *(putting its chin on its left paw)* This is a well used path - see the snow is almost worn off with the feet of many travelers - its all stone.

SANTA: I can see that. That's why if I fall off I'll get hurt.

CAT: *(scratching its left armpit with its right paw)* Yes, but look on the bright side - there's so many people pass this way - someone is bound to come along soon who can get you down.

SANTA: *(cheerily)* Well, that's a thought.

CAT: *(jumps about)* See, there's no need for me to get anyone to help you, then.

SANTA: Oh now wait a minute. I can't see anyone else coming at the moment. *(looking around in desperation)*

CAT: *(to audience, smiling and purring to himself)* Santa *(meow)* doesn't need anyone, does he?

AUDIENCE: *(in unison)* OH YES, HE DOES.

Cat scratches his ears, puzzled.

CAT: Oh no, he doesn't.

AUDIENCE: *(in unison)* OH YES, HE DOES.

Cat jumps and squirms and scratches itself and lopes all around on all fours.

CAT: Oh no, he doesn't.

AUDIENCE: *(in unison)* OH YES, HE DOES.

SANTA: Push, wush, push, wush, wush be a good cat and get me a friend.

CAT: *(reconsidering)* Oh, well, maybe you do need someone *(meow)* to get you out of that tree. *(meow)* After all, *(thinks and scratches his ear)* it happens to cats too. Why come to *(meow)* think of it I remember once my Uncle Tom was trapped high up . . .

SANTA: Oh please, pussy. It's so cold here. Please get me a tree climber with a ladder.

CAT: *(to audience)* Does he really need a ladder? *(hinting in a stage whisper behind a paw)* No, no, no.

AUDIENCE: *(in unison)* YES, YES, YES.

CAT: *(loping off, meowing, following the path to off stage left)* Oh, all right. Cheerio, Santa. I'll try to *(meow)* remember to get a ladder. *(to audience, waving a paw and grinning)* Everyone needs a ladder to succeed in life. Cheerio children.

AUDIENCE: *(in unison)* CHEERIO.

Cat bows and lopes off stage left, waving again to audience.

SANTA: Oh, I'll never hang on until that cat gets back. He's a spaced out lunatic - he is - a nut case - imagine - a talking cat! *(shakes his head)* Help me down from here somebody!

Enter Dick Whittington *right. Tall, slim, carries a stick on his shoulder with a small round bag at the end. He is wearing English medieval* *dress, i.e., cocked hat, short jerkin with large cuffs, tights, turned down boots. He is whistling and cheerful.*

DICK: *(casually)* Hello, Santa. Have a nice tree-climbing day. *(waves and walks on)* Not really cold is it?

SANTA: What's the hurry?

DICK: I'm trying to catch up with my cat. I suppose you haven't seen the truant. He ran off just a little ways back - what a rascal.

SANTA: Yes. He passed here. Said you were in London on business.

DICK: *(laughing and shaking his head)* What a naughty cat. Why, he just ran off from me only a few minutes ago and this is nowhere near London. That cat's a tomfool and a fibber as well as a runaway.

SANTA: Anyway, can you help me down from here?

DICK: Down? You look just fine up there - very impressive - besides, I need to dash on and catch the cat first.

SANTA: *(grumbling)* Oh, very well, catch your nasty, silly cat first.

> *Dick marches merrily on, waves to Santa and leaves stage left.*

SANTA: *(shouting after Dick)* Don't expect my vote when you run for Lord Mayor. *(muttering and rubbing his hands together with the cold)* Catch the cat - what an excuse! *(he buries his head in his arms and shivers)*

Enter the Cat once again.

CAT: Hello again, Santa.

SANTA: Pussy Cat, Pussy Cat where have you been?

CAT: I've been to London to visit the Queen.

SANTA: Pussy Cat, Pussy Cat, what did you there?

CAT: I chased a wee mousie under a chair. But *(wistfully)* alas it got away!

SANTA: *(glumly)* Oh you purr purr thing. That was a very praiseworthy effort on your part but how is that going to help me down from here.

Cat begins to lope and frolic around.

CAT: *(mockingly)* Santa, why are you up there?

(in the following sequences emphasizing the letter "L" at the start of each word)
Are you a look-out or a lodger?

SANTA: Now, you be good. You know I'm neither.

Cat grins playfully at Santa and continues to frolic.

CAT: Then why are you loafing, loitering, layabouting, lounging, lurking, louting, lazy-ing, lingering, leisuring and lolling around up there?

SANTA: *(agitated and furious)* You know I can't get down - I'm not loitering and loll - and all that stuff. What are you doing?

CAT: *(loping about and laughing)* I'm leaping and limbering-up and loping around and laughing at you and loving it and *(smugly)* you can like it or lump it.

SANTA: Well, look, I'm loathing it and longing for a liberator - you cat-faced lunatic. Oh now you've got me at it. Oh, please get the "L" out of here. *(to audience)* get it, get the "L" *(cringes and covers face)* - oh well, I'm sorry about that - but *(pointing to cat)* he started it. *(then pleading with Cat who is still laughing and jumping)* Please help me, dear Mr. Cat.

Cat squats under Santa on the path, washes its face.

CAT: Old King Cole and Dame Liveinashoe are coming to help you. *(points offstage left)*

<u>Curtain</u>

ACT THREE
ALL GO HOME
SCENE ONE: OLD KING COLE MEETS JILL

Scene: The Palace of Old King Cole. Old King Cole, dressed in a satin tunic and Tudor hat, is sitting on his throne. Behind him stand his three fiddlers.

Enter Jack (Principal Boy) *into the palace of Old King Cole (possibly a curtained-off sub-section of the stage). Jack wears jacket with wide turned up sleeves, pantaloons, socks and big boots. His head is bandaged with brown paper. Old King Cole is sitting on his throne. He is very fat and is dressed as a medieval king in robes and with a chain around his neck, trews or tights and heavy boots, a well secured crown on his head.*

OLD KING COLE: I am Old King Cole.

Old King Cole
Was a merry old soul
And a merry old soul was he
He called for his pipe
And he called for his bowl
And he called for his fiddlers three
Every fiddle, he had a fine fiddle
And a very fine fiddle had he
Twee tweedle dee, tweedle dee, went the fiddlers
Oh, there's none so rare as can compare
With King Cole and his fiddlers three

JACK: Old King Cole, my name is Jack, the waterboy. I want to report that Jill has been arrested and her abductor is JackFrost who is pretending to be a sheriff and demands £100 police bail for her release. Can you and your good men rescue her?

OLD KING COLE: This is just kidnapping and extortion, pure and simple. But before we punish the thief we want to make sure that Jill is rescued.
He motions to one of his attendants.
Here, use this £100 to pay her bail and set her free. In fact, send for this rogue and bring him here with Jill. We'll soon mop this up.

One of the fiddlers salutes Old King Cole and leaves stage left.

JACK: Thank you Old King Cole, *(looking around)* this is a nice warm palace. You are very cozy here, your majesty. *(he bows to Old King Cole and steps back)*

Dame Liveinashoe enters *the palace and shakes her broom at the king. She is followed by her children who will dance.*

DAME LIVEINASHOE: *(shaking her broom at the fiddlers and throwing it after them as they retreat, then addressing Old King Cole)* How dare you not rescue old Santa Claus? All you do is sit around and smoke and listen to your fiddlers. Why can't you help your poor subjects in distress? Don't you know that all the children are waiting for Santa Claus' presents and JackFrost has blown him out of his sleigh with a north wind. There he is, Father Christmas, in the middle of a freezing wood, stranded in an icy tree, thanks to JackFrost.

She thumbs her nose at Old King Cole and shakes her fist and dances around.

Come on, stand up and fight like a man or I'll knock the living daylights out of ye. Come out fighting now.

Old King Cole is astounded. He takes off his crown for a moment and wipes the perspiration from his brow.

OLD KING COLE: Nobody ever tells me nothing. How was I supposed to know that Santa Claus was getting stranded in trees instead of handing out presents to the children? Hmm . . . So JackFrost, that old scoundrel, has been at it again. I'll soon put something in his pipe for him to smoke.

Old King Cole puts his pipe in his mouth and plucks a grape out of his bowl.

I hear that you've so many children
You don't know what to do.
So you gave them some broth without any bread
And scolded them soundly
And sent them to bed

Is that so? Well, we have plenty of food here.
What would you all like to eat? Have
anything at all.

DAME LIVEINASHOE:
We'd like some fish and chips, please
If that's alright with you

All sing the **FISH AND CHIPS SONG**. *Individual
verses can be apportioned by the stage manager.*

THE FISH AND CHIPS SONG
Sung: Fast

VERSE ONE AND REFRAIN:

s   d - d   m   s d^1 t
O I'll have some fish and chips please
d^1 r^1 l - l - l - l
If that's all right with you
  f   r - r - r   f   t - t - t
Not too much grease - some mushy peas
l   s   s s - f m
And salt and vinegar too
s   d - d   m - s d^1-d^1 t
No more the dainty dinner do
d^1 r^1 l - l - l - l
No more them dunking dips
l s s - s s - t   t l
I say if it's all right with you
  s - s   s   f r d
I'll have some fish and chips

VERSE ONE AND REFRAIN:
O I'll have some fish and chips please
If that's all right with you
Not too much grease - some mushy peas
And salt and vinegar too
No more the dainty dinner do
No more them dunking dips
I say if it's all right with you
I'll have some fish and chips

VERSE TWO:
Now the Admiral was in the pink
His ships were spiffy clean
Your Majesty what do you think?
He asks the blooming Queen
Says she I absolutely love
This fleet of men and ships
The only thing they need more of
Is good old fish and chips

VERSE THREE:
Well my Uncle Ray drops dead one day
We lay him down in flowers
Then we start a good wake right away
To brighten those sad hours
Ahh . . suddenly he bolts upright
And fear and terror grips . . .
We ask, What brought you back? He cried
I smell some fish and chips

VERSE FOUR: *(male singer)*
See I knew a glamour girl I say
As pretty as the moon
Says she, Come visit me some day
So I showed up right soon
She asked, What would you like to do?
And smiled those lovely lips
I said, If it's all right with you
We'll have some fish and chips

VERSE FOUR: *(female singer)*
See I knew a handsome man I say
As cheerful as the moon
Says he, Come visit me some day
So I showed up right soon
He asked, What would you like to do?
We've some nice river trips
I said, If it's all right with you
We'll have some fish and chips

Enter JackFrost and Jill, still carrying her pail of water. King Cole beckons them to stand before his throne.

JACKFROST: I'm so pleased to be able to hand over this criminal to you, your majesty. I caught her red-handed stealing water from the well on the hill. She had no written authorization from your majesty. Like a good and dutiful subject of your majestys, I immediately placed her under a citizen's arrest and put her on police bail of only £100. I hope your majesty is pleased. I will accept this £100 as a reward. You are most generous, your majesty.

Old King Cole shakes his head and waves JackFrost aside. He beckons to Dame Liveinashoe and Jill, still with her bucket of water, to come forward.

OLD KING COLE: I hope you didn't suffer from the cold. Why don't you go down to my kitchens for a warm-up.

The Grand Dame and Jill leave stage right.

JACK *(Principal Boy):* Thank you for rescuing Jill, Old King Cole. I'm sure she could do with something warm to drink. *(he glances slyly, sideways, at JackFrost who suddenly leaps forward)*

Old King Cole winks understandingly as JackFrost jumps up, startled and in fear.

JACKFROST: *(becomes nervous and suspicious)* Did somebody say warm water? Oh, no! Warm water could make me melt away. Anything but warm water.

Old King Cole, you can have back your £100. I don't think I need it. I'll just be going home now to my ice castle in the Arctic. If that's alright with you.

OLD KING COLE: Just a minute, JackFrost. I'd like you to stay here for a little while.

JackFrost begins to make a dash for the door but is seized by two of the fiddlers

JACKFROST: *(to audience)* Tell them to let me go. You appointed me sheriff, didn't you?

AUDIENCE: *(in unison)* OH NO, WE DIDN'T.

JACKFROST: Oh yes, you did. You do want me to escape, don't you, so that I can come back next year?

AUDIENCE: *(in unison)* OH NO, WE DON'T.

JACKFROST: *(shaking his fist at audience)* I'll be back anyway and then I'll get you. I'm JackFrost.

AUDIENCE: *(in unison)* BOO. HISS.

Just then the Grand Dame and Jill (Principal Girl) return, both holding a bucket of steaming warm (__not hot__) water. They throw it over JackFrost who falls on the floor and begins to melt, with some of his disguises falling off. He runs away, howling in dismay and leaves left.

<u>Curtain</u>

ACT THREE
ALL GO HOME
SCENE TWO: SANTA'S CLIMBDOWN
Scene: Same as Act Two, Scene Three. Santa Claus is still stranded in the tree. Waiting to be rescued.

CAT: I told you that Old King Cole and Dame Liveinashoe were coming to help you and here they are. *(points offstage right)*

SANTA: *(slowly and clearly to Audience)* Oh, no they're not!

CAT: *(leading the audience like a music conductor)* Oh, yes they are! *(meow)*

AUDIENCE: *(in unison)* OH YES THEY ARE!

SANTA: *(grumpily)* Oh, no they're not!

CAT: Meow. Oh, yes they are!

SANTA: *(to Cat)* Well, I can't see them.

CAT: Well, there's many a thing one can't see that's there after all. I know that Dick thinks that I'm a fibber but I'm really a good truthful cat - ahem, meow - *(coughs)* most of the time. I never, never, never tell a lie - hardly ever nowadays. Isn't that true *(to audience)* children? *(leads in a 'Yes' nodding)*

AUDIENCE: *(in unison)* YES!

CAT: *(points offstage)* Look, here comes Old King Cole, now.

Enter from left Old King Cole, cheerfully puffing, panting and carrying a ladder. He is accompanied by Dame Liveinashoe and her dancing children.

OLD KING COLE: Cat, you're so fast, I couldn't keep up with you.   Where's Santa? *(puffs and blows - whew)* Oh, yes there you are Santa.   Hang on we'll have you down in a jiffy.

SANTA: Oh, I'm afraid of jiffies - what is it anyway?

OLD KING COLE: I just mean - in a minute - you'll be back down on terra firma.

SANTA: *(cheering up)*   Great! Oh, I'm so pleased you came - Old King Cole.
Old King Cole was a merry old soul
And a merry old soul was he

During the rest of the action, the Cat lopes about happily meowing and licking his hands (paws) and a washing of his face in circular fashion. He grins at the audience.

SANTA: *(continuing his rime about Old King Cole)*
He sent for a pie in the middle of the night
And he sent for his fiddlers three.

Enter stage right, Simple Simon, still dazed, blinking open-mouthed and looking all around hopefully.

SIMPLE SIMON: Did somebody say "Pie"?

OLD KING COLE: Sorry, that was a mistake Simon. No pie.

SIMON: *(aside, to audience)* I do deserve a pie, don't I?

AUDIENCE: *(in unison)* YES.

Enter Little Jack Horner from left, jumps and stomps his feet in a bad temper.

LITTLE JACK HORNER: No, No, No. No pie for Simple Simon. *(to audience)* He doesn't deserve a pie, does he? *(in a stage whisper)* Say No.

AUDIENCE: *(in unison)* YES.

LITTLE JACK HORNER: No, No, No. He doesn't deserve a pie.

AUDIENCE: *(in unison)* OH YES, HE DOES.

LITTLE JACK HORNER: Oh no, he doesn't.

AUDIENCE: *(in unison)* OH YES, HE DOES.

LITTLE JACK HORNER: *(leaving stage left)* No, No, No.

AUDIENCE: *(in unison)* YES, YES, YES.

Simple Simon turns away disappointed and leaves right. Old King Cole places the ladder against the platform - tree branch and beckons Santa to descend. But Santa in the tree limb to the right of the ladder is stiff and timorous.

SANTA: Oh, please Old King Cole, I'm stiff and afraid of falling, come up and help me down.

OLD KING COLE: Of course, of course, no problem.

Old King Cole climbs the ladder and stands on the platform on the left at the other side of the ladder, reaches out to Santa and leads him to ladder. Dame Liveinashoe holds the ladder firm and Old King Cole sits on the tree to the left of the ladder puffing and panting with great merriment. Santa climbs down the ladder joyfully.

SANTA: Oh, thank you Old King Cole and friends - now I'll be able to get all these presents out on time. Quick, there's no time to lose.

Cat and Santa dash off, along pathway to the right waving to the audience and carrying the ladder between them.

SANTA: See you, children. *(waving to Old King Cole)* Thanks a whole bunch Old King Cole and Dame Liveinashoe. Cheerio, Kids. Cheerio everybody.

OLD KING COLE: Cheerio Santa. Cheerio Cat. Give my regards to Dick Whittington, Cat.

Cat nods, meows, waves. Santa and Cat leave right.

OLD KING COLE: Hee, hee, hee. It was so nice of me to help out. *(looking down)* Hey, what about me? Help. Come back. Now I'm up a tree. Cat, come here - bring back that ladder.

Dame Liveinashoe and her children dance around.

DAME LIVEINASHOE: We'll entertain you, Old King Cole, till we get the ladder back.

Curtain

ACT THREEE
ALL GO HOME
SCENE THREE: AND EVERYONE SINGS

A brief curtain may be used here but the timing is optional as the purpose is merely to enable the cast to reassemble quickly. All the nursery rime characters return - followed by Santa and the Cat. Dick and his Cat are reunited happily and hold hands.

All characters coming on stage bow to the audience and then to Old King Cole. Enter JackFrost, his whiskers restored and waves at the audience and towards his moustache and laughs. They all range around Old King Cole looking up to him in the tree. Old King Cole is now happily holding court from his tree and has forgotten to come down. Dick holds Cat briefly as the Cat mimes a lick on his face.

They all recite or sing - with audience joining in - and repeat as time permits.

ALL SING (*I SAW AN OLD MAN, see p. 309*)

VERSE ONE
I saw an old man in
The crabapple tree
The crabapple tree
The crabapple tree
I saw an old man in
The crabapple tree
On a snowy and shivery morning

VERSE TWO
Guess who the old man was
The old man was
The old man was
Guess who the old man was
On a snowy and shivery morning

Cat approaches off stage and is handed a pie which he presents to a grateful Simple Simon.

LITTLE JACK HORNER: *(stomping his feet)* That's my mammy's pie. It's mine. Give it to me. It's mine.

SIMPLE SIMON: *(to audience)* Will I let him have it?

AUDIENCE: *(in unison)* YES.

SIMPLE SIMON: *(to audience)* Are you sure? I don't know. I'm only a simple country boy. Will I <u>really</u> let him have it?

AUDIENCE: *(in unison, yelling)* YES.

Little Jack Horner looks pleased and happy, jumps up and down in joy.

LITTLE JACK HORNER: Yah. Boo. See Simon. Let me have it.

SIMPLE SIMON: *(to Little Jack Horner)* Are you sure?

LITTLE JACK HORNER AND AUDIENCE: YES.

Simple Simon breaks pie over Little Jack's head and face.
Little Jack Horner begins to blubber and cry and clean his face.

ALL SING *(I SAW AN OLD MAN, see p. 309)*

VERSE FOUR
Old King Cole the old man was
The old man was
The old man was
Old King Cole the old man was
On a snowy and shivery morning

All tip their hats and point towards Old King Cole. They bow in his direction, then turn and bow to the audience.

Curtain

END OF PANTOMIME

Professor Luck

SHORT STORY AND
THREE-ACT PLAYSCRIPT

The Story

Once upon a time there were three young goldbugs - Hardwork Harry, Hopeful Hal and Honest Hank. Dressed in broad-brimmed hats and old clothes they toiled away searching for gold, year after year, in the bitter backwoods of the remotest mountains.

Each of the young goldbugs had come out to the hills by his own unique path and so each one saw something different in the shadows and in the light.

Of the three, by far the greatest believer in honest toil was Hardwork Harry. The one who was most surprised at their failure was the idealist, Hopeful Hal. The most confused and least able to explain their dead-end was Honest Hank who had always believed that honesty was the best policy.

So, one evening, the three goldbugs sat around their campfire drinking stream water and eating beans and stewed rabbit out of aluminum dishes.

Feeling that they were all in a mood to reminisce, Hardwork Harry remarked thoughtfully, "I wonder where did we go wrong in this life? We've all worked hard and yet we've found nothing but work and rock."

Hopeful Hal shook his head, "My old uncle used to say, 'Think Big' – that's the key to success.

So I thought big and here I am . . a real big, fat, flat failure."

Honest Hank agreed, "Is there a missing link? Something people can't or won't or don't tell you . . a secret that they keep for themselves."

"Like what?" asked Hopeful Hal. "How about just plain luck?"

"Well, where do we find it? How do we get it?" asked Hardwork Harry.

"Pray for it," said Hopeful Hal. "The only true secret of success - LUCK."

"Listen," answered Hardwork Harry, "we've been looking for gold all these years - if we can't find gold, how can we find luck?"

"Furthermore," agreed Hopeful Hal, wagging a finger at Hardwork Harry, "If we were lucky people we'd have found gold long ago. There's no point in looking for Luck. Luck would find us just as we are sitting here, if we were lucky people."

Hardwork Harry cried out loudly into the hilly forest, "We're here, come and find us, Luck, Luck." His voice echoed, "Luck, Luck, Luck."

"LUCK, LUCK, LUCK," cried the spirit of the hills and fainter . . .

"Luck, Luck, Luck."

"Here's someone coming," said Honest Hank.

"Maybe it's luck," cried Hopeful Hal.

"Maybe it's a bandit," whispered Hardwork Harry. "Let's stand aside and ambush him."

As the three young goldbugs slid silently into the shadows, a tall, slim, bearded backpacker leaning on a stout staff, entered the clearing and began poking around with his stick.

"Why are you sniffing and poking around here?" asked Honest Hank suspiciously as the three goldbugs sidled carefully out of the shadows.

"Ah, my good friends, nice to meet you. I'm Professor Stargazer. I've come here to observe the heavens from this wonderful vantage point, this panoramic pinnacle of astronomical advantage . . ."

"Very pretty speech," growled Hopeful Hal, "but why not go to look at the stars somewhere down there? Why up here in our little lonely spot?"

"As I said, up here for a better view," replied the professor.

"Oh, so that was what you meant to say," muttered Honest Hank, "why couldn't you just say so in plain lingo?"

"What, speak plainly and lose my lucrative professorship with all its bank balancing bonus and pecuniary perquisites? Ha, ha, plain lingo, indeed. Not a chance. That would never get a fellah a steady job."

"Well, why don't you just go up thatta there mountain?" suggested Hopeful Hal. "You can see for a million miles from the top of the hill."

"Sir, I am a man of more than threescore years and ten. I need rest. Am I not welcome here? Have you found gold and do not wish me to know? I assure you I am silence and secrecy personified."

"We're all broke . . ." muttered Honest Hank, despondently.

"You might as well sit down and have a few beans stranger, it's about all that's left," invited Hardwork Harry.

The professor asked each of the goldbugs how they came to be out in the middle of nowhere.

Honest Hank replied, "I was fired for admitting that the food in the restaurant where I worked wasn't as good as it used to be. So much for being honest."

Hardwork Harry said, "I was fired for working too hard. My fellow workers thought I was trying to make them look bad."

Hopeful Hal responded, "I was so hopeful and optimistic that I put all the takings on a horse. It won at 100-1 but the bookie refused to pay. The boss claimed I had stolen the money so that they could get it back from the bookie. But the bookie didn't pay out any winnings."

Honest Hank addressed the stranger, "What do you think, Professor? Should we bail out or hang around here some more?"

The professor poked around in the dirt as he considered the question. "Let's think," he said. So they all sat around the fire. They looked into the fire and old memories and hopes arose out of the flames.

Still looking far into the distance, the professor spoke, "As a teacher I always advise my students to persevere. So, stick it out, hang in there and . . er . . so on.

"O yes, I told you my profession. I forgot to mention my full name. Professor Stargazer N. Luck. N for numbers. I'm the one you summoned from the echo and the echo called me. Remember?"

Hopeful Hal cried out, "No. I don't believe it. You're him, for real?"

Honest Hank sighed, "Well here we are, getting old and getting nowhere . . ."

The professor replied, "No one is going nowhere in my presence."

Honest Hank replied, "Then perhaps meeting you now has been worth the wait?"

"Yes, I'm Professor Luck, the man with all the destiny numbers and the magic pointer."

"But you'll help us?" asked Hopeful Hal.

"Yes, of course. I'm always willing to give at least a little help to the hardworking, the honest, the hopeful. You should have sent for me sooner."

The professor poked his lightie-up stick at the three goldbugs. "I can't bring back your wasted time looking for gold but I can give you the luck that you have longed for in this mine. Here and now."

The stick glowed like a star and the three goldbugs began to dance around like three year-olds, crying, "Luck. Luck, Professor Luck has come at last."

And then the three goldbugs spoke more slowly and soberly . . .

"Alas, alas, the torments and tortures of searching are all gone away."

The professor pointed his stick at some of the high rocks nearby and jumped around and danced and cried, "There's gold, see gold, more gold. All you need to do is break it up and sluice it. There's millions in gold all around you."

The three goldbugs danced around Professor Luck in joy and song.

Hardwork Harry beamed, "Any kind of gold is success and will certainly do me."

Then they all danced around and Hopeful Hal pointed to the fire and said, "See in the flames the faces of old friends filled with love and laughter and the faces of former foes frowning and cast down with disappointment."

Hardwork Harry cried, "See up there the sun struggles free from his nightchains, drags his face up out of the far hills."

Then Hopeful Hal cried, "And hear the high blue dawnbird beginning to sing a new song that no one has ever heard before."

Then the mysterious professor slowly slipped into the trees, waving his magic stick to the goldbugs and calling out, "I must travel on. I hear someone else crying for me out there."

Professor Luck disappeared into the shortening shadows of the daybreak that crept slowly up upon the old camp and mine.

Honest Hank asked, "Where has Professor Luck gone?"

And Hopeful Hal answered him, "Out there into the great winds and forests and rivers and seas."

Hardwork Harry looked far into the distance, "Yes and there he is still, wandering at his will with his magic stick and destiny numbers, alive and willing to help those who have courage and goodness and faith, somewhere out there far along the little known and lonesome trails of the mind."

THE END

The Playscript

OUTLINE OF THE PLAY

ACT ONE: WE'LL SHOVEL AND SLAVE
Scene One – Looking for Gold
Scene Two - Brains and True Love
Scene Three – The Goldbugs hear Weddingbells
ACT TWO: WHAT A GOOD DOG I WILL BE
Scene One – A Professor Visits
Scene Two – A Squaredeal Arrives
Scene Three – Time Wasted
ACT THREE: DREAM BACK THE GOOD DREAMS
Scene One – Day of the Goldbug
Scene Two – Fit to be Tied
Scene Three - Green Leaves Fall
Scene Four – Weddingbells for Georgie

PLACE: Somewhere in the Great Outback among the great trails of autumn.
TIME: The Present
TIMESPAN: A few weeks
ACTORS: Five male and three female, plus a chorus of singers and dancers.
STAGE TIME: About 120-180 minutes, depending on treatment of the eight songs and dances.
AGE GROUPS: All.
MUSIC: Eight songs with simple, catchy tunes for all good voices - trained or untrained:

Professor Luck's Song; Gold Bugs; I'll Love You Till the Coyote Gives a Howl; Food Ain't as Good as Before; The Gambler's Orphan; Squirrel Song; What a Good Dog I Will Be; Dream Back the Good Dreams.
SET: One. Three Acts, each with four Scenes.

CHARACTERS IN THE PLAY
PROFESSOR STARGAZER NUMBERS LUCK
- a traveling man
GEORGIE SQUAREDEAL GRUBBINGRABBER
- the Villain - a fast-talking salesman
DAME WEDDINGBELLS
- Grand Dame - a matchmaker
HARDWORK HARRY   )   The Goldbugs
HOPEFUL HAL   )   - 3 Principal Boys
HONEST HANK   )
THE GIRLFRIENDS – 3 Principal Girls
ESCAPIST EVE , Harry's girl
PLAYAROUND POLLY, Hal's girl
WET EARS WILMA , Hank's girl
A CHORUS OF DANCERS AND SINGERS

Professor Luck

ACT ONE
WE'LL SHOVEL AND SLAVE
SCENE ONE: LOOKING FOR GOLD

Enter the professor in front of curtain. He takes off his hat, bows to the audience then walks up and down briskly in time to the song.

He sings: **PROFESSOR LUCK'S SONG**
Sung: Fast (Slow for last 3 lines of Chorus)

REFRAIN:

r   t₁   s₁ - s₁   s₁ - s₁
I'm old Professor Luck

r   r   t₁   s₁ - s₁   fe₁ - l₁
I count the magic numbers

r   t₁   s₁ - s₁   s₁ - s₁
Professor Luck will see

l₁   t₁   d - t₁   l₁   s₁   fe₁ - l₁
Who will jump up and who tumbles

s₁ - s₁   t₁   r - r - r
My sums must all agree

r   r - t₁   r   r   t₁ - r
Who rises or who crumbles

r   m - m - r   r   d - t₁   l₁
For Professor Luck will always be

l₁ - t₁   d   t₁   l₁ - s₁   fe₁ - l₁
The man with magic numbers

r   m - m - r   r   d - t₁   l₁
For Professor Luck will always be

r - m   m - r   r - d   d - t₁
(That's me, that's me, that's me, that's me)

l₁ - t₁   d   t₁   l₁ - s₁   fe₁ - l₁
The man with magic numbers.

REFRAIN:
I'm old Professor Luck
I count the magic numbers
Professor Luck will see
Who will jump up and who tumbles
My sums must all agree
Who rises or who crumbles
For Professor Luck will always be
The man with magic numbers
For Professor Luck will always be
(That's me, that's me, that's me, that's me)
The man with magic numbers.

VERSE ONE:

$r \quad t_1 - s_1 \quad\quad s_1 - s_1 - s_1$
The finest brains have tried

$r \quad t_1 \quad\quad s_1 - s_1 \quad s_1 - fe_1 \quad l_1$
To find success without me

$r \quad t_1 - s_1 \quad\quad s_1 - s_1 - s_1$
And many have denied

$l_1 \quad t_1 \quad\quad d - t_1 \quad l_1 \quad s_1 - fe_1 \quad l_1$
That there's any help about me

$r \quad\quad s_1 - s_1 \quad\quad t_1 - r - r - r$
(Yet) Success depends on me

$r \quad r \quad t_1 \quad r \quad\quad r - r - t_1 - r$
And on all my calculations

$r \quad m - m \quad r \quad r \quad d$
For only I can see

$l_1 \quad t_1 \quad\quad d - t_1 \quad\quad l_1 - s_1 - fe_1 - l_1$
All the number combinations

VERSE ONE:
The finest brains have tried
To find success without me
And many have denied
That there's any help about me
(Yet) Success depends on me
And on all my calculations
For only I can see
All the number combinations

VERSE TWO:
Now Hope is not all bad
And I'm inclined to favor
Any honest, decent lad
Or a lass who likes hard labor
But there's one guarantee
I'll give and I'm not bluffing
Without me you will see
All your hard work comes to nothing
All your upright honesty
And your hope will come to nothing
(lines 9 and 10 use the same music as lines 7 and 8)

Then the professor recites.
Here is a case in point
Here are three luckless Henrys
Any one could be your pal
There's Honest Hank, Hardwork Harry
And good old Hopeful Hal
Back in them thar hills, those goldbugs dig

And pan for gold, this many a year
These goldbugs have really strange ideas
About things that we hold dear
Things like hard work and hope and honesty
And brains and true love too
They must be raving crazy mad
To say the things they do
So let them ramble on and off
And rant and rave again
It's all in fun, dear ladies
Just joking, gentlemen.

Professor removes his hat, holds it to his chest, bows and **leaves stage.**

The curtain opens to reveal the setting of Scene One. Somewhere in the far backwoods and hills it is the fall, time of reminiscence, recall, looking back, nostalgia and these feelings are reflected in the dramatic mood.

Left-stage is an old mine, a brick-ringed campfire and a broad creek or a small river. There are a few tools, wheels, pots, utensils, a few ropes, including an old lasso, alarm clocks, bedding, pillows, blankets and similar odds and ends lying around.

Professor Luck

Center-stage is a fairly level field with a few large rocks here and there, merging into the backdrop of autumnal, multicolored, mostly green wooded hills, with some hill-sheep grazing. Squirrels, birds, hogs, deer, turkey or other wild animals may appear here and there on the backdrop.

Right-stage is a small orchard with a few fruit trees and bushes. There are a few logs arranged to substitute as picnic tables and benches.

In the following scene lighting should emphasize whoever is singing each verse. The center-stage will be for general action and dancing. The three goldbugs, Hopeful Hal, Hardwork Harry and Honest Hank live here and work their old mine, so far without success.

Curtain rises on the three goldbugs, in broad brimmed hats, rough beards and old clothes. They are seated around the campfire, drinking coffee and eating beans out of aluminum dishes.

Enter Chorus dressed as goldbugs. Most of the singing and dancing takes place around the old mine and creek. Leading dancer is a dowser with a divining rod who searches for treasure, stopping when the rod twitches and beckoning *the others to come. All are costumed as goldbugs with broad-brimmed hats, plaid shirts and boots.. Their strutting and dancing is enthusiastic. About half of the dancers carry picks and shovels and the other half carry large panning dishes. When the dowser indicates a spot, they rally round and either pan or pick with zeal.*

The three goldbugs: Hal, Harry and Hank introduce themselves to the audience.

HARRY: I'm Hardwork Harry. *(takes off his hat and bows)*

HAL: I'm Hopeful Hal. *(takes off his hat and bows)*

HANK: And I'm Honest Hank. *(takes off his hat and bows)*

They join the Chorus to sing GOLDBUGS and follow the last of the dancers with slight awkwardness and jerky expectancy as though looking for the gold.

GOLDBUGS
Sung: Jerkily and Cheerfully

VERSE ONE:

d   f   l   f   d   f   l   f
We shovel and slave, we rant and rave
d - d   f   f   f   m   r   m   f   s
As we scratch each patch for the wealth we crave
d   f   l   f   d   f   l   f
Ho, ho, hee, hee, ho, ho, hee, hee
l d^1 l   s   s   f
We'll bug all day for gold
d   f   l - l   f   d   f   l   f
It's more than a joke, we've all gone broke
d   f   f - f - f   m - r   m - f   s
It's not just a fad, we're raving mad
d   f   l   f   d   f   l   f
Ho, ho, hee, hee, ho, ho, hee, hee
l d^1 l   s   s   f
We'll bug all day for gold

VERSE ONE: *(Hardwork Harry)*
We shovel and slave, we rant and rave
As we scratch each patch for the wealth we crave
Ho, ho, hee, hee, ho, ho, hee, hee
We'll bug all day for gold
It's more than a joke, we've all gone broke
It's not just a fad, we're raving mad
Ho, ho, hee, hee, ho, ho, hee, hee
We'll bug all day for gold.

REFRAIN: *(all Sing)*
Some little bugs come, some big bugs go
That's just the way of the world you know
But the only bugs who never grow old
Are the bugs who bug for gold
Smash up the stones, give them a kick
One more shovel load might do the trick
Ho, ho, hee, hee, ho, ho, hee, hee
We bug all day for gold

VERSE TWO: *(Honest Hank)*
And when we've found the gold we love
We'll bug some more for treasure trove
Ho, ho, hee, hee, ho, ho, hee, hee
We'll bug for treasure trove
The search for treasure never ends
We may strut all around and impress our friends
Ho, ho, hee, hee, ho, ho, hee, hee
Then we'll bug for treasure trove

VERSE THREE: *(Hopeful Hal)*
If you live in hope you'll never grow old
It'll keep you alive just a digging for gold
Ho, ho, hee, hee, ho, ho, hee, hee
We'll bug for silver and gold
But when we've made our very last try
We'll dig some more in the sweet bye and bye
Ho, ho, hee, hee, ho, ho, hee, hee
We're bugs for treasure trove

*Harry, Hank and Hal each take off their hats and bow to the audience. **Chorus leaves the stage followed by the three goldbugs.***

Curtain

ACT ONE
WE'LL SHOVEL AND SLAVE
SCENE TWO: BRAINS AND TRUE LOVE
Scene: The same. **Enter Harry, Hal and Hank.** *They walk toward the distant hills center-stage and look out over the creeks and woods.*

HAL: What a romantic place! See, those rolling hills slope up and down like waves. Here's a truly romantic spot for us to talk about the good times gone by and about the true love of the old days . . for that was really something.

Seems like there are strange things happening in these haunted hills and woods tonight. There are visions and spirits in these mountains that come alive . . sights that come and go in starlight that looked the same back when the world was young. Starlight that lit these musical hills a thousand years ago.

HANK: You're very romantic Hal. But, as for true love, there was no such thing in the old days. We just could not afford it. We were too poor.

The three goldbugs cheerfully slap each other on the back.

HAL: *(undeterred)* Ah, love survives poverty. That is part of the mystery of it.

HANK: I thought mysteries only happened to me. *(wistfully)* My oldtime gal was a mystery too . . at least to me she was a mystery. I never realized that she was going to ditch me. She sure fooled me.

HAL: So you had a girl. Then you can't mean it when you say that there was no true love in the old days.

HANK: Well, maybe that's a slight exaggeration. But like I always say, there are three steps to girlfriending; number one, going out - like romancing and getting to know ya; number two, finding out - what they're really like, I mean and number three - getting out.

HAL: Getting out? How do you mean?

HANK: Well, for instance, on horseback or on a boxcar or on a bus or the like. A car would be fine if you have that much money left after a real good episode of girlfriend dating. Strange things happen in young romances. First, I nearly drowned my girl, then she left me. I can't understand it. Now I somehow feel her presence once again.

Enter Wet-Ears Wilma (Hank's girl). Unnoticed, she dances around scooping up and splashing water from the creek, here and there.

HAL: *(to Hank)* Oh come on, you're not serious but still I like that bit about going out, finding out and getting out. I usually get as far as number one.

HARRY: Me too. In fact, I never really got beyond step number one.

HAL: How not?

HARRY: Well, my gal left me early in our friendship. I never saw her again. But I can see her now, in memory. *(lights dimmed)* She was beautiful. At least I can say that . . that's something. It's better to be walked out on by a beautiful girl than by a hard-looking one. You know what I mean fellahs, it's better for one's self-esteem. *(others laugh)*

Enter Escapist Eve (Harry's girl). She dances in the spotlight.

Enter rest of Dancers and Playaround Polly (Hal's girl). Spotlight remains on Hopeful Hal's girl (Playaround Polly). She and the rest of the dancers wear a ponytail and bow hairstyle and are dressed in the 50's style with wide skirt, starched, wide flared underskirts, broad belt and blouse with puffed sleeves. She dances center-stage then moves to right as the spotlight fades away and the stage lighting highlights right-stage. Male dancers wear 50's style (e.g., white shirts, velvet ties, drain pipe trousers)

Harry's girl (Escapist Eve) dances around.

HAL: *(to his girl, Polly)* What happened? Why did you leave me? Why did you not care for me?

POLLY: I always cared for you Hal. I just thought that you were too clever ever to be a success. It's only dumb men who make good. So I went my way and you went your way. Why can't we be friends in memory?

HAL: *(smiling)* Why not indeed?

HANK: Harry, now I remember what it was like to be in love. *(ruefully)* Some oldtime loves were quick to drift away. I wonder why?

HARRY: Well . . I never thought my great love would leave me. I think, on the whole, I got to the number two step, finding out. I found out what made my gal do the things she did. It was simple, she liked to escape from guys. It made her feel smarter than them. Though it's still a mystery to me what kind of strange satisfaction she got from it all. Yes, you've heard of girls who like to trap men and hold on to them. My girl liked to be captured and then make a break for it. I suppose she was a kind of female escape artist.

> *Harry plays with a lasso on the end of a rope, which he aims at Escapist Eve*
> *Hank and Hal also join in the dancing, pursuing the Chorus but never being able to capture them.*

HARRY: I wonder why they left us all? Perhaps these ghostly memories will tell us.

POLLY: *(to Hal accusingly)*
Brains
I hate'em
If I know that a man has brains
I won't date'em
Now <u>kindness</u> I can take
(Not that I'm on the make)
Indeed, <u>kindness</u> reigns
Not brains
<u>Kindness</u> is all
At least as far as I can recall
Well, let me see now. Oh yes, I know

There's also dough
But brains - wit
Who needs it
I really truly can
Stand almost any kind of man
Except one who has brains
That's the kind of guy who gives me pains
Pains here and there
Everywhere
I get pains and pains and pains
When I even think of a man with brains
I will sometimes date a guy
Sure, let's give it a try
But only if he has <u>not got</u> brains
(quickly and decisively)
Men with brains
Shouldn't date dames.

EVE: *(to Harry)*
I agree with Polly
Kindness is the thing
Kindness is king
Any man who is dumb
O.K. come
Along with me, I say
But if the guy is brainy and smart

He'd better get off to an early start
Before I help him on his way
In fact any guy with a brain
Is only fit for pouring down the drain
As far as I am concerned
That's one foxy smart lesson I've learned
Brainy guys are far too wise
To deserve to win me as a prize
(quickly and decisively)
Men with brains
Don't get dames

WILMA: *(to Hank)*
Yes, some guys are just too clever
To have any part
In a normal girl's simple fate
Some guys are just too witty
To get down to the nitty gritty
Of showing a girl a good date
All you brainy men really need
Is a good book to read
And no matter how many books you've tried
(accusingly)
You're never, never, never satisfied!
Are you, are you? *(disgustedly)*
All you do, is go look

For another book
In fact, men with brains
Don't need dames

POLLY: *(to the audience)*
I don't mind a little dishonesty
In fact, a roguish smile can fan the flames
And as for a man being mean *(shrugs)*
Well, that's part of the male scene
(stamping her foot)
But I can't stand a man with brains

ALL GIRLFRIENDS TOGETHER:
(aside to audience)
In fact, men with brains
Don't need dames.

EVE:
Kindness and money
Go together like milk and honey
But brains and true love go together (Oh Yeh)
Like winter storms and spring day weather
Brains, bah!
I agree with the girls - I hate smart guys too
(aside) Don't you?

All three girlfriends look aggressively with their hands on their hips at the three goldbugs who are only a little intimidated. The lights dim and waver briefly.

HARRY: Weird happenings are here tonight, for sure.

HANK: Is this all real?

HAL: *(musingly)* These girls can't be real! What memories are these? Certainly not ego-boosting and how can these images speak? Is it magic? Or is it all just broken pictures coming to life to haunt us from the old rummaging attic of our past lives?

> *Harry lassoes Escapist Eve and tries to tie her but she escapes from the rope and continues to dance. She beckons to him and retreats. Dancers emulate her actions and retreat. Harry wildly and desperately tries to lasso her but without success. He throws aside the rope and tries to rush forward to capture any of the other retreating dancers but he is restrained by Hal and Hank as the*

dancers exit, ushered out by Harry's girl, Escapist Eve

EVE: My old and golden love, come let us go to the high mountains. Come, follow me, Harry.

Chorus and Girlfriends Leave Hal and Hank restrain Harry by holding him back forcibly

HARRY: Let me go with her, my oldtime true love.

HAL: Don't go, it's only a memory. She seems to be real but it's all an illusion. Strange things are going on.

HANK: That's right. Hang on Harry. She's just a memory, now. There's magic in these hills around here tonight that is bringing these memories alive to us. It's as though at times our minds need to bring alive our memories of the past and think about the old days. But though there's a magic in the air, these things are only in your mind. They seem to be real, the way ghosts are said to be real on Halloween. Yet, a ghost is still a ghost, a memory is still only a memory even though it seems to have a life of its own.

HARRY: *(sighs lightly and then nods agreeably)* You're right. There are times when memories seem alive. You all can sense it and now I think that I can sense it too. It's in the air. It's magic but it is only a dream of days gone by, a ghost of younger days. We cannot capture it with a rope.

He wraps up his rope, smiling with just a hint of sadness

HANK: I wish that I had had that rope, Harry, the night I lost my girl . . the evening she dared to walk out on me. I could have used that rope on her.

HAL: O, no, surely not, Hank. You wouldn't have done that?

HARRY: Would you?

HAL: You know that ain't right, Hank. The punishment should fit the crime . . . I mean, it was only you she left . . not Henry VIII.

HANK: *(mystified)* What are you all ranting and raving about?

HARRY: *(sadly)* Hanging her.

HANK: *(puzzled)* Hanging who?

HAL: Your girl.

HANK: *(blankly)* Why?

HARRY: *(at a loss, querulously)* For leaving you, of course.

HANK: *(understanding)* Oh that. Don't be silly. I meant to say, if I had had that rope I could have saved my girl's life more quickly and, as a result, maybe she and I would still be together today.

HAL: O we really should apologize. I'm so sorry we misunderstood you, Hank. Tell us

about her.   It seems like we've all been
deserted by our true-loves or perhaps I
should say by our untrue loves.   What
happened Hank?

Re-enter the Chorus and the Three
Girlfriends. All are dressed in 50's style
as in previous appearance.   One of the
Chorus represents young Hank, many
years ago. The dancer (young Hank) and
his girl, Wet-Ears Wilma, go through the
*events of the song, **COYOTE**, left-stage on*
the river bank as the Chorus dance, left-
stage and center.   Yodels and howls and
yelps after each verse may be made by the
live Chorus or by sound effects with
miming by the Chorus.

Hank, Harry and Hal, hands on chins,
sit on the logs in the shadows, right,
*watching the events of the song, **COYOTE**.*

*Polly sings **COYOTE** and the rest give*
vocal backing and join in the song's chorus
as the young Hank and his girl, Wet-Ears
Wilma, act out the events of the song. Polly
and Eve join in the singing and dancing
with the Chorus.

POLLY: Let me tell you the story of a young man not a million miles from here who used to believe in true love but who doesn't anymore. *(she sings)*

I'LL LOVE YOU TILL THE COYOTE*
GIVES A HOWL
*or Dingo or Wild Wolf

I'LL LOVE YOU TILL
THE COYOTE* GIVES A HOWL
Sung: Lively

VERSE ONE:

m   f - s   l   s   m - d
Far away and long ago

d t_1 l_1 - r   d - l_1 s_1
Where the windy waters flow

s_1 d - d   d   d - d   d t_1 d - *r*
A goldbug took his girl out to propose

m - f   s   l   s - m   d
Down by that mighty river

d - t_1 l_1 r   d l_1 - s_1
He swore his love forever

   m - f   s   s - s   s   f   r t_1 - s_1 *d*
Holding her so close right where the water flows

VERSE ONE:
Far away and long ago
Where the windy waters flow
A goldbug took his girl out to propose
Down by that mighty river
He swore his love forever
Holding her so close right where the water flows

```
    d - m   s - s   s - s   l - s
    Yodel  odel  odel  odel
     f - f   f - f   taw - l
    Yodel o ah laydel ee,
    d - m     d - d - d - d    m  s - s  f
    Yodel  Yodel odel odel ay delee
```

REFRAIN: (same tune + the last 3 lines)
O please be my sweetheart
You and I will never part
You're so beautiful I'll love you every day
Then the coyote gave a howl *(howls, yaps, barks)*
An old dog did bark and growl
And a traveling singer yodeled on his way
Yodel odel odel odel
Yodel o ah laydel ee,
Yodel Yodel odel odel ay delee *(howls, yaps, barks)*

```
    d - m   s - s   s - s   l - s
    Yodel  odel  odel  odel
     f - f   f - f   taw - l
    Yodel o ah laydel ee,
    d - m     d - d - d    m  s - s  f
    Yodel  Yodel odel odel ay delee
```

VERSE TWO:
Well the goldbug got so shaken
By the noise the dogs were making
That he dropped his girl into the flowing tide
When he tried to pull her out
Her makeup all washed out
And her wig went floating off away from sight

VERSE THREE:
When her eyebrows washed away
Her face looked kind of gray
And the water soon destroyed her padded top
Then her tight belt split in two
And her waist inflated too
When that poor girl came ashore she was a flop

VERSE FOUR:
There she stood in that cold place
And slapped him in the face
She walloped him real hard with all her might
(slowly) Oh, how quickly love departs
In the stream of broken hearts
As beauty floats away upon life's tide
(howls, yaps, barks, yodels)
The last three lines "O how quickly etc" are sung again slowly and then the refrain is repeated briskly. Lights fade briefly

HAL: Ah, yes, beauty floats away upon life's tide and so rarely and sparely returns.

Chorus leaves followed by Wet-Ears Wilma, young Hank, Escapist Eve and Playaround Polly

HANK: Yes, its strange to see alive again the memories of the past. Life was good then, in the good old days.

HARRY: Still, here we are, trapped in the horrible present, brains and all but still no girls and no gold.

They remain standing still, as

Curtain

ACT ONE
WE'LL SHOVEL AND SLAVE
SCENE THREE: THE GOLDBUGS
HEAR WEDDINGBELLS

Scene: The same. Opens just as the three girlfriends leave stage. Dame Weddingbells calls to the girls and shakes her fist after them.

DAME: Don't forget . . it's mostly the men with brains who make the money.

Dame Weddingbells dressed in a long skirt and boots, wears a shawl over her grey hair and carries a large umbrella. She is middle-aged and speaks with a loud voice

DAME: *(opens up her umbrella)* My name is Dame Weddingbells and my job is to bring couples together who like each other and might want to get married. I'm just an oldfashioned matchmaker. This brolly is for a rainy day.

HANK: Then you've come to the right part of the country.

She joins the goldbugs and listens as they daydream.

HAL: *(dreamily)* Sometimes I wonder if these mountains are real. It's like they lie somewhere in the great outback far along the lonesome and little known trails of the mind. What an otherworldly place!

HARRY: Yes, these are trails that lead to certain success or total failure. Here there can be no in-between, half-way home, no safe retreat.

HANK: *(sighing)* Yip, there is only gold or silver or treasure trove or useless toil, foul soil and the coil of the snake.

HARRY: This is a landscape where any traveling man might come. A fortress for only the brave. A graveyard of dry bones with only toil at the end of the trail.

HANK: We're all here to avoid the bossman, the tyrant, the Genghis Khan.

All three of the goldbugs become sad and philosophical as they see the darkness out there beyond their campfire.

HANK: *(sadly)* I see the shadows of wasted years thinly shimmering beyond the fire's fainting illusions of soon success. See, there in the campfire's flames, the faces of old friends are frowning and the faces of former foes are filled with a loathsome joy.

HAL: Each of us has come out here along his own path. So each of us is bound to see something different in the shadows and in the light. You are the one who trusted hard toil, Hardwork Harry.

I am the one who is most surprised at our failure. That's why you call me, Hopeful Hal. *(he smiles)* And you, Honest Hank, have always believed that honesty is the best policy.

HARRY: So maybe this evening we should all just sit around the campfire, drink good old creek water and eat wild beans and stewed rabbit. *(he sets aside some aluminum dishes)*

HAL: *(thoughtfully)* Indeed, the very idea makes me wonder where did we go wrong in this life?

DAME: *(interrupting)* Why don't you make it up with your girlfriends – those gold-diggers. I'll set up a good little get-together for you all. How's about that?

HAL: Sure. That would be fine but right now we're all broke. If we're going to get married, we need money for the rent.

Harry and Hank agree with Hal.

DAME: I'll find a moneyguide to advise you all.

HANK: Then you should find us a money-advisor with only one arm.

DAME: *(surprised)* Why only ONE arm?

HANK: The last one we visited kept saying, on the one hand I'd advise this and on the other hand I'd advise that. So we ended up doing nothing. Maybe a one-armed advisor would be best.

DAME: At least he was honest with you. The other day I got mugged by three octogenarians in squeaky wheelchairs.

HARRY: How could you allow yourself to be mugged by old-age pensioners?

DAME: I was taken unawares.   I never suspected them.

HAL: Unexpected? I thought you said they were in squeaky wheelchairs.

DAME: Yes, that's true.

HANK: Then why didn't you hear them coming?

Dame Weddingbells moans and strikes her forehead with her palm in agony as she leaves the stage. The three goldbugs look at each other in amazement, as

Curtain

ACT TWO
WHAT A GOOD DOG I WILL BE
SCENE ONE: A PROFESSOR VISITS

Scene: The same. The three goldbugs are still sitting around their campfire.

HARRY: Well, we're told to think big and that hard work leads to success. That honesty is the best policy.

HANK: But I say no to all that <u>be a good boy and you'll do well</u> nonsense. I insist on being a bad boy. I feel somehow that it's my only hope for success.

HARRY: I know. What we need is luck!

HAL: *(walking up and down agitatedly)* Well, where do we find it?

HARRY: That I do not know but whether you find it or don't find it, now or never, that's what you need. The one and only true secret of success - LUCK.

HANK: Listen, we've been looking for gold or silver or jewels all these years . . that's a kind of hard, glinting, shining LUCK. If we can't find treasure, how can we find luck?

HAL: Furthermore, *(wagging a finger at Hank)* if we were lucky people we'd have found treasure long ago. There's no point in looking for Luck. Luck would find us just as we are sitting here, if we were lucky people.

HARRY: *(loudly into the hilly forest, his voice echoing)* We're here . . come and find us. Luck, luck, luck.

ECHO: *(the spirit of the hills)* LUCK, LUCK, LUCK. *(growing fainter)* Luck, Luck, Luck.

HANK: Here's someone coming.

HAL: Maybe it's luck.

HARRY: Maybe it's a bandit. Let's stand aside and ambush him.

*As the three goldbugs slide silently into the shadows, a tall, slim, bearded **older gentleman** in* *white shirt and black coat with tails, **enters the clearing from right-stage** and begins poking around with his stick.*

The three goldbugs sidle carefully out of the shadows.

HANK: *(suspiciously)* Whatderee poking and sniffing around here for?

PROFESSOR: Ah, my good friends, nice to meet you. I'm Professor Stargazer. I'm here to observe the heavens and the fates, past or future, from this wonderful vantage point. This panoramic pinnacle of astronomical advantage . . . By the way, what is the elevation of this camp?

HANK: You mean, how high up are we?

PROFESSOR: Yes, how high?

HARRY: 6000 feet.

PROFESSOR: *(shaking his head)* That's very high.

HAL: Since we're friends, I'll make it 5500. But that's my last offer. *(he laughs)*

PROFESSOR: I'm pleased to know that I am among financially rational friends.

HANK: *(muttering)* Why can't you just speak in plain lingo?

PROFESSOR: What . . speak plainly and lose my lucrative professorship with all its bank balancing bonus and pecuniary perquisites. Ha, ha, plain lingo, indeed. Not a chance. That would never get me a job for life.

HAL: *(growling)* Those are all very pretty speeches Professor. But why not go to look at the stars somewhere down there? Why up here, in our little lonely spot?

HARRY: Or, why don't you just go up, up thatta there mountain? You can see for a million miles from the top of the hill.

PROFESSOR: Sir, I am a man of more than threescore years and ten. I need rest. Am I not welcome here? Have you struck gold or silver or other treasure and do not wish me to know? I assure you that I am silence and secrecy personified. No amount of torture or tribulation or titillation would ever induce me to reveal your secret. *(his eyes narrow as he grows intense)* They could put me on the rack itself and turn it so mercilessly that . . .

HANK: *(shaking his head despondently)* O save yourself all the pains and aches, Professor. There's nothing to reveal. We're broke . . .

HARRY: You might as well sit down and drink some creek water. Here, have a few beans too, stranger - it's about all that's left.

PROFESSOR: What a great place to look for gold or silver or treasured memories and plenty of them.

HANK: Well, we just need the gold or silver or treasures and never mind the memories but sure enough, Professor, it's good to share remembrances. We do a lot of reminiscing here about the old times. How we came to be goldbugs and put all our time and money and hard work into this here mine and creek. Yes, a lot of our money has disappeared into the ground.

HARRY: But none has come back out. *(shakes head)* All we do is grub for gold and reap no return.

PROFESSOR: Well, that's hard graft and I am glad to hear about your hard work, Harry.

HAL: Hope, hard work and honesty have always been the three surest ways to get fired.

HANK: Absolutely! Hard work, hope and honesty are the three worst things you could do except, of course, for having brains - which is the number one reason for failure in life, judging from what our gold-digger girlfriends seem to think.

Hal and Harry chortle and guffaw and slap one another on the back.

HARRY: *(morosely)* Perhaps we need luck as well, Professor.

HANK: Yes, that's it. Luck is what we need. I was fired for honesty.

PROFESSOR: *(to Hank)* Rubbish! How on earth could they have fired you for being honest? It's against the law. It's an outrage against humanity. *(Professor pretends to faint, facetiously)*

(interested) So, what happened?

HANK: Simple! I was fired for being honest. I worked for a restaurant. I had to keep the costs down. When I admitted to the diners that the food wasn't as good as it used to be, I was fired. But I still say that cheap food ain't as good as it used to be or as good as it ought to be. Just fired that's all, fired. That's when I came out here to goldbug and eat some plain ornery, mean tasting food.

Enter Chorus who dance right-stage among the fruit trees and logs.

Professor Luck

Hank, Professor, Hal and Harry sit at separate log tables. Dancers are dressed as waiters and waitresses each carrying a small tray and wiping cloth hung over one wrist. They dance among the log tables and trees of the orchard, bow to each of the four patrons and place invisible, imaginary food and drinks on the log tables.

Hank leads in singing
FOOD AIN'T AS GOOD AS BEFORE
Sung: Slow

VERSE ONE:

t_1 - r   m   m   m - m   r   m   s s   s - l
I   ain't shed no tears over onions in years
s - l   t   l   s   m   r t_1 r
It   seems that good smells have been banned
t_1 - r   m   m   m - m   r   m   s   s   l
My taste bud's a dud when I eat a new spud
 s - l   t   l   s - m   m   m - m
And the eggs are so weak they can't stand
 t r^1 t   t - t   l - s   l   l - l   l
The dog that I had went a stark staring mad
 s - l   t   l   s - m   r t_1 r
When it smelt a fresh steak from the store
  t_1 - r   m   m   m - m   r - m   s   s   s - l
Now the meat has no smell and the dog sleeps so well
 s - l   t   l   s - m   m m - m
Oh the food ain't as good as before

VERSE ONE: *(Hank sings)*
I ain't shed no tears over onions in years
It seems that good smells have been banned
My taste bud's a dud when I eat a new spud
And the eggs are so weak they can't stand
The dog that I had went a stark staring mad
When it smelt a fresh steak from the store
Now the meat has no smell and the dog sleeps so well
Oh the food ain't as good as before
No the food ain't as good as before

VERSE TWO: *(Hal sings)*
The tomatoey smell was so strong I could tell
It had grown up on all loving care
And the scarred ugly fruit was so sweet and so cute
I was eager as a bee for my share
So let's get the good oldtime taste back in food
Must we wait for a pie in the sky?
Tell me, O tell, where is sharp taste and smell?
Where's the catfish that made the cat cry? *(sniff, sniff)*

REFRAIN: *(all sing)*
I'm a-looking for good and plain old fashioned food
With a crunch or a munch I declare
With a smell and a smack and a tang and a crack
I'm as keen as a bee for my share
(tune: same as last 4 lines of verse)
     As song ends, **Chorus retreat to periphery**
of the orchard and leave stage.

HARRY: Yes, there's plenty of plain natural food around here - like that rabbit-steak. *(he points to a dish of some kind)* I think I'll put off eating this delicious rabbit meat until tomorrow so that I'll have something wonderful to look forward to.

HAL: Why don't you just eat it now so that tomorrow you'll have some beautiful memories . . if you live.

HARRY: *(undecided, confused)* Why yes, on second thoughts, what a good idea. Let me see. But no, it's better to look forward than look back. On third thoughts, I'm hungry. *(he shrugs and begins to eat)*

HANK: *(to Harry)* You're not as thrifty with food as you are with soap, are you Harry?

Hal laughs. Harry looks offended.

HARRY: *(indignantly)* What do you mean?

HANK: Why don't you have a bath? A bath, a good wash, see?

HARRY: What and risk catching a chill! I'd rather be dirty and have my health.

HANK: We agreed to wash once a week in the interests of friendship. That is, so as not to stink and your week is up tonight, O.K?

HARRY: Well I have to conserve our soap. If I wash tonight I'll clean up only seven day's dirt and filthy sweat but if I save up another day's dirt I'll get eight days dirt off for the same amount of soap, see? Let's be thrifty. This is a business, all right? Remember? A business deal. *(nods significantly)* O.K? See? Save money.

HAL: Oh, all right, you two. Wrap it up.

HANK: Oh, a wild rabbit stew is so good.

OTHERS: If you'd eat that, you'd eat an old boot.

HANK: All I want is good oldfashioned food!

OTHERS: *(shaking heads)* No, no, ugh, ugh!

PROFESSOR: What about you Hal?   What brought you to these hills?

HAL: *(walking up and down, reminiscing)*   I was fired for being hopeful.   Fired for having big ideas.   How come?   I put the shops' entire weeks takings on a horse at 100 to 1.

PROFESSOR: And it lost?   So you deserved to be fired for your big ideas.

HAL: No.   It's not as simple as that.   The horse won at 100 to 1.

PROFESSOR: Well, what was the complaint then?

HAL: The complaint was – the bookie would not pay.

PROFESSOR: You should know that the bookie does not have to pay.   All bets are binding in honor only.

HAL: Well, what kind of honor is that?   Of course, the firm got their money back but no winnings. They declared that I'd stolen the money. I was lucky to get out of town before the sheriff got hold of me.

PROFESSOR: It was your own fault for making a deal like that.

HAL: I don't like bookies. They're untrustworthy criminals, including those who call themselves insurance men. But especially the ones who deal with horses. They're a bad lot.

> *Enter Chorus dressed as in their previous appearance but with no dishcloths or trays. They join in the singing. Dude-gambler style may be substituted or evening dresses and suits/tuxedoes.*
>
> *Hal leads in singing GAMBLER'S ORPHAN and the others join in singing and dancing.*

THE GAMBLER'S ORPHAN
Sung: Slow and Pathetically

VERSE ONE:

d - d f f - f f - m f s r
Will there be any bookies in heaven?

r m - m m d m s f
O Mammy please say that it's so

d - d f f f f m f s r
And does Daddy spend all day out betting

r m m - m d m s *f*
Up there like he did down below?

f d d l l - l s l taw - r
Do the dear saints all tear up their tickets

r d s s s - f s l
And boo and jump wildly and jeer

d - d f f f - f m f s r
When the jockeys hold back the hot favorites

r - r d taw l s *f*
The way they do down here?

VERSE ONE: *(Hal sings)*
Will there be any bookies in heaven?
O Mammy please say that it's so
And does Daddy spend all day out betting
Up there like he did down below?
Do the dear saints all tear up their tickets
And boo and jump wildly and jeer
When the jockeys hold back the hot favorites
The way they do down here?

REFRAIN:

l_1 taw$_1$ d - d   r   m   f

Yes the gamblers still run rash

d^1 - d^1 d^1 d^1 taw   l   r

When the bookies scream for cash

r   d - d   m   f   l   l - s

And the blessed ones all holler

s   d   d d - d   f   s   l

When the favorite makes a dash

r   d - d   r   m   s - f

Yes Daddy still picks horses

l d^1 d^1 taw l   r

That fade or fall or die

d - d   f   f   f - f   m   f   s r

As he loses his last dime and dollar

r   r   d taw   l   s   *f*

At the racetrack in the sky

REFRAIN: *(all sing)*
Yes, the gamblers still run rash
When the bookies scream for cash
And the blessed ones all holler
When the favorite makes a dash
Yes, Daddy still picks horses
That fade or fall or die
As he loses his last dime and dollar
At the racetrack in the sky

VERSE TWO: *(Hal sings)*
If all things are free up in heaven
O Mammy, the dear saints would fret
If there weren't any bookies to help them
Get rid of their cash in a bet
O say, there'll be bookies in heaven
All laying odds just like below
Where else would a good bookie settle
Than the place where gamblers go?

REFRAIN: *(all sing)*
Yes, the gamblers still run rash
When the bookies scream for cash
And the blessed ones all holler
When the favorite makes a dash
Yes, Daddy still picks horses
That fade or fall or die
As he loses his last dime and dollar
At the racetrack in the sky

Chorus leave stage

HARRY: *(chortling)* My tale is as sad as theirs, Professor. The reason why they call me Hardwork Harry is because hard work was my ruin and downfall. Hard work caused all my failure in life and made me a penniless derelict crawling bitterly on the face of the earth, scavenging for pennies and crusts. That's why I came here as a goldbug.

PROFESSOR: *(concerned)* Surely not! Surely honest toil never hurt anyone. Why, my grandmother used to say "hard work never killed anyone" . . hmm . . but then she mostly sat in her armchair until she took her first and last flying lesson.

HARRY: If you work hard, you sometimes work yourself out of a job but you always work yourself out of promotion. I wanted to get promotion and do well but alas I was a compulsive hard worker, a workaholic. Why, I even went to counseling on it, in the billiards room around the corner. But I was hooked on work. My fellow workers thought that I was working hard just to make them look bad. Promotion always went to someone who was lazy but popular with the boys. So that's why I became self-employed, digging for gold.

PROFESSOR: Well, if only you could find what you're looking for as easily as some of these woodland critters. Why it <u>should</u> be as easy for you as for a squirrel finding a nut or a bird finding a worm.

HARRY: Yep, these critters could sure give us a lesson.

Enter the Chorus dressed as goldbugs. Harry leads as they all sing

SQUIRREL
Sung: Rollicking

VERSE ONE:

m   m   m - m   m   m - m
I'd like to be a squirrel
  m r - d   d   r - d
A-jumping high and low
m   s - s   l   s - s   m - m
He always finds a way to get
f   s - s   f   m – r
To where he wants to go
  m   f   s - s l - s - s   s – m
Now, if such a skittery critter
m - f   s - s   m   d - r
Can find a way that's new
d - r   m - m s_1 - s_1 l_1 d - d
Then we can skip the crumbling dreams
  m   r   d - d   d - d
And find our own way through

VERSE ONE:

I'd like to be a squirrel
A-jumping high and low
He always finds a way to get
To where he wants to go
Now, if such a skittery critter
Can find a way that's new
Then we can skip the crumbling dreams
And find our own way through

REFRAIN:

d   r   m - m - m   m - m - m   m - m
O the squirrelly - iddelly-iddel
  m - m   r - d   d   d - d
Goes a bouncing with a bump
    m   s - s   l - s - s   s - m
Through bushes into the middle
  f - f   s - s - s   f - m - m   r
With a jittery, flittery jump
   m   f   s - s - s - l   s - s - s - m
He's a trickery-dick and a riddle
   m   s   s   m   d   r
He's there and then he's gone
  d   r   m - m - m   m - m - m   m - m
For the squirrelly - iddelly-iddel
  m   m   r - d - d   d - d - d   d
Goes a squirrelly- iddeling on

Professor Luck

REFRAIN:
O the squirrelly-iddelly-iddel
Goes a bouncing with a bump
Through bushes into the middle
With a jittery, flittery jump
He's a trickery-dick and a riddle
He's there and then he's gone
For the squirrelly-iddelly-iddel
Goes a squirrelly-iddeling on.

VERSE TWO:
Now the squirrel has a passport
That always gets him by
It's a slippery zippery bluster
And it makes his engines fly
Though the woods are slick and thickety
And weeds are worrying high
We'll dig the good things out of the hills
If we give it a squirrelly try.

At the line, "he's there and then he's gone" Harry points at an invisible squirrel then spreads his hands and shakes his head as it "disappears". **Chorus leave the stage**

HANK: Well, Professor. What do you think?

PROFESSOR: Of hopefulness, hard work and honesty? Well, these are things that I used to recommend to my students. But now I can see that it's only luck that counts. You were right to put all your energy into working for yourselves out here in this old mine.

Hank wags his head sadly and the others shake their heads in sympathy and agreement with him. **The Professor and the three goldbugs remain on stage, as**

Curtain

ACT TWO
WHAT A GOOD DOG I WILL BE
SCENE TWO: A SQUAREDEAL ARRIVES

Scene: The Same. The three goldbugs and the professor are sitting at the campfire.

Enter Georgie Grubbingrabber (*the villain*) *a short, broad-shouldered man sporting a large moustache. He steps out of the shadows and is dressed as a dude cowboy in fine western gear.*

GRUBBINGRABBER: Oh beans. If there's beans going, can I have a share? I'm Georgie S. Grubbingrabber. (*in a friendly way, shaking hands all around*) Trust me, you guys, for a square deal. That's what most folks call me, Squaredeal. That's my middle name.

The three goldbugs look at each other and shrug in puzzlement.

HANK: *(mystified)* A square deal on what? We've nothing to sell and no money to buy.

GRUBBINGRABBER: Of course you have a lot to buy or sell, my dear young fellahs. That's where you're wrong. You could get a pretty penny for this quaint old mine, you know. A place like this could be rented out to holidaymakers. Of course, I know there's no gold here. Nobody ever finds gold nowadays but I could sure pack in the gawkers and gapers. You see I sell dreams . . dreams are worth good money and I'm the original wheelerdealer.
(to the audience, twirling his large moustache)
Selling this place to me. That is a good idea, isn't it?

AUDIENCE: *(in unison)* OH NO IT ISN'T.

GRUBBINGRABBER: *(to audience)* I'm offering them a square deal. An honest break.

AUDIENCE: *(in unison)* BOO, HISS.

HARRY: *(morosely)* Well this place ain't for sale, so forget it.

GRUBBINGRABBER: Didn't you say your money was going down?

HAL: Like apples in the fall.

HARRY: Like rainwater going down a drain.

HANK: Yes, going down like an absent-minded parachutist. *(he signals with his right hand a falling plane)*

HAL: But we're still not selling out and we don't need no tourists neither, stepping nor stomping around here. Not to mention their spying and reporting.

HANK: Tourists would interfere with the treasure troving.

GRUBBINGRABBER: *(pacifyingly)* No, no, of course not, outsiders and visitors would be a menace to you all. I mean to buy you boys out completely so that you can try something else . . like an honest trade for instance. How's that? How's about a steady job?

HAL: A job? You mean you want us to go panhandling, scrounging and begging? That doesn't sound like a square deal to me. There's no such thing as a good job. The only good job is working for yourself.

Squaredeal sits down with a small plate of beans and begins to eat ravenously.

GRUBBINGRABBER: Consider it boys. There's no hurry for a quick decision. How about a lump sum up front and a good job working for a chemical company? No problem. A paycheck every month. Gee, what about earning enough to buy a small house in a mere 50 year's time or a nice little car to help you go buy the groceries.

HANK: Here, just a minute, Squaredeal, are you trying to buy us out with regular jobs? We don't want a wage-earning career. We came out here because we all believed that <u>truly</u> there is no such thing as a good paycheck. Paychecks all cost too much in stress. Working for a big firm is like buying a lottery ticket. Yes. A few - one or two - a few hit it big and make real money. But the thousands and millions lose their lot. That's what a lottery is all about. It's big biz with a swiz to rip you off. Of course, there are always daydreams to entertain you.

GRUBBINGRABBER: *(reassuringly)* You don't mean to say that you want to BE YOUR OWN BOSS? *(the three goldbugs nod keenly)* Bah! You'll likely starve. And don't forget that a regular paycheck puts you in the way of meeting some real nice people and you become socially acceptable, see?

HANK: So's I can mix and match with all and sundry.

HARRY: *(cynically)* That's all I need. A way to meet with more people.

HAL: I have met all the people I ever want to meet in this life. And good riddance to them.

HANK: I have always said that a shotgun is the best neighbor you'll ever have.

GRUBBINGRABBER: *(insisting)* Come on now fellahs, you need money. *(wide-eyed with disbelief)* You've got to eat some kind of food.

HAL: Food? We don't need to buy food. It's all here in these here hills for free. We've got snakes, rabbits, berries, raw beans, wild birds, cacti. Not a great variety but it's all good food.

GRUBBINGRABBER: Yes, but think about it - a TV in your living room! Here, you don't even have a living room never mind a TV in it. And that's not all. No, no, no, of course not. Chairs and all. All conceivable helps and gadgets. Piped water, electronic screens, electric lights, windows to see through . . .

HANK: *(scanning the horizon with hands shading his eyes)* Yes, windows to see who's coming.

HAL: *(laughing)* Yes I see. To arrest us, rob us, murder us or bore us to death . . . Yes I see. Oh yes, windows to let the burglars see in advance what they're getting.

GRUBBINGRABBER: *(assuring them keenly)* Lookee see, fellahs. It's great to have all your comforts. It's a hard life out here in these here hills.

HANK: Here we have all the running water, all the starlight, all the views free. Listen here stranger, Mr. Squaredeal, what you are offering us is just what we all ran away from - being terrorized by the boss. Yessir, nosir, three bags full sir. That's not a life . . that's a sentence to fear for life.

HARRY: Yessir to you, Hopeful, and Nosir to you Mr. Squaredeal. O what good dogs we would have to be to earn our scraps, begging,

trembling and jumping. We'd have to sit up
and beg.

*Harry begs like a dog as Hank tumbles
and Hal jumps up and down. Then
Harry, Hal and Hank each act out their
role in the following song - WHAT A
GOOD DOG.*

WHAT A GOOD DOG I WILL BE
Sung: Cheerful and Rollicking

VERSE ONE

d   r   m   m   m - m   r   d   m   s   s - s
Now the bad dogs today just won't do as we say
l   s   m   d - d   r   m   l₁
But still they expect to get food
d   m   m   m - m   r   d   m   s   s - s
Why should they get fed and why should they get bed
 l - l   s   m   d   r   m - r   d
When their manners are not very   good.

REFRAIN:

m - m   s   s   s   s   l   t   d¹- d¹   l - d¹
I will sit up and beg and then hold up a leg
l   s   m   d - d   r   m - l₁   m   l₁
I'll stick out my tongue and agree (you'll see)
d   m   m   m   m   r   d   m s   s   s
O please let me do all you're asking me to
l   s   m   d   r   m   r   d   r   d
O what a good dog I will be (you'll see)

HANK: *(singing)*
Now some dogs are so bold they won't do what
they're told
But still they expect to get food
Why should they get fed and why should they get bed
When their manners are not very good?

HARRY *(singing and shaking his head in sorrow)*
I'll go round in a loop or I'll jump through a hoop
I'll crawl on the ground and lie low

> *(Harry crawls and rolls over and covers his
> eye with his hands)*

I'll cover my face and pretend to say Yes
I'll bring back whatever you throw

HAL *(singing)*
It is quite an affront if you can't do a stunt
Like cringe away down and play dead
*(Hal cringes, then lies down as though dead,
playing possum)*
If you can't earn your pay in some groveling way
I don't think you ought to get paid

HANK *(singing)*
I will sit up and beg and then hold up a leg
I'll stick out my tongue and agree *(you'll see)*
(Hank puts out his tongue and nods)
O please let me do all you're asking me to

O what a good dog I will be *(you'll see)*
(Hank holds his hands before him like
begging paws)

HANK: *(addressing Professor Stargazer who has been listening without comment)* What do you think, Professor? Should we bail out now or hang around here a little more?

The professor pokes around in the dirt, as he considers the question.

PROFESSOR: Let's think.

They all sit around the fire, looking into the flames.

HAL: I seem to see old memories and hopes rising up and flying away out of these flames.

PROFESSOR: *(still looking far into the distance)* As a teacher I always advise my students to persevere. So, stick it out, hang in there and sure enough one day you will be a success.
     Seek and you will find
     Knock and the door will open
     Nothing ventured, nothing gained

GRUBBINGRABBER: *(looking confused and thoughtful, then muttering)* Well yes. I see what you're saying but . . .

HANK: You can't <u>see</u> what he says. You mean you can <u>hear</u> what he says?

GRUBBINGRABBER: Well, whatever, anyway. My advice to you all goldbugs is to sell up and become predictable professionals like the rest of us . . enjoy the good things of life . . like music, plays, stories.

HAL: *(astonished, jumping up and stomping his feet)* But why do those things have to be laid out on a plate in your silly world down there. We sing to ourselves. We tell stories to each other and we dream up plays about what we would do if . . .

PROFESSOR: *(yawning)* Let us practice those perambulations sometime soon. Meanwhile I'm going to secure some somnolence.

HANK: He means snatch some sleep.

GRUBBINGRABBER: Oh no, anything but that.

HAL: Why, no?

GRUBBINGRABBER: No one should ever sleep, unless he wants to drop dead. See, no one can ever be sure of wakening up. Besides, that's when the bandits catch you unawares. *(he draws his hand sharply across his throat)* When <u>you</u> sleep, <u>they</u> creep.

They all ignore Georgie S. Grubbingrabber and remove their hats, boots, outer jackets and coats. All lie down on their blankets and one by one they all fall asleep. As the others sleep, Squaredeal opens up first one eye and then another, rises and begins to mutter and search and surreptitiously rummage around. First, he finds a few trinkets and sticks a few tools and utensils in his backpack. Then, searching their pockets, he finds their small change, watches and clocks, holds them up in the air, sniggering, rubbing his hands and jumping for joy.

GRUBBINGRABBER: Ah, ha, this is what I want most . . their timepieces . . their time-schemes . . their time.

Grubbingrabber chortles and giggles as he sneaks off into the shadows.

GRUBBINGRABBER: *(to audience)* I'm not really stealing, only borrowing, yes?

AUDIENCE: *(led by conductor using hand-signs)* NO!

GRUBBINGRABBER: *(outraged, to audience)* I'm not a thief, am I?

AUDIENCE: OH, YES YOU ARE.

GRUBBINGRABBER: *(to audience)* Oh no I'm not a thief, not that. I'm just a borrower, right?

AUDIENCE: OH, NO YOU'RE NOT.

GRUBBINGRABBER: Oh, no, no. I am not a rogue, a liar, a thief, am I?

AUDIENCE: OH, YES YOU ARE.

GRUBBINGRABBER: *(to audience)* Now, be fair, be honest, tell the truth. What do you really think of me?

AUDIENCE: BOO. BOO. HISS.

Grubbingrabber panics, falls into the dying embers of the fire, then as sparks are flying from his clothes, runs offstage left. The others sigh and moan and toss in their troubled dreams but fitfully continue to sleep for a while. All the lights on stage go out and there is a pause, as

Curtain

ACT TWO
WHAT A GOOD DOG I WILL BE
SCENE THREE: TIME WASTED

Scene: *The same, later in the night.*   **All continue to sleep.** *Slowly a faint light creeps up above the western hills and reveals a still shadowy and bleak old mine site.*

Hal is the first to waken up and looks around in fear and confusion. He stretches his limbs and appears full of aches and pains as he moves around.

HAL: What's happening?

Slowly and stiffly the others get up, limbs creaking, moaning and groaning.

HARRY: *(nervously)* What's going on?

The others rekindle the fire and shiver in the dark, cold, thin dawn. They look each other up and down.

HAL: You look so old.

HARRY: It's only the faint dawn light.

HAL: But last night I felt so much younger.

The professor has by now wakened up and is stretching his limbs.

HANK: Professor, you don't look any older than the night before.

PROFESSOR: *(proudly)* Well, we tall, thin people usually age better than the short and stocky.

HARRY: What is happening, Professor? How long have we been sleeping? It feels like decades.

PROFESSOR: *(looking at his watch)* Decades? Rubbish! We've all been asleep about eight hours, indeed seven hours and forty six minutes precisely.

HARRY: Then why do we feel so old and achy?

PROFESSOR: Don't you see it? Don't you see why? It's your own fault. You trusted a conman - George S. Grubbingrabber. He has stolen everything he could lay his thieving hands on including wasting your time.

HARRY: I would never have believed it possible *(exercising his arms and shoulders)* except that I feel older.

HAL: Me too. And I can see you look the way I feel, Harry. It must be true as the professor says. We seem to have grown older.

PROFESSOR: This is becoming such a sad place. I think we need to get a little more rest. We'll probably feel better in the morning.

HAL, HARRY AND HANK: *(to each other)* We're going to bed. This must be just a bad dream. A good sleep will bring us all back to normal.

They all bed down for some sleep..

Enter Georgie S. Grubbingrabber, now dressed as a lumberjack in checked shirt and jeans with an axe in his hand. Stealthily, he creeps past the sleepers and begins to hack with his axe at some of the mine machinery in the shadows. He sniggers and chortles.

GRUBBINGRABBER: *(aside)* This'll let them know about some of the problems of being self-employed.

Wood cracks and splits and the sound almost awakens the three goldbugs. He swings his axe again and again and there is the loud crunch of breaking wood and smashing metal. The three treasure bugs now waken up fully with a start and cry out. They rise up.

HAL: What was that noise?

HARRY: Sounded like a tree falling.

HANK: *(puzzled)* More like metal breaking.

Grubbingrabber steps into the light of the fire.

GRUBBINGRABBER: *(swinging his axe on his shoulder)* I was just breaking up some firewood for you old pals of mine.

HANK: Oh, it's you again. Since when did you want to help anyone, Mr. Bossman?

GRUBBINGRABBER: Oh, come on. Hello fellahs. Let's be pals. *(ingratiatingly)* I'm your old pal Squaredeal but you can call me Georgie, this time. I was just waiting until that old weirdo went away. I don't trust anyone who says he's a professor. *(looks around furtively)* Who does he think he's kidding?

The three treasure bugs are astonished.

HAL: You're a rogue. What are you up to?

HARRY: You scoundrel, you liar.

HANK: You thief of time.

GRUBBINGRABBER: Thief of time? I don't get it. I never stole anything in my life.

HAL: It was like you wasted 40 years of our lives with all your talk about nice safe jobs.

Grubbingrabber laughs and laughs and shakes his head.

HANK: And some of our gear and pots and pans and watches and odds and ends and small change as well.

HAL: Not to mention other goods and chattels.

GRUBBINGRABBER: *(outraged)* How could I do all that? I'm just a poor, simple cowboy wheeler-dealer and honest tree-chopper. How could I steal 40 years of your lives? Anyone, <u>anyone</u> will tell you that just ain't possible. That's fantasy. And stealing your goods? Who, I'd like to know, told you that? Who had the gall, the mendacity to accuse me? I'm just an honest, hardworking, decent soul. Never in my life have I been so humiliated and wronged by being accused of stealing miserable pennies. Why, if I ever wanted to lose my hard-earned reputation for honesty and decency I would steal a million not your silly old pots and pans and tools and small change. Not that I ever would rob or steal but grant me, credit me, with the common sense at least to steal something big and worthwhile.

HARRY: Yes . . like the best part of our lives, for instance.

GRUBBINGRABBER: *(laughing again and shaking his head)* One more time. That ain't no go, noways. Only <u>you</u> can spend <u>your</u> lives. Nobody else can steal time, the way you say. Who told you that cock and bull story? WHO? I want to know. My good name counts to me. I demand to know . . Who is my accuser . . eh?

Grubbingrabber clenches his fist and glowers from one to another. The three bugs look sheepishly at each other. Hank digs his foot in the ground and appears to be worried.

HANK: *(to the other two bugs)* I suppose we need to tell him?

Hal and Harry sadly nod their heads.

HANK: Well it was Professor Stargazer who gave us that impression.

GRUBBINGRABBER: *(with outrage)* Him! That old fraud. He knows nothing. He's a deceiver, a cheat and a rogue. I wondered what he was up to, poking around here. *(nodding his head thoughtfully)* So that's what he was up to . . hmm . . snooping around and lying about decent old Georgie Squaredeal Grubbingrabber. Why, the squaredeal I offered you would have paid you off with getting you a small down-payment admittedly but you would have gotten a big fat paycheck every month for life. Boy, were you boys taken in by that old ripper-offer. *(aggressively)* How could you have believed him against me?

HARRY: *(looking Grubbingrabber up and down suspiciously)* Well, we quite like the old professor and besides we all felt like 40 years older after you left.

HAL: (*also suspiciously*) And besides we'd nothing but aches and pains.

GRUBBINGRABBER: Of course you did. But lookee here fellahs. It's cold here and the dampness of the creek was bound to get you feeling old and achy sooner or later.

HANK: (*looking Grubbingrabber up and down, slowly*) Nothing is as stressful and mean and ornery as working for someone else and sitting at a machine in a bad smelling factory. Oh, no thanks. I like to be my own boss. I don't want to be your pet poodle, Georgie.

HAL, HARRY, HANK: (*as they cringe and crawl and roll over and play dead and hold up one paw*) WOOF, WOOF, BOW WOW, HOWL, HOWL, YELP, YELP.

HAL: Me too. I'd rather have me for a boss than you. We trusted you once just for a little while and you slunk off like a thief in the night with our goods and gear.

GRUBBINGRABBER: Look guys, I didn't steal anything from you. Honest. I swear . . .

HANK: How come the goods vanished with you when you ran off?

GRUBBINGRABBER: Well, digging for treasure is bound to make you feel old and tired. As for getting out of here, I had no choice. I ran off because the old professor chased me. Yes, that's it. He had a gun and he ordered me off so that he could steal you blind. It was all the work of Professor Stargazer . . falsely so-called if you ask me.

Professor Luck suddenly awakens..

The three bugs roll up their sleeves to tackle Mr. Squaredeal. He holds up his hands and backs away towards the nearby woods, right-stage.

GRUBBINGRABBER: Now, please fellahs, take it easy. I was only offering you a fair deal. A fair offer of three good jobs. What's wrong with that. You can always turn me down. I don't mind. *(as they still advance towards him grimly)* Lookee here, gentleman, bosses, captains, professors. I tell you what, I'll bring back the things I borrowed from you . . all of them.

(to audience) I only borrowed them didn't I?

AUDIENCE: OH, NO YOU DIDN'T.

GRUBBINGRABBER: I didn't steal anything did I?

AUDIENCE: OH, YES YOU DID.

GRUBBINGRABBER: I'm not a liar or a thief am I?

AUDIENCE: OH YES YOU ARE.

GRUBBINGRABBER: *(slowly)* No - no - no.

AUDIENCE: BOO, BOO, HISS.

*The three treasure bugs continue to slowly advance towards **Grubbingrabber** as he **turns and begins to run offstage left**. He drops his axe and plunges into the creek, coming up soaked, scared and yelling.*

GRUBBINGRABBER: See, I'll just go and get those things that I borrowed. I'll bring them back to you real soon. Just let me go, fellahs.

*Grubbingrabber **runs off**, dripping wet and terrified into the woods, **exiting left**. The Professor and the three bugs all laugh and shake hands and clap each other on the back.*

PROFESSOR: *(shaking his head)* You almost believed him but I admit he's a plausible rogue. He states his case well I'll say that for him.

They continue to laugh as

Curtain
End of Act Two

ACT THREE
DREAM BACK THE GOOD DREAMS
SCENE ONE: DAY OF THE GOLDBUG

Scene: The Same. **Enter the professor**, *as before, carrying a walking stick, lit at the pointed end. It is late at night, the stage is dimly lit.* **The three goldbugs are sleeping.** *The figure of the professor is lightly spotlighted and dances all around stage waving the walking stick like a wand.*

PROFESSOR: At last the mine is quiet and deserted. Now I can work my magic on these rocks and touch a golden gleam into these streams. *(he laughs)* Ha, ha, little did those goldbugs see through my disguise. Little did they realize that I am the one some call Professor Luck and others know as the Gold Bug King. An old professor, yes, *(shakes his head)* but Professor of Luck. But no one has suspected me. *(he points his stick here and there)*

Here! Let gold crawl up from far beneath the earth. Let the gold lie just beneath the surface. *(he points his stick)*

The professor dashes about the stage pointing his lighted stick here and there.

This is the only way anyone ever found treasure, by good luck and hard work. Here and here is the luck. Tomorrow the three goldbugs will find what they have been digging for. Suddenly they will be rewarded *(he straightens up proudly)* by me, the great Professor Luck, who worked my magic in these dreary diggings. Good luck to the digger, here and there.

Professor Luck struts up and down with his coat tails held behind his back, lighted cane in hand, shaking it here and there.

PROFESSOR: I am Professor Luck . . the master of math. I choose who passes and who fails, who succeeds and who slaves away with little or no reward. I make my decisions purely on the basis of my own system of mathematics.

That's why I'm the Professor of Luck. Of course, when I was young, a mere 800 years ago or so, I studied for a doctorate in the field of Luck. But call me whatever you like, Professor or Mathematician, I am the only one who understands the math of win or lose. A combination of numbers that, believe it or not, approaches infinity. *(nods)*

Yes, indeed. Ha, ha, goldbugs indeed - Hardwork Harry, Honest Hank and Hopeful Hal, all your efforts are of no avail except with my help.

Professor Luck raises his arms wide in magnificent self-pride, then shakes his cane in the air and smiles as he struts back and forth across the stage, then bows to audience. The three goldbugs waken up.

HAL: Just a minute now Professor, what are you doing there with those lights?

HARRY: Is this a joke? What are you up to, Professor?

HANK: Is this a dream or are you somehow doing strange things?

PROFESSOR: Well, I did tell you'all my profession. I forgot to mention my full name. Professor Stargazer N. Luck. N for Numbers. I'm the one you summoned from the echo and the echo called me. Remember?

HAL: No. I don't believe it.

HARRY: You're LUCK, for real?

HANK: *(sighing)* Well that's amazing you're LUCK and here we were, getting nowhere . . .

PROFESSOR: No one is going nowhere when I'm around.

HANK: Then perhaps meeting you now has been worth the wait?

PROFESSOR: Yes, I'm Professor Luck, the man with all the destiny numbers and the magic pointer.

HAL: But you'll help us?

PROFESSOR: Yes, of course. I'm always willing to give at least a little help to the hardworking, the honest, the hopeful and perhaps even the clever on rare occasions. You should have sent for me sooner.

The professor pokes his lightie-up stick at the three goldbugs.

PROFESSOR: I can't bring back your wasted time but I can give you the luck that you searched for in these diggings.
The professor's stick glows like a star and the three treasure bugs begin to dance around like three year-olds.

ALL THREE: Luck. Luck, Professor Luck has come at last.
Enter Dame Weddingbells dressed as before, with her brolly.

DAME: Hello boys, I see you've got company.

PROFESSOR: Oh yes. Permit me to introduce myself, dear lady. I am Professor Luck.

Enter the Chorus, dressed as goldbugs in gold hats, shoes, coats and pants. They join the professor in singing:

PROFESSOR LUCK'S SONG
(see p. 349)

REFRAIN:
O Professor Luck – that's me
I count the magic numbers
Professor Luck will see
Who will jump up and who tumbles
My sums must all agree
Who rises or who crumbles
For Professor Luck will always be
The man with magic numbers
For Professor Luck will always be
That's me, that's me, that's me, that's me
The man with magic numbers

VERSE ONE:
The finest brains have tried
To find success without me
And many have denied
That there's any help about me
(Yet) Success depends on me
And on all my calculations
For only I can see
All the number combinations

VERSE TWO:
Now Hope is not all bad
And I'm inclined to favor
Any honest decent lad
Or a lass who likes hard labor
But there's one guarantee
I'll give and I'm not bluffing
Without me you will see
All your hard work come to nothing
All your upright honesty
And your hope will come to nothing

Chorus exits stage right.

PROFESSOR: I am helping these goldbugs to find treasure.

DAME: Did I hear you say you're a Professor? I'm so pleased to meet you Professor Luck. I don't mind men with brains if they know where to find a little gold. Of course, the gold is not really necessary. I'll overlook it if you've forgotten where the gold is. Although, I'm saving up for my mid-life crisis. I'm only 65 you know.

She curtsies to the professor with her index finger under her chin.

HANK: What do you mean – mid-life crisis? *(aside to audience)* What age does she expect to live to?

DAME: Professor, I'd like to read you a little advertisement I put in the personal column of the internet.

> Young lady, blond hair, blue eyes, well-dressed would be interested to meet mature, educated gentleman with means.

(she flutter her eyelids coyly)

The only reply I have gotten so far is from an old-age pensioner with white hair. He dropped his stick and then he fell on the floor. I had to help him up and he apologized for dropping his car keys. I said to him, don't forget your car keys, you'll need them. No, I won't need them, he replied, I get around in a wheelchair theseadays. He promised me a date when his pension came through so I'd be prepared to consider another date if you are available, naturally. By the way, are you married?

PROFESSOR: I always remember the old proverb:

> If you want to be praised drop dead
> If you want to be criticized get married

DAME: Oh, its so fortunate that you're still available Professor. *(she curtsies and holds out her wide skirt and bows)*
I'm just a poor widow myself you know.
(sobs and cries)

PROFESSOR: I always say never marry a widow – she might be planning to make a habit of it.

DAME: Anyhow, *(brightly)* I'm trying to encourage these three goldbugs to get back with their gold-digger girlfriends.
> *She staggers backwards, falls and kicks*
> *up her legs.*
Oh dear, I think I've fallen for you, Professor.

> *Two of the goldbugs pick her up and stand*
> *her up straight.*

PROFESSOR: One of you goldbugs needs to take her off my hands. Phew!

HANK: *(looking closely at Dame)* She's as old as these hills.

HAL: Why, she doesn't have any teeth.

HARRY: *(shrugging)* Well, she's not a cat – you don't want her for catching rats, do you?

Dame draws herself up and begins to whack the three goldbugs around the shoulder with her umbrella.

DAME: How dare you all insult me. No teeth indeed. Not for catching rats, eh? I'm sending your gold-digger girlfriends back to get you and all the gold you've got.

Then she leaves stage right, shouting as she goes. The others remained stunned, as

Curtain

ACT THREE
DREAM BACK THE GOOD DREAMS
SCENE TWO: FIT TO BE TIED

Scene: The Same. The three goldbugs are still celebrating their gold find.

From the shadows, *slowly and sneakily,* **enters Georgie Squaredeal Grubbingrabber (the villain).**

He is dressed in a business suit, striped shirt, bright red tie, gray socks and black shiny shoes. His hair is neatly trimmed and brushed. There are pens in his top jacket pocket and he carries a briefcase.

GRUBBINGRABBER: *(smiling)*Hi there, fellahs. Remember me, your old pal Squaredeal. Hee, Hee. I hear you've struck it lucky.

HANK: Oh yes, you're the crook who stole our goods, chattels and money. Hi, Pal. *(with sarcasm)* Then, after your last visit, we found some of our machines broken.

HARRY: *(edging closer to Grubbingrabber)* Oh sure we're nuts. You didn't really rip us off.

HANK: Yes, we've all gone treasure-trove. *(he sticks his thumbs in his ears and wags fingers)*

HAL: *(sinisterly approaching Grubbingrabber)* Why, it's our esteemed associate, Georgie. It's dusty around here. Let me brush your lapels, old chap.

GRUBBINGRABBER: *(relieved)* Phew yea. I have a great deal for you guys. Now that you have a business and all, maybe you'll be worrying a little. Now you need security, peace of mind, guarantees against a rainy day. Have I got an insurance policy for you all. Low, low payment per month and covers you against sickness, hospitalization, loss of business profits and in case of sudden death a large bonus goes to your next of kill, I mean kin. Bad things can happen . . you need protection from them now that you're going into business.

HAL: *(edging closer to Grubbingrabber)* Always on the make, eh? But, for once, yes, I agree with you, Squaredeal.

GRUBBINGRABBER: *(eagerly)* Yes, it makes sense.

HAL: Sure it does. We all need guarantees of security such as a good insurance policy against what could happen to anyone - like injury or hospitalization.

The three goldbugs have now surrounded Grubbingrabber.

HANK: *(calmly and pacifying)* Sure, Mr. Squaredeal. No doubt you have such a real good insurance policy to cover your own needs.

GRUBBINGRABBER: *(nervously)* Oh sure, boys. Me and my loved ones are well covered for all risks.

HAL: Great, Georgie, old boy. Then you won't mind us seizing you . . .

They seize Georgie right-stage and bind him to a tree with some old rope or the lasso. Grubbingrabber begs for mercy.

GRUBBINGRABBER: Help. Let me go, this is kidnapping.

(to audience) Call the mountain rangers. Tell them to let me go.

(to silent audience) Well . . they're kidnappers, aren't they?

AUDIENCE: OH NO THEY'RE NOT.

GRUBBINGRABBER: Oh yes they are.

AUDIENCE: OH NO THEY'RE NOT.

HAL: You don't mind us tying you up here, do you?

HANK: And . . ah . . inflicting a few well-insured against injuries?

HARRY: Then leaving you here for the wild-dogs to perform their cute little tricks and hoop jumps and bow wow begs for you. We'll leave it to them. We don't want to become your poodles . . your performing dogs. Let the wild dogs do that for you.

GRUBBINGRABBER: *(to audience)* You've no right to treat me like this.

AUDIENCE: OH YES WE HAVE.

GRUBBINGRABBER: Don't you want me to escape?

AUDIENCE: BOO. BOO. HISS.

All three goldbugs dance around the streams of water, then march offstage right, leaving Grubbingrabber tied to the tree.

GRUBBINGRABBER: Hey, come back.

(to audience) This is kidnapping. You can't leave me here all tied up.

AUDIENCE: OH YES WE CAN. BOO. HISS.

Curtain

ACT THREE
DREAM BACK THE GOOD DREAMS
SCENE THREE: GREEN LEAVES FALL

Scene: The Same. Grubbingrabber is still tied to the tree and yelps at times. **Enter from left the professor,** *looks around, walks about. Music of* GOLDBUGS *(see p. 355) is played at a brisk march.*

Enter Hal, Harry and Hank from right *(each to the music of his former song). They are all dressed as before.*

By way of self-introduction, Hopeful Hal sings the refrain of **THE GAMBLER'S ORPHAN** *(see p. 393).*

Hardwork Harry sings the refrain of **SQUIRREL SONG** *(see p. 397).*

Honest Hank sings the refrain of **FOOD AIN'T AS GOOD AS BEFORE** *(see p. 387).*

The Professor sings refrain of **PROFESSOR LUCK'S SONG** *(see p. 349).*

They are carrying bags of gold dust and piles of dollar bills (dollar bills continually fall or are thrown away by the goldbugs) as autumn leaves symbolically fall from trees. At this point the dramatic mood is one of exuberance. The professor jumps with joy, in greeting the three goldbugs.

PROFESSOR: Here I am back again. Where have you been . . deserting the mine?

HAL AND HANK: We're enjoying gathering the motherlode.

HAL: Whoever you are Professor, you've brought us luck.

PROFESSOR: *(dancing and delighted)* This is what the cat really wanted all along . . the smell of money.

HARRY: Yes, this is just what the pussycat ordered. In the past day or so we've been found by so many old friends in need and we've come to find out about so many good causes that we were afraid we would have given away all our newfound treasure.

> *Enter Chorus taking up the background, center, dressed as goldbugs as before.*
> *Enter Playaround Polly (Hopeful Hal's Girl) she is costumed as before, sees Hal and approaches him.*

PLAYAROUND POLLY: *(to Hopeful Hal)* Hal, it's me, Playaround Polly. I've come back to you.

Hal is delighted. They embrace and dance to the refrain of DREAM BACK THE GOOD DREAMS.

> **REFRAIN:**
> m s s s s l t - d^1
> We'll sing of the good songs gone by
> l - d^1
> And cry
> l s m d d r m l$_1$
> We'll sing all the songs we sang then
> d m m m m
> For all the day long
> r d m - s l - s
> We were singing a song
> l s m d r m r *d*
> We'll sing back the good songs again

HAL: It's great to see you again. It's just like oldtimes.

PLAYAROUND POLLY: It's great to know you've struck it rich, Hal. For I sure need a couple of hundred dollars.

HAL: Why? Oh, never mind. What does it matter? Who cares? (*gives Polly some dollars and throws some money around*)

Polly joins the Chorus to the music of **DREAM BACK THE GOOD DREAMS.**

Enter Harry's girl, Escapist Eve *as the dancers continue singing the refrain. Eve is costumed as before, she looks around, sees Harry and approaches him.*

ESCAPIST EVE: It's me, Escapist Eve. I've come back to you, Harry.

Harry is delighted. They embrace and dance to the refrain of **DREAM BACK THE GOOD DREAMS**

> **REFRAIN:**
> We'll sing of the good songs gone by
> And cry
> We'll sing all the songs we sang then
> For all the day long
> We were singing a song
> We'll sing back the good songs again

ESCAPIST EVE: (*to Harry*) Let me tell you my story. I was kidnapped by woman-torturing dwarfs, tied up, taken to sea and dumped overboard. But lucky for me a passing shark cut my ropes and I escaped, swam ashore, and now I'm looking for a good private eye to track down my kidnappers and find out who done it.

HARRY: What about the police?

EVE: *(considering)* Yea, they were the first suspects I thought of but . . naw, I don't think it was them that done it. *(shakes her head rejecting the idea)* See, those undersized kidnappers were too short to be cops. Like I said, they were dwarfs. What I need is a good private eye to catch the culprits . . agreed - Harry?

HARRY: *(uncertainly)* Well . . sure I would think so.

ESCAPIST EVE: Some first-class detective who will put those ornery torturers where they belong - behind bars.

HARRY: *(with more enthusiasm)* Right, Eve. Now you're talking.

EVE: O.K. Harry, let's have your share then.

HARRY: *(at a loss)* My share of what?

EVE: *(smiling innocently)* Of the detective's fee, of course. You just said I should hire one. I'll need money, honey, for the private eye's fee - naturally .. and you said . . .

HARRY: *(shaking his head and laughing)* Sure .. here, have a few hundred. *(dances around)* Are you sure this is true love?

EVE: Sure, I truly love both you and the big dollar bills. Don't you believe me?

HARRY: I believe you, ha, ha, ha, ha. You gold digger.

EVE: What's wrong with being a gold digger? Why, remember, you've been doing it for years yourself, ha, ha, ha, ha. We're all goldbugs together.

They dance around together, dollar bills flying. Escapist Eve joins the Chorus and sings to the music of DREAM BACK THE GOOD DREAMS..

Enter Wet Ears Wilma *(Hank's girl). The dancers continue singing the refrain. Wilma is costumed much as before but her arms and legs are bandaged and she hobbles pitifully on crutches. She heads painfully for Hank, groaning and moaning and appearing to be in pain.*

WET-EARS WILMA: Why, its Honest Hank. I see you're doing well, Hank. Don't you remember me, I'm Wet-Ears Wilma from way back on the old river bank?

Hank is happy to see her and he dances briefly. Wilma hobbles pathetically on her crutches. The three goldbugs each take turns in singing **DREAM BACK THE GOOD DREAMS.** *Everybody dances except Wilma who hobbles around.*

DREAM BACK THE GOOD DREAMS
Sung: Medium Slow and Nostalgic

VERSE ONE:

d   m   m   m   m   r   d   m - s
We'll dream of the good dreams gone by

l   *s*
And sigh

l   s   m   d - d   r   m l_1
We'll dream of our dreams way back then

d   m   m   m   m
When all of our days

r   d   m - s   l - s
We were dreaming always

l   s   m   d   r   m   r   *d*
We'll dream back the good dreams again

REFRAIN:

m   s   s   s   s   l   t - d^1
We'll sing of the good songs gone by

l - d^1
And cry

l   s   m   d   d   r   m l_1
We'll sing all the songs we sang then

d   m   m   m   m
For all the day long

r   d   m - s   l - s
We were singing a song

l   s   m   d   r   m   r   *d*
We'll sing back the good songs again

HAL:
We'll dream of the good dreams gone by
And sigh
We'll dream of our dreams way back then
When all of our days
We were dreaming always
We'll dream back the good dreams again

HARRY:
We'll sing of the good songs gone by
And cry
We'll sing all the songs we sang then
For all the day long
We were singing a song
We'll sing back the good songs again

HANK:
The dancers of night will dance by
And fly
Too quickly old dancing does end
But we'll dance until dawn
And the night fear is gone
And we'll dance the old dancing again

HANK: You're not dancing Wilma. What's the matter?

WILMA: O think nothing of it, Hank. It's just that I'm suffering from the crippling effects of arthritis and rheumatism as a result of a terrible fall into the river, long ago. Yes, "delayed effect" the doctor said. Yes that's what the silly old doctor said. *(laughter)*

HANK: *(tongue in cheek)* It's too bad I can't help you out with your doctor's bills, Wilma. I'm sorry the money and all has been earmarked for high living and dancing and gallivanting around. Since you're not fit for song and dance and flying around . . then I'm afraid my accountant would never let me give you anything. I would never want to squander good-times money on doctor bills. Naw! I hate doctors. Every time I see a doctor I feel sick.

WILMA: Oh why should I pretend. *(throws away crutches, rips off bandages and begins to dance with Hank. She catches some of the money that Hank throws away).*

I can see you're still fond of me Hank *(picking up more money)* but how long will it last?

HANK: Wilma, we're all treasure trovers together.

True love is very well and good.
But it doesn't take the place of food.
So let's just forget about money most foul.
I'll love you for sure till the coyote gives a howl.

A coyote howl is heard in the background

WILMA: *(alarmed and seizing Hank's arm)* But how can I stop him howling, Hank?

HANK: Why you just grab him by the throat baby! Ha, ha, ha, ha.

> *He gives a coyote howl. The others are shocked, some faint and are fanned by others with their hats.*
> *Wet-Ears Wilma joins the Chorus as they sing **COYOTE** (see p. 371). The Chorus playfully hold out their hands to the goldbugs who throw some money into the air as they dance.*
> *This sequence ends as they all dance and sing **GOLDBUGS** (see p. 355).*
> *Gradually the professor, three girlfriends and the Chorus fade somewhat into the background but remain around the stage*

perimeter as the lights focus on the three goldbugs who prance and strut around the tree where Grubbingrabber, moaning and yelling, is still tied. The music of **GOLD BUGS** *(see p. 355) gradually fades away.*

All remain on stage standing still as

Curtain

ACT THREE
DREAM BACK THE GOOD DREAMS

SCENE FOUR: WEDDINGBELLS FOR GEORGIE

Scene: The Same: Grubbingrabber is still tied to the tree. The three goldbugs pretend to be dogs and bow wow and bark and jump and beg as they join hand-in-hand and dance around the tree. Grubbingrabber, still bound, begs for mercy with wailing and howling, twisting and turning. He struggles free from the tree and tries to escape toward the forest, shaking his fist and shouting as he limps away.

GRUBBINGRABBER: *(twirling his moustache)* I'll get you all one day. I'm the boss. See? So you want to be your own boss, do you, eh? Then ha, ha, I'm telling you I'll get you for rent or taxes or gas or service charges or something. No one ever escapes me.

Enter Dame Weddingbells and pursues Grubbingrabber as he runs towards the forest.

DAME: *(keenly)* I think I'll just get you to marry me. There's no one else available.

GRUBBINGRABBER: Help! Help! Anything but that.

Dame whacks his bottom with her umbrella, seizes him by the scruff of the neck and marches him off stage left.
The others all dance around the fire and Hopeful Hal points to the flames.

HAL: See in the flames the faces of old friends filled with love and laughter and the faces of former foes frowning and cast down with disappointment.

HARRY: See up there the sun struggles free from his nightchains, drags his face up out of the far hills.

HANK: And hear the high blue dawnbird beginning the new day by singing a new song that no one has ever heard before.

Then the professor slowly slips among the trees, waving his magic stick to the goldbugs.

PROFESSOR: I must travel on.   I hear someone else crying out for LUCK just like you all did.

Then Professor Luck disappears into the shortening shadows of the daybreak that creeps slowly up upon the old mine camp and the fountains of clear spring water.

WILMA: Where has Professor Luck gone?

POLLY: Out there into the great winds and forests and rivers and seas.

EVE: *(looking far into the distance)* Yes, there he will travel for evermore . . somewhere out there . . far along the little known and lonesome trails of the mind. Wandering at his will with his magic stick and destiny numbers. Alive and willing to help those who have courage and goodness and faith.

All remain on stage and are joined once again by the Professor, the Grand Dame Weddingbells and the villain Georgie Squaredeal Grubbingrabber as they all sing some of the choruses from the pantomime.

They all bow as . .

<u>Curtain</u>
End of Playscript

APPENDIX
FIVE FINGER EXERCISE
Simple Instructions on
How to Play the Tunes

Music is presented in the form of tonic sol-fa. Tonic sol-fa is the written form of music for both beginners and virtuosos – those who do not need guidance on timing, arrangements or chords – those who need only the basic tune.

1. Hitting the Right Note
2. White Keys - Stick-On Labels
3. Black Keys - Stick-On Labels
4. Getting the Timing Right
5. Summary

HITTING THE RIGHT NOTE

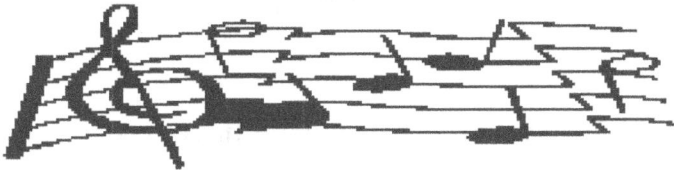

C is the white note just to the left of the two black notes side by side. Find Middle C on your keyboard. A register is the level of a set of tonic sol-fa. Here is the location of Middle C on a standard three register keyboard. The white note in the exact middle of any keyboard is Middle C (in staff) and Doh (in tonic sol-fa).

The tunes in this songbook can all be played on these three middle registers. Larger keyboards may have additional higher or lower registers but these will not be needed for the simple basic tunes in this book.

C is always Doh and going up from Middle C is the central set of tonic sol-fa:

Doh, Ray, Me, Fah, Soh, Lah, Te.

The next note is also a C and is the Doh higher than Central Doh. This starts off the next register of tonic sol-fa notes.

The Middle Set of tonic sol-fa have no subscript or superscript: d, r, m, f, s, l, t.

The Lower Register (set of tonic sol-fa) have subscripts as follows: $d_1, r_1, m_1, f_1, s_1, l_1, t_1$.

The Higher Register (set of tonic sol-fa) have superscripts as follows: $d^1, r^1, m^1, f^1, s^1, l^1, t^1$.

Here is a complete set of labels, for the white and black keys, to stick onto your central basic keyboard.

WHITE KEYS: STICK-ON LABELS
FOR YOUR KEYBOARD

LOWER REGISTER	**Doh$_1$**	**Ray$_1$**	**Me$_1$**	**Fah$_1$**	**Soh$_1$**	**Lah$_1$**	**Te$_1$**
MIDDLE REGISTER	**Doh**	**Ray**	**Me**	**Fah**	**Soh**	**Lah**	**Te**
HIGHER REGISTER	**Doh^1**	**Ray^1**	**Me^1**	**Fah^1**	**Soh^1**	**Lah^1**	**Te^1**

WHITE STICK-ON NOTE INSTRUCTIONS

These are to be stuck on to your keyboard to show you which notes to play as you follow the Tonic Sol-fa music set out in each song.

1. The seven white notes with subscripts (lower register) lead up to Middle C.

2. Middle C starts off the middle register of seven white notes that have neither subscripts nor superscript.

3. The seven white notes with superscripts (higher register) follows on after the middle register.

Only the last three white notes of the lower register and the first white note of the higher register are shown with the middle register in the above diagram *(p. 360)*.

THE BLACK KEYS

The black keys in each register are as follows:
de, maw, fe, law, taw.

The five black keys in the lower register
    have subscripts
The five black keys in the middle register
    have no subscripts or superscripts
The five black keys in the higher register
    have superscripts.

Here are the three sets of labels to stick onto the black notes on your keyboard.

LOWER REGISTER	De_1	Maw_1	Fe_1	Law_1	Taw_1
MIDDLE REGISTER	De	Maw	Fe	Law	Taw
HIGHER REGISTER	De^1	Maw^1	Fe^1	Law^1	Taw^1

GETTING THE TIMING RIGHT

(1)   Notes that are grouped together have hyphens between them - to show that they are played together. (eg: d - f - l). This does not mean that such notes are speeded up, only that they are joined together.

(2)   Notes that are to be held longer than average are written in italics - that is to say they are sloped to the right (eg: *d* or *s*).

(3)   Try to follow the hints at the head of each tune (eg: slow and simple or fast and warlike).

(4)   Keep a steady and regular beat whether the tune is fast or slow (eg: tap your foot or get a friend to tap out an even measured beat).

SUMMARY

Below is a diagram of all three registers - Lower, Middle and Higher. Of course, on many keyboards and pianos there are more than these three registers but these keys are all that you will need to play the simple tunes in this songbook

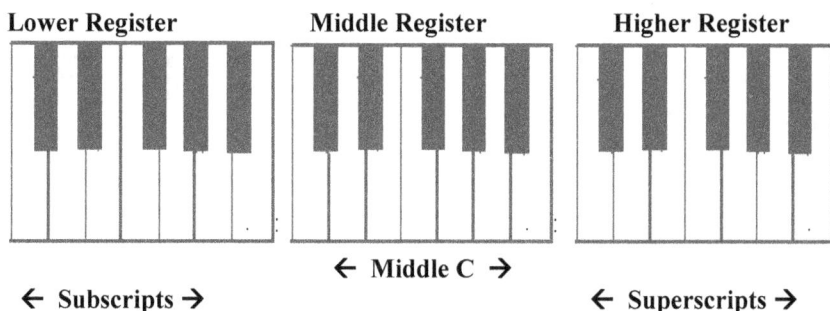

Lower Register   **Middle Register**   **Higher Register**

← Middle C →

← Subscripts →   ← Superscripts →

BRIEF INSTRUCTIONS

1. Cut out the squares and stick them on to the black and white keys.
2. Hit the notes asked for in the tonic sol-fa tunes, trying to hear each melody as a whole and keeping a steady beat.

Key to Tonic Sol-fa Notes
D = doh
R = ray
M = me
F = fah
S = soh
L = lah
T = te

WHITE KEYS: STICK-ON LABELS
FOR YOUR KEYBOARD

LOWER REGISTER	Doh_1	Ray_1	Me_1	Fah_1	Soh_1	Lah_1	Te_1
MIDDLE REGISTER	Doh	Ray	Me	Fah	Soh	Lah	Te
HIGHER REGISTER	Doh^1	Ray^1	Me^1	Fah^1	Soh^1	Lah^1	Te^1

BLACK KEYS: STICK-ON LABELS
FOR YOUR KEYBOARD

LOWER REGISTER	De_1	Maw_1	Fe_1	Law_1	Taw_1
MIDDLE REGISTER	De	Maw	Fe	Law	Taw
HIGHER REGISTER	De^1	Maw^1	Fe^1	Law^1	Taw^1

HOW TO IMPROVE YOUR SINGING

In singing these songs there are seven main aspects of singing to check out and practice towards perfection. (There are also several more subtle, complex and minor aspects which only a real-life music teacher could explain. Each aspect of singing calls for separate exercises as well as putting all six together.

1. Voice Quality

Largely a given, quality can be developed by practice, healthy diet and deep breathing.

2. Diction

Concentrate on sharp clear pronunciation to achieve understanding on the part of the listener. Aim for sounds that most people with standard English, not accents, will understand.

3. Projection

Throw out the voice until all the audience can hear it. Every word must always reach the listener.

4. Phrasing

A phrase is a group of words and notes that are grouped together. Watch how the sounds and words hang together and change the combinations until it sounds right to you in your opinion. What is right for one singer may not be right for another.

5. Feeling

Try to imagine how the sender of the message would feel and think. Develop a dramatic empathy, a oneness with the message of the song so that it comes over as genuine.

6. Rhythm

Keep an even beat or a creative subtly uneven one. Tap your foot on the ground or follow a drummer, or hand claps (see also the section on timing).

7. True Notes

Make sure that the note you play is the right one. Listen to a self-tape and compare your notes with those sung by a friend or played on a keyboard or other instrument. Sometimes it helps to close your eyes and listen well.

8. Find a Teacher

If you can, find a good singing teacher with top credentials or at least get a musical friend to critique you.

THE END